W9-AOD-600

Feminist Ethics

Feminist
Ethics

EDITED BY CLAUDIA CARD

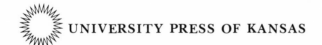 UNIVERSITY PRESS OF KANSAS

© 1991 by the University Press of Kansas

"Feminist Ethics: Problems, Projects, Prospects," © 1990 Alison M. Jaggar

All rights reserved

Published by the University Press of Kansas (Lawrence, Kansas 66045), which was organized by the Kansas Board of Regents and is operated and funded by Emporia State University, Fort Hays State University, Kansas State University, Pittsburg State University, the University of Kansas, and Wichita State University

Library of Congress Cataloging-in-Publication Data

Feminist ethics / edited by Claudia Card.
    p.   cm.
  Includes bibliographical references and index.
  ISBN 0–7006–0482–0 (alk. paper) — ISBN 0–7006–0483–9
(pbk. : alk. paper)
    1. Femininity (Philosophy)—History.   2. Feminism—Moral and ethical
aspects. 3. Social ethics.   I. Card, Claudia.
BD450.F43   1991
170'.82–dc20   91–6753
                                                    CIP

British Library Cataloguing in Publication Data is available.

Printed in the United States of America
10 9 8 7 6 5 4 3 2 1

The paper used in this publication meets the minimum requirements of the American National Standard for Permanence of Paper for Printed Library Materials Z39.48-1984.

To Emily
1923–1965

Contents

Introduction

1 / *The Feistiness of Feminism*

CLAUDIA CARD

This introduction is addressed to the general scholarly reader, which is a challenge, as no one person is that reader. And so I have kept in mind a variety of possible readers. I think especially of women entering the study of philosophy who are curious about the excitement and creativity of feminist ethics and of philosophers discovering feminist scholarship after two decades during which feminist philosophy has been growing—especially any who may be a little wary of the feistiness of feminist voices but are curious enough to read on. What follows introduces this volume's contributors (and some friends) through their connections with me, by way of a reflective narrative meant to illustrate some themes of contemporary feminist ethics as it discusses developments in this area. In the quiet of your library, turn the volume to what feels good, and let your imagination play with these stories.

RETROSPECT

In May and August 1957, *The Ladder*, a new lesbian magazine with a national circulation, printed two letters from a woman in New York City initiating critical feminist ethical discussion. The first letter compared the writer's experience as "a Negro" with the magazine's stated policy of advocating "a mode of behaviour and dress acceptable to society," commenting on the "shallowness" of the views of those who are "forever lecturing to their fellows about how to appear acceptable to the dominant social group." The writer ever so politely agreed with the magazine's policy "to the degree of wanting to comment on it." The second letter, "speaking personally as well as abstractly" about the situation of "heterosexually married lesbians," concluded with the following:

> I think it is about time that equipped women began to take on some of the ethical questions which a male dominated culture has produced and dissect and analyze them quite to pieces in a serious fashion. It is time that "half the human race" had something to say about the nature of its existence. Otherwise— without revised basic thinking—the woman intellectual is likely to find herself trying to draw conclusions—moral conclusions—based on acceptance of a social moral superstructure which has never admitted to the equality of women and is therefore immoral itself.

She went on:

> In this kind of work there may be women to emerge, who will be able to formulate a new and possible concept that homosexual persecution and condemnation has at its roots not only social ignorance, but a philosophically active anti-feminist dogma.[1]

The letter writer, signing herself "L.H.N." and "L.N.," is reported to have been Lorraine Hansberry (1930–1965), soon to be famous for her award-winning play, A Raisin in the Sun.[2] Had her life extended another decade, she would have been joined by other feminists "equipped" with activist experience and philosophical training, eagerly taking on such ethical questions, eventually the superstructures also, even exploring her hypothesis about interconnections of the persecution of homosexuals with antifeminism.

Feminist ethics is born in women's refusals to endure with grace the arrogance, indifference, hostility, and damage of oppressively sexist environments. It is fueled by bonds among women, forged in experiments to create better environments now and for the future, and tried by commitments to overcome damage already done. Ethics benefits from reflection upon our own experience, upon choices we have actually faced. Scarcely uniform, still women's options defined by legacies of sexual politics differ enough from men's to warrant different identifying labels for our reflections and commitments in this area. Thus I apply the term "feminist" only to women, referring to men who support feminism as "profeminist."[3] When feminists and profeminists confront comparable life choices, there may no longer be a need for feminism or for feminist ethics.

I always found it hard to draw lines between ethics and political philosophy. Kate Millett gave me a new slant on political philosophy with the concept of sexual politics, which helps. Before reading her *Sexual Politics*, I thought political philosophy was defined by questions of authority to make certain kinds of decisions.[4] Afterward, I understood it as a study of the uses and abuses of power. Political philosophy traditionally studies norms governing power relationships among members of nation-states and between or among nation-states themselves. The notion of sovereignty within a geographical area is crucial to the idea of a state. Political philosophy includes the issue of anarchy: Should there *be* states? *Sexual* politics is not a subtopic under political philosophy so conceived. It is not the study of laws regulating sexual conduct, for example, although it can include that. Nor is it philosophy of the bedroom conceived as a mini-state, although it has exposed bedroom politics. If anything, the state becomes a subtopic (not necessarily indispensable) under the more general study of sexual politics. Sovereignty in sexual politics pertains to our bodies, not to geographical territories. Sexual politics is about norms governing power relations among members of *the sexes*, considered as such (also not considered simply as such but often considered as masculine, feminine, gay, lesbian, and so on). Lesbian politics is likewise concerned with norms defining power relations among individuals. Few of these norms pertain to erotic behavior. There are analogues to the anarchy questions: Should there be norms systematically governing power relationships among and between members of the sexes? This, if not an ethical question itself, leads quickly to ethical issues such as those explored in this book. For it invites reflection upon character and social relationships developed under oppressive sexuopolitical norms and upon possibilities of bringing about change or, as Sarah Hoagland puts it, "making a difference." Thus oppressive sexual politics sets the stage for ethical inquiries into character, interpersonal relationships, emotional response, and choice in persistently stressful, damaging contexts.

Over the past two decades, the image of feminist ethics in the

United States has changed radically. At first it was viewed by non-feminist philosophers as marginal to philosophy, as applied ethics examining implications of canonical theories and principles for fairly public matters protested by feminist activists. It is now widely recognized as a family of approaches to ethics at all levels of theory, no more marginal than Kantian ethics. Feminist ethics extends philosophical inquiry into areas not ordinarily public as well as addresses central issues of theory, including assessments of what counts as central. Alison Jaggar finds that not only has it enlarged the ethical domain but also it has brought into sharp focus deep problems in moral epistemology not adequately addressed by nonfeminist theorists.[5]

There are at least two kinds of history in the development of feminist ethics. One is a history of reflection upon existing ethical theory by philosophers within academies, criticizing, modifying, and extending it in light of feminist appreciations of history, rejecting some views, defending others, using one's own experience as a kind of checkpoint. The other kind of history comes from a politically active experience of building new relationships in the world and engaging in new social practices as an alternative to full participation in sexist society. Reflection upon the raw data of such experience serves more often as a starting point for theorizing, not simply as a checkpoint. These two lines of development do not coincide with particular "isms." Many philosophers have participated in both, the latter in two ways. On the one hand, many have engaged in alternative social experiments outside the academies, including community work to repair and contain the damage of oppression. Some contributors to this volume have worked in rape crisis centers; some have sheltered women and children against battery; some have counseled incest survivors; some have taught women and children self-defense; some are engaged in building lesbian communities and hispanic communities in the United States. On the other hand, and at the same time, many have experimented with teaching practices and new forms of professional interaction within the academies. Reflection upon active experimentation, both within and outside the academies, is primarily responsible for the development of feminist ethics as a family of approaches to ethical theorizing at all levels, as feminist philosophers either integrate or contrast the results of such reflection with other traditions in philosophical ethics. I will trace some of these developments as I have witnessed them and as they have af-fected my own teaching and research during the past decade and a half.

In October 1976 I first participated in a conference of the Midwest Society of Women in Philosophy (SWIP) as a panelist on the question "Are Virtues Sex Related?"[6] There I met Joyce Trebilcot, who hosted the conference at Washington University, St. Louis, and also Sandy (Sandra Lee) Bartky and Marilyn Frye, geographical and spiritual neighbors with whom I have maintained more or less continuous contact. Since 1976, I have missed only one Midwest SWIP confer-ence. At the next one I met Alison Jaggar, and at the Eastern SWIP in 1977 and 1978 at December APA conventions, Christine Pierce, Bat-Ami Bar On, and Vicky (Elizabeth V.) Spelman. In October 1977, I met Sarah Hoagland at an interdisciplinary conference in Madison, Wisconsin, called "The Prism of Sex," at which I presented a short narrative on feminists in philosophy, following Kathy Addelson's (Kathryn Pyne Parsons) "Moral Revolution." There I first heard Mary Daly speak on clitoridectomy. There I also met my colleague Evelyn Beck, who coedited a volume based on that conference.[7] In May 1978, again on the stage with Kathy Addelson in deliberate defiance of the custom of isolating a speaker in front of the room, I delivered my "coming out" paper, "Feminist Ethical Theory: A Lesbian Perspec-tive," to a standing-room-only audience of philosophers, women's studies faculty, and others at the University of Minnesota, distribut-ing it afterward to colleagues at Wisconsin and in the fall to the Faculty Seminar for Feminist Inquiry at Dartmouth College, where I visited for a year.[8]

In 1977, I began inventing a course, "Feminism and Sexual Poli-tics," which I taught every semester for many years at the University of Wisconsin as well as at Dartmouth (spring 1979) and at the Univer-sity of Pittsburgh (winter 1980)—which, by the way, is where I met Lynne McFall, who writes fiction as well as philosophy.[9] "Feminism and Sexual Politics" involved experiments with class format, not only the usual breaking into small discussion groups but forms less usual. For example, we used "rotating chair" for parts of class discus-sions, we sometimes did a round of "check-in" at the beginning of class or "check-out" at the end, and everyone was encouraged to use the chalkboards. In rotating chair, the chair is passed (rotated) to the next speaker each time someone is called on to speak, thereby offering an experiment in the possibility of order without hierarchy, taking the focus off the instructor, revealing to members of the class from whom others wished to hear, and challenging the line between content and form by encouraging consciousness of "form" and bringing the ethics of process into subsequent discussions. When I raised my hand during "rotating chair," students had no obligation to call on me. They knew that when I felt it necessary (because of my responsibility for the class), I would seize the chair. (Occasionally others seized it, too, and we began with someone seizing the chair by being the first to speak up). "Check-in" and "check-out" consisted of going around the class so each person could say briefly what was on their mind or how they were feeling, or, if they chose, simply pass.

Encouraging people to talk about feelings in a class dealing with heavy topics, such as sexual assault and sexual orientation, led to new responsibilities, for which my major preparation was not graduate school but three years of weekly meetings in a consciousness-raising (CR) group organized in 1971 by María Lugones, whom I have known longest among contributors to this volume. I did not learn rotating chair, check-in, and check-out in graduate school either or even at SWIP. I encountered them at lesbian collective meetings in Minneapolis and at local (Madison) branch meetings of the short-lived National Lesbian Feminist Organization.

Feminist teaching experiments of the 1970s often adopted and adapted values, attitudes, and practices from CR groups and collectives: noncompetitiveness and antihierarchialism (manifested, for example, in the preference for sitting in circles rather than in lines); rejection of adversarial structures; suspicion of rules and abstractions; preference for narrative style and encouraging analytical verbalizations of motivation, feeling, and emotion (a step toward defiance of conventions meant to keep such things out of "rational" discussions); habits of self-criticism, self-revelation, and peer evaluation; collective problem-solving; discussion of process. Such experiments yielded data upon which many feminist philosophers reflect ethically today. Some have criticized practices involving self-revelation, for example, as presupposing safer environments than feminist classrooms can ordinarily provide.[10]

When I began teaching "Feminism and Sexual Politics," I found relatively little contemporary material by philosophers, aside from Ti-Grace Atkinson's *Amazon Odyssey,* that was engaging enough and reflective enough of my newly erupted discontent to use as texts.[11] Most relevant journal articles by men were on abortion or preferential hiring and assumed unquestioned interventionist powers to define major life choices for others.[12] An informal bibliography, "Philosophy and Feminism: Recent Papers," compiled in 1976 by Janice Moulton and backed by SWIP and the APA Committee on the Status of Women, revealed that articles by women were more widely distributed over a spectrum that included critiques of classical texts, inquiries into sexist language, discussions of sex roles and androgyny, the nature of women, and women in the history of philosophy. Academic journal essays, however, tended to be guarded and highly qualified compared with the uncensored happenings on SWIP programs. At first, I taught more from informally circulated drafts and from publications of women who were not known as or trained as philosophers—poet Adrienne Rich's "Women and Honor: Some Notes on Lying," for example, and essays by neurophysiologist Ruth Bleier (1923–1988), vegetarian activist Carol Adams, science fiction novelist Joanna Russ, freelance writer Andrea Dworkin—women who were trying to say what was wrong and explore new ideas without fitting into philosophical traditions or submitting to the scrutiny of philosophical establishments.[13] Some academically trained philosophers followed the example of Ti-Grace Atkinson, publishing with small presses, in interdisciplinary women's journals, or in grass-roots periodicals.[14]

Small feminist periodicals became a source of stimulating theoretical exchange. Less academic than philosophy journals, sometimes edited by former academics, they have often been receptive to philosophical essays, typically designated as "theory." From 1974 into the 1980s, there was *Quest: A Feminist Quarterly* from Washington, D.C., with articles by Charlotte Bunch, Mary Daly, Marilyn Frye, Nancy Hartsock, and Janice Raymond, and from 1977 to 1980, ten wonderful issues of *Chrysalis* from Los Angeles, offering advance chapters from books soon to be published.[15] *Sinister Wisdom,* originally "for the lesbian imagination in all women," has published essays, poems, and graphics since 1976; since 1977, *Conditions* and *Heresies: A Feminist Publication on Art and Politics,* both edited by collectives, have published writings in a variety of styles.[16]

By the late 1970s, academic philosophers had produced anthologies in response to the growing needs of new feminist philosophy courses. Two such widely used collections are *Feminist Frameworks*, (currently in its second edition), edited by Alison M. Jaggar and Paula S. Rothenberg, which organizes by political persuasion a wealth of short pieces on many topics, and *Feminism and Philosophy*, edited by Mary Vetterling Braggin and others, which has fewer but longer papers than *Feminist Frameworks*; both have extensive bibliographies.[17] *Feminism and Philosophy* included in full several engaging papers with ethically significant content, among them early work by Alison Jaggar, Joyce Trebilcot, and Marilyn Frye (with Carolyn Shafer), as well as Janice Moulton's "Myth of the Neutral 'Man' " and Sandra Bartky's "Toward a Phenomenology of Feminist Consciousness." Perhaps for the first time ever in an academic philosophy book, there was an entire section on rape, including Susan Griffin's "Rape: The All-American Crime," originally from *Ramparts* magazine (1971) and used in rape crisis training programs from coast to coast.

A few large publishers, finding themselves with feminist editors, began issuing books with radical feminist content that raised ethically provocative questions. In the fall of 1978, two such books, which made a great impact and which I have used many times as texts, were poet Susan Griffin's *Woman and Nature: The Roaring Inside Her* and theologian-philosopher Mary Daly's *Gyn/Ecology: The Metaethics of Radical Feminism*.[18] Utterly different in style, each joined the holistic concerns of environmental ethics with a historical perspective. *Woman and Nature* juxtaposed the words of Plato, Aristotle, Descartes, and others with milestone historical events in the subordination of European women and nature, illustrating in a long section called "Matter" the taming of spirit involved in the dualisms of mind/body, reason/feeling, culture/nature, and man/woman. *Gyn/Ecology*, a double ax splashed across its front dust jacket, may have been first to put "ethics" into its (sub)title along with "feminism" (surely with "radical feminism").[19] More significant, Mary Daly put the global scope of a history of lethal environments for women at the heart of her treatise, with heavily documented chapters on Chinese footbinding, European witchburning, African genital mutilation, Indian suttee, and American gynecology.[20]

Gyn/Ecology may have generated more controversy among feminist scholars than any other work in feminist ethics of the past two decades. Its courage, scholarship, feistiness, humor, and innovation were an inspiration.[21] Yet its enthusiasm to rescue women from the charge of evil betrayed serious limits to the complexities of women's characters that it was prepared to explore, if not to its empathy with victims of cruelty. Although such limitations were not unique, the book's circulation of its visions was unprecedented, as were some of the examples it used in introducing the concept of "token torturers": women carrying out the dirty work of men who are only too glad to have women be the focus of misogynist attention. *Gyn/Ecology* compared American gynecology to the Nazi medical experiments—here was yet another example of physicians, with the apparent blessing of the state, using their skills to kill and maim rather than to save lives and promote health. Its discussions of women's roles did not acknowledge female accountability to anyone for anything but referred to Nazi women, including doctors, as "tokens," a trivializing term that, coupled with "torturers," is dizzying.[22] Not outright denying women's responsibility for abuse, the book refused to discuss it, pointing instead to what men have done with what women have been willing to do for them. Thus it did not confront, among other things, women's accountability to other women. When and how to confront such issues in public remains a source of continuing concern. No doubt in part as a result of controversies surrounding *Gyn/Ecology*, such accountability, as well as other histories of women's abusiveness, has significantly complicated contemporary feminist ethics.

Poet and essayist Audre Lorde, in an open letter to Mary Daly, objected that *Gyn/Ecology* exposed only negative aspects of African culture for women, that it did not mention African goddesses, for example, who might be inspirational for women of African descent.[23] In the spring following the publication of *Gyn/Ecology* and *Woman and Nature*, the first volume of Adrienne Rich's collected essays appeared, concluding with "Disloyal to Civilization: Feminism, Racism, Gynephobia," which discussed, from a Euro-American woman's perspective, Euro-American women who have collaborated with Afro-American women in U.S. history, using racialist privilege to resist and undermine rather than to support racialism.[24]

Jewish feminists and antipatriarchal women of color invited and urged white, non-Jewish feminists to become equally conscious of the extent and complexities of racialism, racialist privilege, and the history of anti-Semitism and to confront ethical issues at the intersections of such oppressions with misogyny. At the same time, many Afro-American women activists in the United States were addressing Afro-American readers on male privilege. In 1978, the *Black Scholar* published a special issue, "Blacks and the Sexual Revolution," with articles by Assata Shakur/Joanne Chesimard, Angela Davis, Audre Lorde, Johnnetta Cole, and Elizabeth Hood, addressing not only sexual revolution but also feminist issues, including lesbian eroticism and rape.[25]

In the fall of 1979, upon my return from Dartmouth, I met Nellie McKay, professor of literature in the Afro-American Studies Department, who had been hired at Wisconsin (from the English Department at Simmons College in Boston) while I was away. She was the first woman colleague from another department on my home campus to look me up and visit my office.[26] Her bibliographies on Afro-American autobiography and Afro-American women's literature showed me new worlds, forever altering my reading habits and, consequently, perceptual habits.[27] As a result of this friendship, I added to the ethics courses I taught regularly a course in philosophy and literature with a multicultural base of texts and a feminist focus on ethical issues in and about literature. Many feminist philosophers have found fiction, especially by women with bicultural experience, important sources of data and of reflection upon ethical issues.

That year I joined the Women's Studies Program, and a decade later, Environmental Studies. Such interdisciplinary programs offer philosophers immersed in humanities important contacts with ethically significant developments in science. They are also an important intersection for developments in many ethnic area studies on the campus.

Published theoretical exchanges on feminist issues among women of color in the United States, as well as exchanges between women of color and white women, appeared more frequently in the next decade. Multicultural innovations turned up in feminist periodicals, anthologies, and styles of composition, as in the essay by María C. Lugones and Elizabeth V. Spelman, "Have We Got a Theory for You! Feminist Theory, Cultural Imperialism, and the Demand for 'the Woman's Voice,' " which had a Spanish prologue and, in English, now alternating voices, now joint ones.[28] *This Bridge Called My Back: Writings by Radical Women of Color*, edited by Cherríe Moraga and Gloria Anzaldua, included poems, narratives, and analyses by

African-American, Asian/Pacific American, Latin American, and Native American women, with extensive bibliographies in each ethnic cluster.[29] Women's Studies curricula offered courses with focuses on women of color. Kitchen Table: Woman of Color Press began publishing books in New York City. In 1983, Alice Walker wrote, "Womanist is to feminist as purple to lavender."[30] Five years later, Katie G. Cannon published *Black Womanist Ethics*, taking Afro-American women's literary traditions as her source with special attention to the life of anthropologist and novelist Zora Neale Hurston (1901–1960).[31]

Before the 1980s, the only Afro-American woman philosopher I had heard lecture was Angela Davis. During the 1980s, I heard papers by American women philosophers of diverse ethnic heritages on a variety of topics at ethics conferences and feminist conferences. Some, especially at feminist conferences, wrote with an explicit analytical and critical consciousness of an often mixed ethnic heritage. Midwest SWIP conferences offered presentations from philosophers of Latin American, Native American, Asian/Pacific American, and Afro-American identity or ancestry on topics ranging from friendship and separatism to ecofeminism. Recently, Jacqueline Anderson, of Olive Harvey College in Chicago, explored the significance of popular ignorance of the historical perspectives of indigenous peoples upon such events as the arrival of Christopher Columbus (discovered by a group of Arawakian Lucayos on the island of Guanahani on October 12, 1492).[32] Some papers by women of Euro-American ancestry exhibited a new and critical consciousness of white heritages. In 1986 at a University of Cincinnati feminist moral, social, and legal theory conference, I met my colleague, logician and philosopher of mathematics La Verne Shelton, who was a panelist in a symposium, "Theorizing Differences." Two years later, I heard moral philosopher Adrian Piper read her paper "Higher Order Discrimination" at a conference on moral psychology at Radcliffe.[33] On both coasts, conferences on moral character offered papers by philosophers with diverse ethnic heritages who have not turned up at Midwest SWIP but have clarifying things to say on issues central to feminist scholarship.[34]

Courses in lesbian studies have also produced a growing body of ethically relevant literature, increasingly multicultural and multidisciplinary. The Lesbian and Gay Studies Newsletter of the Modern Language Association (MLA) is an excellent source of reviews and relevant information.[35] Before leaving Wisconsin, Evelyn Beck introduced a course on lesbian culture into a variable-content women's studies offering in 1978. I helped turn it into a permanent course, from the ancient Amazons to the present, and have taught it many times, with Evelyn Beck's *Nice Jewish Girls: A Lesbian Anthology* among the texts.[36] In 1988, Sarah Hoagland and I met with John Pugh at the APA convention in Cincinnati in response to his call for a caucus and together founded the Society for Lesbian and Gay Philosophy and the Gay and Lesbian Caucus. In 1990, we held our first session of papers on topics in lesbian and gay philosophy at the Central APA in New Orleans, and another is planned for the Pacific APA meetings in San Francisco in 1991.[37]

In 1983, three books were published by contributors to this volume. Marilyn Frye's incisive and compact *Politics of Reality: Essays in Feminist Theory* grew out of her feminist philosophy course at Michigan State University. Its nine interrelated lectures defined a radical woman-centered perspective on such topics as oppression, separatism, anger, gay rights, being white, and being lesbian.[38] Alison Jaggar's *Feminist Politics and Human Nature* defended a socialist feminism and offered a wealth of detailed analysis and critical examination of major trends in feminist political philosophy in the United States of the 1970s and early 1980s.[39] Joyce Trebilcot's anthology, *Mothering: Essays in Feminist Theory*, in the tradition of Adrienne Rich's *Of Woman Born*, challenged the glorification of motherhood as an institution and explored the lessons of actual mothering experience.[40]

In the early 1980s, the term "feminist ethics" was still new. Feminist writings in ethics were not yet collected in volumes identified as such but were scattered in works called "feminist theory" or "feminist politics." Joyce Trebilcot's book on mothering may have been the first to gather philosophical essays explicitly addressing the idea of an ethic growing out of the mothering experience. The early 1980s produced more small journals—*Trivia* and *Lesbian Ethics* in the United States, followed by *Gossip: A Journal of Lesbian Feminist Ethics* in London,—that have encouraged work in ethical theory.[41] During this period at SWIP I met Marilyn Friedman, whose passions for both justice and friendship struck a responsive chord, and at Wisconsin, Terry Winant, Victoria Davion, and Ruth Ginzberg, whose lively presences as critics, instigators, and visionaries are now missed in Madison.

At an East Coast conference on character and morality in the late 1980s, I met Michele Moody-Adams, whose paper dealing with responsibility for character defended a "roughly Kantian skepticism" about the worth of natural inclinations. Annette Baier presented a piece at that conference also, on honesty as "a hard virtue," to which I improvised a response when the original respondent was unable to come.[42] As Annette Baier was on leave when I visited at Pittsburgh in 1980, we became acquainted with each other's feminist work in ethics mainly through hearing each other's papers on women and ethical theory one Saturday morning in 1985 at Central APA meetings in Chicago.[43]

Not until the second half of the 1980s were there many book-length works dealing explicitly with feminist ethics. *Hypatia: A Journal of Feminist Philosophy*, named for an Egyptian woman philosopher, mathematician, and astronomer (370–415 C.E.), became an independent journal in 1986 with Peg (Margaret) Simons as editor. The Institute of Lesbian Studies was also launched that year in Palo Alto, California, with the publication of Jeffner Allen's *Lesbian Philosophy: Explorations*, which included searing essays on motherhood and rape. The next year, three important anthologies explored issues in and around gynocentric ethics. The most genteel, *Women and Moral Theory*, edited by Eva Feder Kittay and Diana T. Meyers, grew out of an East Coast conference on the philosophical implications of Carol Gilligan's hypotheses about women's moral development.[44] From Canada, *Science, Morality, and Feminist Theory*, edited by Marsha Hanen and Kai Nielsen, explored in a politically bolder vein feminist gynocentrism in ethics and epistemology.[45] More interdisciplinary, multicultural, and feistier yet, *Competition: A Feminist Taboo?* edited by Californians Valerie Miner and Helen Longino, gathered new essays by women examining values and scruples underlying the widespread reluctance and outright refusal among many feminists to support competition or at least to admit to doing so.[46]

In 1988, Beacon published Elizabeth V. Spelman's *Inessential Woman: Problems of Exclusion in Feminist Thought*, its ambiguous title referring both to women's history of being treated as unimportant and to current anti-essentialist struggles to make sense of the concept "woman" (and thereby of feminism) without doing injustice to cultural, ethnic, and class differences.[47] That year also, the Institute of Lesbian Studies published Sarah Lucia Hoagland's *Lesbian Ethics: Toward New Value,* which received in June 1989 one of the first annual Lambda Literary Awards.[48] This treatise was the culmination of a decade's thought and experience in defining an ethic that takes relationships among lesbians as its paradigms of caring, explicitly rejecting mother-child bonding as a paradigm for ethics between adults.[49] The following year, Beacon published Sara Ruddick's *Maternal Thinking*—likewise the culmination of years of thought and political experience—proposing a feminist peace philosophy based on ideals argued to be implicit in the caretaking tasks of mothering.[50] Suddenly there was more than enough published material for advanced courses and graduate seminars devoted to feminist ethics.

Today, feminist ethics has many layers and traditions of its own. Its readership is rapidly expanding. Graduate students are working on dissertations in the area. Some writers continue examining implications of older theories and principles (such as John Rawls's principles of justice) for focal points of feminist activism—pornography, battering, childcare, and so on. Others continue exposing misogyny and stereotypes in writings of historically influential philosophers (such as Aristotle and Kant) or, more cheerfully, reclaim past defenses of women against sexist practices and attitudes (by Mary Wollstonecraft, Margaret Fuller, and John Stuart Mill, for example).

Although there is endless work to be done here, feminist ethics has also become more sophisticated, diversified, and creative. Some thinkers examine or re-examine particular ethical concepts and traits—equality, justice, caring, honesty—in light of feminist struggles, sometimes taking up traits that have not enjoyed previous attention from philosophers, as Lynne McFall does with bitterness in chapter 9. Some take a feminist approach to ethical issues not stereotypically associated with women, as Bat-Ami Bar On does with terrorism in chapter 7. Some identify and explore androcentric biases implicit in the theoretical standpoints of historically influential philosophers (as Elizabeth V. Spelman has done with Plato and Aristotle) or identify standpoints that do not appear particularly androcentric (as Annette Baier has done in a series of papers on the ethical writings of David Hume).[51] A few attempt new identifications and formulations of basic concepts for ethical thinking, as Sarah Hoagland does with "attending," Sara Ruddick with "preservative love," and María Lugones with "interactive pluralism," taking activist data of their own lives as starting points.[52] Finally, the material in and related to feminist ethics now includes substantial critical examination of previous work in the field and of other relevant work by women. This book's essays tend to cluster in the latter layers of feminist ethics and include critical examinations of relevant work by women (occasionally by men also).

Since 1982, the idea of feminist ethics has received a certain popular acceptance as a result of the research of developmental psychologist Carol Gilligan. Without drawing upon feminist ideas, she described several themes distinguishing the ethical thinking of many women from that of most men in her experience of many years' listening to mostly white, middle-class speakers reflect upon themselves and upon certain moral problems.[53] From a feminist perspective, the popular reception has been unfortunate in some ways. Carol Gilligan's writings portray everyone as basically honest and of goodwill, although understandably limited in perspective and consequently often misunderstanding one another. From this partial picture, gynocentric and androcentric perspectives in ethics have come to seem more comfortable than they should to many who might have benefited from fuller pictures. A parochial and conservative gynocentrism has become widely confused in the public mind with feminism. Some who formerly frankly opposed feminism now can be found embracing under the label "feminist" certain traditional middle-class conceptions of femininity. Carol Gilligan's research, like feminist research, was born in refusal. But that refusal is not (or no longer?) feisty. Conservative gynocentrism has not found a voice in this volume. Several contributors, however, most notably Michele Moody-Adams and Elizabeth V. Spelman, raise worrisome questions about the broader implications of Carol Gilligan's work and about the lines of thought that such work might be used to support.

The present collection does not disown the feistiness of feminist ethics. Feistiness is often manifested in traditions complementing those represented in the essays here—for example, identifying philosophical issues in topics the discussion of which violates rules of polite society, using vocabularies that transcend conventions of politeness, and relentlessly uncovering and protesting systematic violence against women and girls. This volume, however, does exemplify traditions of turning back on ourselves critiques of the dominations and subordinations sometimes implicit in otherwise feminist scholarship, thereby uncovering racialism, classism, ageism, or ableism. We have learned from experience how assailants manipulate targets of violence by dominant conventions of politeness and how such conventions are used also to suppress criticism by subordinates. A corollary to the observation that feminist ethics is born in refusal may be that politeness is not the first virtue of feminist thought. Feminist conventions of politeness are developing their own roots and forms. The feistiness of insubordination, however, ranks high on my scale of feminist virtues. It is this feistiness that puts off those who want to object that feminist philosophy is ideological or polemical. "Ideological" suggests more unity of thought than one finds in fact. Refusals to accommodate to the subordination of women mislead if they suggest unity of voice; the refusals different ones of us make are often not the same. "Polemical" is a charge hurled where anger shows, simultaneously betraying and protesting an emotion that white, middle-class, Euro-American philosophers of both sexes are conventionally supposed to keep under wraps. That convention is commonly questioned in feminist ethics.[54] My own view is that the sustaining of feistiness by feminist philosophers over two decades is probably a tribute to our integrity, insofar as that touchiness, that readiness to quarrel, has kept alive the traditions I have mentioned. Such vitality gives me hope. The contagious friskiness and excitability of feminist feistiness are also among the qualities that endear some of us to each other.

Certain commitments are evident in most of the essays of this book. The essays demonstrate unwillingness either to denigrate or to glorify women's experience and capacities for moral judgment. Those discussing women's oppression also demonstrate unwillingness either to minimize the effects of that oppression or to acquiesce in the view that women are only what oppression has made of us. Nor do they assume that all oppression leads to sex oppression or that sex oppression is always the worst. For many, awareness of sex oppression was preceded by reflection upon oppression by class or ethnic origin, upon such legacies as those of slavery, imperialism, colonialism, the Holocaust, centuries of christian anti-Semitism. Those with explicitly politically informed perspectives are committed, as

Alison Jaggar puts it, to respecting women's experience in its diversity and to the view that women's subordination is wrong. This much is not argued as often as assumed. Yet a measure of this book's merits may be the extent to which as a whole it supports such commitments.

Beyond such relatively abstract widely shared concerns, the essays may appear at first united more by the absence of themes common elsewhere in feminist ethics than by the presence of themes of their own. They offer a symphony of women's voices in which the theme of care, for example, is not dominant, although neither is it absent. Nor are motherhood and reproductive control much discussed here. When mothers are discussed, it is apt to be from the perspective of daughters—as in Annette Baier's "Whom Can Women Trust?" The Amazon spirit comes closer than matriarchy to capturing the animation of this book. Yet what unites the essays is actually more complex: There are many professional friendships among the contributors, between women with diverse ethnic heritages, women of different generations, women who identify publicly as lesbian or heterosexual or who prefer not to identify publicly as either, women who have long and proudly identified as "feminist philosophers" and women who, for various reasons, have not professionally identified themselves as such.

The contributors were raised in Israel, Argentina, England, and New Zealand, as well as on both coasts and in the middle of the United States. At least one has lived in Canada, another in Panama. As indicated, many have interacted at meetings of the Midwest Society of Women in Philosophy during the past two decades and are familiar with each other's work from that context. A few of the essays in this book were presented in earlier versions at SWIP conferences. Some contributors maintain philosophical correspondence with others. Some know each other from professional conferences. Many follow the publications of others. There is overlap and doubling back in these networks of acquaintance and friendship. Such ties contribute a certain cohesiveness to the essays that is not a matter of agreement in positions or even in points of view but occasionally shows itself as a matter of audience: Where writers are aware of each other's positions and points of view, they tend to take such things into account, sometimes explicitly, sometimes implicitly.

One reason these ties are important is that they create an environment in which it is possible to explore in depth questions of and about feminist ethics without having to justify the inquiry. For those who want such justification, the most persuasive response may be a set of essays not preoccupied directly with addressing that want but engaged, rather, in the nitty-gritty of the work itself. The existence of such an environment also makes it possible to encourage philosophers who have not previously written explicitly on feminist ethics to do so in an atmosphere supportive of women's voices and yet receptive to questioning from many points of view.

A NOTE ON STYLE

Stylistic conventions and experiments are found in some of the essays, including parts of this one, that are commoner in contemporary feminist writing than in other philosophical writing. An introductory word of clarification may be useful to forestall misunderstandings in those unacquainted with such heresies.

First, the demise of the allegedly neutral "man" has led to pronomial experiments in formal writing. For more than a decade, many feminists have used "we" in reference to less than universal subsets of humanity among whom we individually include ourselves, without presupposing that readers will always want or be able to include themselves in the same groups. Many women find it self-alienating to say, as we were academically trained to do, "men . . . we" and "women . . . they." It encourages unsympathetic self-understanding to identify with a "we" who were taught to see us as inferior. At the same time, refusing to refer to ourselves in the third person can counteract seductions to the illusion that we are not like our peers—not one of "them." Thus it can be both healing and clarifying to say "we" where we *are* among those we discuss. When such a "we" refers to women, it seldom, if ever, refers to all women. Context is usally relied upon to give a sense of more specific fields of reference.

This reliance has problems of its own and often justifiably provokes the "What do *you* mean by 'we'?" question. "We" used in feminist writing has come under feminist criticism, first, for suggesting false generalizations or categories imperialistically constructed across ethnic and class differences and, second, for presuming to include readers with whom the writer does not in fact engage. Thus some writers prefer to stick as much as possible with "I," avoiding "we" constructions altogether.[55] Others use "we" as often for ethnic as for gender identifications. In spite of real dangers of false construction, many of us still find that ethically a continued use of "we," with responsible attention to its implications, is crucial to our bearings, as we continue to define ourselves interactively and even sometimes find we have, significantly, more than one such self.

The first person plurals encountered in these essays are sometimes thus limited but not totally arbitrary even if their boundaries are neither clear nor uniform. Two further things are worth noting for readers not familiar with the consciously less than universal "we" in formal writing. The practice is not meant to define a readership. First, a reader need not be included in a writer's "we" in order to be addressed by the writer; the reader can just as respectfully be a "you." In the autobiographical spirit explored by Joyce Trebilcot's "Ethics of Method" (chapter 3), many of us often mean to communicate to others what we take to be true specifically of ourselves and assume that this does not mean others will be uninterested. In the spirit of María Lugones's " 'world'-traveling," we may expect readers to enter into points of view not their own.[56] However, at times there is also a significant sense in which a writer does *not* address all intended readers. I refer to the "audience in one's head" as one writes. As targets of oppressive practices, many of us were encouraged to develop what Adrienne Rich calls an "internal censor," learning to communicate only what (one assumes) listeners in positions of social dominance want or are able to hear.[57] Such censorship, habitually practiced, endangers a writer's integrity. In a volume such as this, it would also result in a less interesting set of essays. Many of us discovered in CR groups that some truths emerge more readily in addressing others who, if not situated exactly as we are, at any rate do not occupy positions of social power over us. This means neither that the value of the emergent truths is similarly restricted nor that they are not to be shared. Some readers, used to commanding the attention of at least philosophers, experience a new self-consciousness upon realizing that they are not part of the audience in a writer's head. Such self-consciousness, creation of which can offend if the writer also creates a conflicting expectation of inclusion, can be salutary if combined instead with a realization of inclusion among intended readers.

Second, the demise of "Miss" and "Mrs." has led to experiments with proper names in formal contexts where titles are not used. Some of us prefer to avoid referring to women by patronyms only. In practice this means that even after the first citation, a given name may be used in addition to the surname. For example, I may remain "Claudia Card" instead of becoming just "Card." This practice maintains a lively sense of gender, appropriate enough in this context, as well as avoiding identifying women solely by naming practices that have subordinated us as women. It is, of course, a compromise and thus predictably controversial. It does not come to terms with all subordinating naming practices. And we can seldom identify women nonintimately in this society by names other than patronyms without communicating still greater subordinance (as first names alone do in a society that subordinates children that way).[58] To some of us full names for women in these circumstances seem to come close to communicating the formality and respect that surnames command for men.

CONNECTING THREADS AND A BIRD'S-EYE GLIMPSE

The next five chapters together with this one set a context for those in parts 2 and 3. In "On the Logic of Pluralist Feminism" (chapter 3), María Lugones invites interactive theorizing. She argues that "the problem of difference" is not well understood by those who cast it as a problem of false generalization or of the category construction involved in theorizing. She argues that the most serious problem has been a failure of *interaction* and urges taking seriously a culturally pluralist "we" in the *activity* of theorizing. Joyce Trebilcot supports an autobiographical method of writing, exemplified in her own essay as well as in those immediately preceding and following it. She argues that understanding a writer's history, motivations, and perceived situation in the universe can be crucial to appreciating what the writer has to say. Marilyn Frye's response to (Sarah Lucia Hoagland's) *Lesbian Ethics* and to the idea of lesbian ethics questions whether *ethics* is really what Sarah Hoagland's book offers and whether ethics is really what women need. Probing her own history of concern with being good, she develops a hypothesis about why feminists may sometimes be so desperate to have ethics. The next chapter by Christine Pierce on postmodernism and other skepticisms picks up themes from the preceding essays in pursuing implications of the importance of historical consciousness for the possibility and desirability of theory. Although she sympathizes with certain skepticisms about rationality, she also argues that because the universalization of ethics is unlike that of science, the skepticism of postmodernism should not be assumed to threaten it. Alison Jaggar's survey of problems, projects, and prospects for feminist ethics offers a historical overview and critical analyses of recent styles of ethical inquiry identified by various audiences as "feminist." She argues that some of these appear viable, whereas others are not promising.

Because oppression molds women, we are almost invariably preoccupied with our identities, our selves—in more traditional ethical language, our characters. The essays in part 1 manifest this concern to a considerable extent. The essays in parts 2 and 3 fall perhaps even more clearly into what many call, in the idiom of Anglo-American philosophy, "character ethics." Etymologically, a character is a mark. We are marked in various ways in our attitudes and our habits of choice. Questions about which marks to own with pride, which to try to reclaim, which to reorient, and which to try to erase or submerge are the materials that compose much of feminist ethical reflection. These kinds of questions and related matters are considered in parts 2 and 3.

The essays in part 2 are connected by themes of the possibility of agency, the development and maintenance of character and integrity, and conceptions of the moral self and its concerns. Bat-Ami Bar On, reflecting upon the impact of terrorism on her own life, examines contemporary debates on the ethics of terrorism. Hers is the only chapter with an explicit and direct focus on violence. Her concern, however, is not with the gender of the victims or perpetrators but, rather, with the kinds of people terrorist regimes produce and with what it means that contemporary philosophical debates about terrorism have not addressed that issue. The theme of terrorism leads naturally to thinking about survival. Ruth Ginzberg examines the place of philosophical ethics in survival values, arguing that philosophy is not a luxury with respect to the development of responsible agency in contexts that threaten our survival. Lynne McFall's "What's Wrong with Bitterness?" takes up a deeply troubling attitude produced by profound and sustained misfortune. She argues that although bitterness can be justified, there is finally also reason to

move beyond it. Marilyn Friedman's "The Social Self and the Partiality Debates" examines two difficulties for a social conception of the
self: the difficulty of providing a basis for social criticism and the
difficulty of finding or providing a basis for global moral concern. She
examines recent feminist and nonfeminist critiques of "impartialism" that appeal to social conceptions of the self, arguing that the
feminist critiques tend to be more sensitive to both difficulties,
although the problem of finding or providing a basis in the socially
constructed self for feminists' evident global moral concern remains
a source of perplexity. Victoria Davion's "Integrity and Radical
Change" continues the theme of the social self, exploring implications of feminist revolutions in consciousness, and thereby in fundamental commitments, for the meaning of integrity. She proposes a
way to reconcile the apparently conflicting views of Lynne McFall
and Sarah Hoagland on integrity. She then tests her proposal by
applying it to María Lugones's idea of the pluralist self of bicultural
feminists who are willing to relinquish neither their roots in an
endangered culture, despite its misogyny and antilesbian hostility,
nor their ties to feminist communities that have roots in the imperialist and racialist cultures responsible for endangering the
former.[59]

The final section addresses issues arising out of debates around
the question whether women's voices yield a viable and distinct
aproach or family of approaches to ethics. These essays consider what
is, or should be, involved in attempts to treat women's experiences as
caretakers as data for ethical thinking. In so doing, they often comment on issues arising from the research and hypotheses of Carol
Gilligan. In "Gender and the Complexity of Moral Voices," Michele
Moody-Adams argues that the attempt to find a single gender-specific
moral perspective masks the diversity of women's moral voices and
the complexity of the moral domain. She finds Carol Gilligan's work
insufficiently critical of stereotypical notions that assume that the
biology of sex exhausts a woman's identity. She concludes that the
moral domain cannot be reduced to one—or even two—measures of
significance. In "The Virtue of Feeling and the Feeling of Virtue,"
Elizabeth Spelman asks for whom women have cared. She reminds us
of painful histories of women's mistreatment of other women—as
overseers of enslaved women, as Nazis, as wielders of economic and
sometimes imperialistic power, in the family, at feminist gatherings.

Annette Baier examines a related issue, whether women can trust each other in societies that have systematically subordinated women. She looks critically at Nancy Chodorow's views on the reproduction of mothering, which have been so influential upon Carol Gilligan's theorizing, and at recent reports on Soviet families. Finally, Sarah Hoagland examines in critical detail a feminine analysis of caring developed by Nel Noddings, contrasting it with models of caring not inspired by mother-child bonding. She argues that "a truly radical ethics will challenge not only the masculine but also the feminine."

WHY FEMINIST ETHICS?

As a graduate student, I studied John Rawls's theory of justice, which he characterized as "ideal" theory. By "ideal," he meant that its principles were framed on the assumption that most of the people most of the time could count upon each other to comply with the rules of their mostly just common practices. With an interest in criminal justice, I pursued for awhile his idea that even an ideal society might need to establish penal sanctions to provide a general mutual assurance of goodwill. As I learned more about who had defined and who had borne the burdens of penal sanctions, who had enjoyed and who had borne the burdens of protection, over the centuries, ideal theory with its focus upon the assurance problem seemed less and less relevant to the most pressing ethical issues confronting me.[60] The present inquiries come from and address social contexts far from ideal in justice or anything else, societies in which large numbers of people can count on little but trouble from large numbers of others, where mutual goodwill is yet to be developed. Such a development requires cognitive losses of innocence, peeling back rather than donning veils of ignorance.

Feminist ethics interests me especially in relation to problems of agency under oppression: If oppressive institutions stifle and stunt the moral development of the oppressed, how is it possible, what does it *mean*, for the oppressed to be liberated? What is *there* to liberate? What does it mean to resist, to make morally responsible choices, to become moral agents, to develop character? I see at least four interrelated needs of feminist ethics. Simple to state, they are difficult to fulfill. I list them as though they form a progression. Yet I think it would be a mistake to assume that they must be fulfilled in a particular order. They no doubt need simultaneous and overlapping attention. One, we need to identify our possibilities for agency in oppressive contexts. Two, we need to distinguish modes of resistance that would make our survival and our deeds worthwhile from those that would not. Three, we need to articulate ideals of the person and community that can acknowledge our histories and yet provide bases for pride in ourselves and each other. And four, we need to be alert to the dangers of becoming what we despise.

NOTES

This chapter has benefited from the essays of the contributors to this volume and from the contributors' comments as well as comments from others named and unnamed herein. None, however, is responsible for, nor should be assumed to share, my perspectives. Each contributor speaks for herself in her own essay. At times, I have adopted a contributor's own words or used a near paraphrase to describe her work.

1. Vol. 1, no. 8, pp. 26–28; vol. 1, no. 11, pp. 26–30. A complete set of *The Ladder* was reissued by Arno Press, New York, in 1975. Begun by the San Francisco Daughters of Bilitis, *The Ladder* appeared monthly from October 1956 through September 1972.

2. See Jonathan Katz, ed., *Gay American History: Lesbians and Gay Men in the U.S.A.* (New York: Thomas Crowell, 1976), 425; and Adrienne Rich, "The Problem with *Lorraine Hansberry*," *Freedomways* 19, no. 4 (Fourth Quarter, 1979): 247–255, reprinted in Adrienne Rich, *Blood, Bread, and Poetry: Selected Prose, 1979–1985* (New York: Norton, 1986). Lorraine Hansberry's play, *A Raisin in the Sun*, won the New York Drama Critics Circle Award for the 1958–59 season and was later made into a movie. She was married to (and divorced from) Robert Nemiroff, who was also her literary executor.

3. I advocate this usage. Calling men "feminist" invariably gets a laugh. Recognizing them as profeminist can evoke a more appropriate tinge of fear.

4. Kate Millett, *Sexual Politics* (Garden City, N.Y.: Doubleday, 1970).

5. Alison M. Jaggar, "Feminist Ethics: Problems, Projects, Prospects," chap. 6 of this volume.

6. Midwest SWIP was founded in 1971 when Sandra Bartky and Nancy Holmstrom called a women's caucus at an American Philosophical Association (APA) convention. Since then, Eastern, Pacific, Canadian, and various metropolitan SWIPs have appeared, and Southwest SWIP appeared briefly. Currently, at least one semiannual newsletter is sent to dues payers in several SWIPs.

7. Julia A. Sherman and Evelyn Beck, eds., *The Prism of Sex: Essays in the Sociology of Knowledge* (Madison: University of Wisconsin Press, 1979). This volume includes Kathy Addelson's (then Kathryn Pyne Parsons) "Moral Revolution."

8. That paper exhibited my sexuality no more than this essay. I have written about how and why I came to do such a thing in "Finding My Voice: Reminiscence of an Outlaw" for a projected volume of autobiographical pieces tentatively entitled *Falling in Love with Wisdom*, ed. Robert G. Shoemaker and David D. Karnos (New York: Oxford University Press, 1991), and about the necessity for "coming out" in "Lesbian Battering," *APA Newsletter on Feminism and Philosophy* 88, no. 1 (Nov. 1988): 3–7.

9. See Lynne McFall, *The One True Story of the World* (New York: Atlantic Monthly Press, 1990).

10. On racism in feminist classrooms, see, for example, Susan Geiger and Jacqueline Zita, "White Traders: The Caveat Emptor of Women's Studies," *Journal of Thought* 20, no. 3 (Fall 1985): 106–120.

11. Ti-Grace Atkinson, *Amazon Odyssey* (New York: Links Books, 1974). The anthologies mentioned below were not yet available for classroom use.

12. Judith Jarvis Thompson's challenge to that perspective, in "A Defense of Abortion," *Philosophy and Public Affairs* 1, no. 1 (Fall 1971): 47–66, is discussed in Kathy Addelson, "Moral Revolution," in Julia Sherman and Evelyn Beck, eds., *Prism of Sex.*

13. "Women and Honor" is reprinted in Adrienne Rich, *On Lies, Secrets, and Silence: Selected Prose, 1966–1978* (New York: Norton, 1979), 185–194. For Ruth Bleier's feminist theoretical work, see *Science and Gender: A Critique of Biology and Its Theories on Women* (New York: Pergamon, 1984). Carol Adams recently published *The Sexual Politics of Meat: A Feminist-Vegetarian Critical Theory* (New York: Continuum, 1990); her early essay "The Oedible Complex" was reprinted in *The Lesbian Reader: An Amazon Quarterly Anthology*, ed. Gina Covina and Laurel Galana (Oakland, Calif.: Amazon Press, 1975), 145–152.

14. Between 1975 and 1978, Christine Pierce, Janice Moulton, and Jane English (1947–1982) wrote review essays on feminist philosophy for *Signs: A Journal of Women in Culture and Society*. Marilyn Frye, Sarah Hoagland, and Joyce Trebilcot have contributed to *Sinister Wisdom*.

15. The *Quest* staff published an anthology, *Building Feminist Theory: Essays from Quest* (New York: Longman, 1981), that included essays by Marilyn Frye, Nancy Hartsock, and Janice Raymond.

16. *Sinister Wisdom*, currently subtitled *"A Journal for the Lesbian Imagination in the Arts and Politics,"* was originally edited by Harriet Desmoines and Catherine Nicholson. It has had many editors since. Issue 39, "On Disability," edited by Elana Dykewomon, appeared in the winter of 1989–90. *Conditions*, subtitled *"a magazine of writing by women with an emphasis on writings by lesbians,"* was begun by a collective consisting of Elly Bulkin, Jan Clausen, Irene Klepfisz, and Rima Shore. In 1989, its sixteenth issue, "A Retrospective," collected favorites from the previous twelve years. Volume

17 (1990) was its final issue as a periodical. Future *Conditions* anthologies are planned.

17. Alison M. Jaggar and Paula Rothenberg Struhl, eds., *Feminist Frameworks: Alternative Theoretical Accounts of the Relations between Women and Men* (New York: McGraw-Hill); the first edition appeared in 1978, the second in 1984. Mary Vetterling-Braggin, Frederick A. Elliston, and Jane English, eds., *Feminism and Philosophy*, (Totowa, N.J.: Littlefield, Adams, 1977).

18. Susan Griffin, *Woman and Nature: The Roaring inside Her* (New York: Harper and Row, 1978), and Mary Daly, *Gyn/Ecology: The Metaethics of Radical Feminism* (Boston: Beacon, 1978).

19. The double ax (labrys), battle-ax of the ancient Amazons, became a popular radical lesbian feminist symbol after the Flying Lesbians, a Berlin *Frauenrockband*, decorated their album cover with it in the mid-1970s.

20. Andrea Dworkin's *Woman Hating* (New York: Dutton, 1974), a shorter volume with memorable chapters on pornography and fairy tales, had earlier chapters on Chinese footbinding and European witchburning.

21. It is tempting to invite any who still think feminists lack humor to laugh with Mary Daly. Her observations on women's laughter are now classic (*Gyn/Ecology*, 17).

22. *Gyn/Ecology*, "Conclusion and Afterword to Chapter Seven: Nazi Medicine and American Gynecology: A Torture Cross-Cultural Comparison," 293–312. My objection is to the term "token," not to pointing out that men have had women conspicuously do their dirty work and take the fall for it.

23. Reprinted in Audre Lorde, *Sister/Outsider: Essays and Speeches* (Trumansburg, N.Y.: Crossing, 1984), 66–71.

24. Adrienne Rich, *On Lies, Secrets, and Silence*. Essays especially in the second half include extensive ethical reflection, as do those of *Blood, Bread, and Poetry*. "Disloyal to Civilization" appeared previously in *Chrysalis*.

The term used by feminist writers during this time has been "racism," a shortening of the older term "racialism." I have come to prefer the older term, as it suggests the verb "to racialize," which conveys more readily the idea that "race" is a social construction.

25. *Black Scholar* 9, no. 7 (April 1978).

26. Two, however, had visited my "Feminism and Sexual Politics" class.

27. Nellie McKay is currently a professor of Afro-American studies, English, and Women's Studies at Wisconsin (despite Ivy League offers). Her bibliographies on black women writers are obtainable from the Women's Studies Librarian-at-Large, Memorial Library, University of Wisconsin, Madison.

It may be difficult for readers who attended college after the 1960s' civil rights movement to appreciate how thoroughly white were the curricula of northern midwestern state universities, such as the one I attended from 1958 to 1962. For example, I do not recall being aware of a single work of fiction, history, or philosophy by a black author, female or male, in the assignments of any of my undergraduate courses or even listed among the collateral readings. My graduate school experience, from 1962 to 1966 in New England, was not a significant improvement in that regard.

28. *Women's Studies International Forum* (*WSIF*) 6, no. 6 (1983): 573–581. This was the first of three special issues of *Hypatia* published by *WSIF* before *Hypatia* became independent. The others were vol. 7, no. 5 (1984) and vol. 8, no. 3 (1985). Most of the papers published in these three issues are collected in *Hypatia Reborn: Essays in Feminist Philosophy*, ed. Azizah Y. al-Hibri and Margaret A. Simons (Bloomington: Indiana University Press, 1990).

29. Cherríe Moraga and Gloria Anzaldúa, eds., *This Bridge Called My Back: Writings by Radical Women of Color* (Watertown, Mass.: Persephone, 1981).

30. *In Search of Our Mothers' Gardens* (New York: Harcourt, Brace, Jovanovich, 1983), xii.

31. Katie G. Cannon, *Black Womanist Ethics* (Atlanta, Ga.: Scholars, 1988).

32. Research on Columbus's diaries and relevant historical documents, with an aim to uncover such perspectives and to expose both racialism and misogyny in accounts of European conquerors, is also being done by Margarita Zamora, professor of Spanish at Wisconsin. See also her *Language, Authority, and Indigenous History in the* Comentarios Reales de Los Incas (Cambridge: Cambridge University Press, 1988).

33. Adrian Piper's paper has been published in Owen Flanagan and Amélie Oksenberg Rorty, eds., *Identity, Character, and Morality: Essays in Moral Psychology* (Cambridge, Mass.: MIT Press, 1990).

34. One such conference on the virtues was sponsored by the Philosophy Department of San Diego State University in February 1986.

35. One need not be a member of the MLA to subscribe. Information as of November 1990 is available from Jack Yeager, Treasurer, Gay and Lesbian Caucus of the MLA (GLCMLA), P.O. Box 415, Kittery, Maine 03904.

36. Evelyn Torton Beck, *Nice Jewish Girls: A Lesbian Anthology*, updated and rev. ed. (Boston: Beacon, 1989).

37. These organizations, welcomed at once by the Pacific Division, received official status in 1990 in the Central Division APA.

38. Marilyn Frye, *The Politics of Reality: Essays in Feminist Theory* (Trumansburg, N.Y.: Crossing, 1983); reviewed by me in *Hypatia* 1, no. 1 (Spring 1986): 149–166.

39. Alison M. Jaggar, *Feminist Politics and Human Nature* (Totowa, N.J.: Rowman and Allanheld, 1983).

40. Joyce Trebilcot, ed., *Mothering: Essays in Feminist Theory* (Totowa, N.J.: Rowman and Allanheld, 1983); Adrienne Rich, *Of Woman Born: Motherhood as Experience and Institution* (New York: Norton, 1976).

41. *Trivia*, three times annually since 1982 from Amherst, Massachusetts, has published work by Jan Raymond and Mary Daly. *Lesbian Ethics*, also three times annually since 1982 from New Mexico, has published work by Sarah Lucia Hoagland, Joyce Trebilcot, Marilyn Frye, and me. *Gossip*, five or six issues by Onlywomen Press, London, from about 1986 to 1988, includes

work by Joyce Trebilcot and British sociologist Celia Kitzinger, as well as reprints from *Lesbian Ethics.*

42. I was originally scheduled to chair the session, and Carol Gilligan was scheduled to respond to Annette Baier's paper.

43. See Owen Flanagan and Amélie Rorty, eds., *Identity, Character, and Morality,* for Annette C. Baier, "Why Honesty Is a Hard Virtue," Michele M. Moody-Adams, "On the Old Saw That Character Is Destiny," and my "Gender and Moral Luck."

44. Eva Feder Kittay and Diana T. Meyers, eds., *Women and Moral Theory,* (Totowa, N.J.: Rowman and Littlefield, 1987); reviewed by me in "Women's Voices and Ethical Ideals: Must We Mean What We Say?" *Ethics* 99, no. 1 (Oct. 1988): 125–135.

45. Marsha Hanen and Kai Nielsen, eds., *Science, Morality, and Feminist Theory* (Calgary: University of Calgary Press, 1987), is supplementary volume 13 of the *Canadian Journal of Philosophy.*

46. Helen Longino and Valerie Miner, eds., *Competition: A Feminist Taboo?* (New York: Feminist Press, 1987), includes "Competition, Compassion, and Community: Models for a Feminist Ethos," by María C. Lugones and Elizabeth V. Spelman.

47. Elizabeth V. Spelman, *Inessential Woman: Problems of Exclusion in Feminist Thought* (Boston: Beacon, 1988).

48. See *Lambda Rising Book Report: A Contemporary Review of Gay and Lesbian Literature* 1, no. 11 (June/July 1989), front page, for the first year's winners.

49. Certain issues that were raised for me as I reflected on Sarah Hoagland's book are discussed in my essay "Defusing the Bomb: Lesbian Ethics and Horizontal Violence," *Lesbian Ethics* 3, no. 3 (Summer 1989): 91–100.

50. Sara Ruddick, *Maternal Thinking: Toward a Politics of Peace* (Boston: Beacon, 1989).

51. See Elizabeth V. Spelman, the first two chapters of *Inessential Woman,* and Annette C. Baier, "Trust and Anti-Trust," *Ethics* 96, no. 2 (Jan. 1986): 231–260, and "Hume, the Women's Moral Theorist?" in Eva Kittay and Diana Meyers, eds., *Women and Moral Theory,* 37–55.

52. On "attending," see Sarah Lucia Hoagland, *Lesbian Ethics,* chap. 3; on "preservative love," see Sara Ruddick, *Maternal Thinking,* part 2. Both cite Simone Weil's concept of "attentive love" and Iris Murdoch's discussion of it in *The Sovereignty of Good* (London: Routledge, 1970). On interactive pluralism, see María C. Lugones, "On the Logic of Pluralist Feminism," chap. 2 of this volume.

53. Carol Gilligan, *In a Different Voice: Psychological Theory and Women's Development* (Cambridge, Mass.: Harvard University Press, 1982). See also her "Moral Orientation and Moral Development," in Eva Kittay and Diana Meyers, eds., *Women and Moral Theory,* 19–33; Carol Gilligan, Janie Victoria Ward, Jill McLean Taylor, and Betty Bardige, eds., *Mapping the Moral Domain: A Contribution of Women's Thinking to Psychological Theory and Education* (Cambridge, Mass.: Center for the Study of Gender,

Education, and Human Development, Harvard University Graduate School of Education, 1988); and Carol Gilligan, Nona P. Lyons, and Trudy J. Hanmer, eds., *Making Connections: The Relational Worlds of Adolescent Girls at Emma Willard School* (Troy, N.Y.: Emma Willard School, 1989).

54. See, for example, Elizabeth V. Spelman, "Anger and Insubordination," *Women, Knowledge, and Reality: Explorations in Feminist Philosophy*, ed. Ann Garry and Marilyn Pearsall (Boston: Unwin Hyman, 1989), 263–273; and Marilyn Frye, "A Note on Anger," *Politics of Reality*, 84–94.

55. See, for example, Joyce Trebilcot, "Dyke Methods *or* Principles for the Discovery/Creation of the Withstanding," *Hypatia* 3, no. 2 (Summer 1988): 1–13, and responses in *Hypatia* 5, no. 1 (Spring 1990): 140–144.

56. See María C. Lugones, "Playfulness, 'World'-Traveling, and Loving Perception," *Hypatia* 2, no. 2 (Summer 1987): 3–19.

57. Adrienne Rich, "Problem with *Lorraine Hansberry*."

58. Some women have dropped patronyms altogether, some substituting a mother's given name, as in "Julia Penelope" and "Amber L. Katherine."

59. María Lugones, "Hispaneando y Lesbiando: On Sarah Hoagland's *Lesbian Ethics*," *Hypatia* 5, no. 3 (Fall 1990): 138–146.

60. Rawls, of course, does not claim that ideal theory addresses the most *pressing* issues of social ethics.

Part One
Contexts, Histories, Methods

2 / On the Logic of Pluralist Feminism

MARÍA C. LUGONES

I wrote this paper from a dark place: a place where I see white/ anglo women as "on the other side," on "the light side." From a dark place where I see myself dark but do not focus on or dwell inside the darkness but rather focus on "the other side."

To me it makes a deep difference where I am writing from. It makes a profound difference whether I am writing from the place of our possibilities as companions in play or from the place "in between," the place of pilgrimage, of true liminality; from the place of La Raza, la gente de colores, the place "within," or from across "the other side" where light and dark are highlighted.

I inhabit the place from across "the other side" with anger, pain, urgency, a sense of being trapped, pounding the walls with speech that hurts my own ears. It is from across "the other side" that I want to explore the logic of pluralist feminism.

I am rereading Lorraine Bethel's (1979) "What Chou Mean We, White Girl?" and June Jordan's (1980) "Where Is the Love?" two pieces written about ten years ago, and a layering of voices of women of color comes to my mind, crowding my thinking space: voices that I have heard keenly, attended to with the gladness that fills one when one learns really good news, voices that have accompanied me sweetly. The voices all speak this knowledge to me: One just does not go around alone (lonely maybe), but not individual-style alone making or remaking anything, ignoring the relations one has, the ones one does not have, the good about the good ones, the bad about the bad ones and the good ones. To know oneself and one's situation is to know one's company or lack thereof, is to know oneself with or against others.

I want to surround you with some of the voices that commit me to this knowledge and ask you to keep them with you as I explain the difference that lacking this knowledge makes while theorizing. When Audre Lorde (1984) tells us that "interdependency between women is the only way to the freedom which allows the 'I' to 'be,' not in order to be used, but in order to be creative," she is offering us her visionary turn on this knowledge. Interdependency between women is the being with others that is necessary if we are to remake ourselves into active, creative selves. Lorde knows the company she wants to keep and why. Lorraine Bethel (1979) also knows the company she wants to keep, what comes from keeping this or that company, who she wants to be, and how that is related to the company she keeps. Bethel says:

I am so tired of talking to others
translating my life for the deaf, the blind,
. . . while we wonder where the next meal, job, payment on our
    college loans and other bills,
apartment, the *first* car, Black woman–identified bookstore,
    health center, magazine,
bar, record company, newspaper, press, forty acres and a mule, or
    national conference
are going to come from.
They will come from us loving/speaking *to* our Black/Third
    World sisters, not *at* white women.

In a calm refusal to assimilate, Ines Hernandez Tovar (1977) tells us about patient, painstaking, interactive self-knowledge and self-affirmation. She tells us of the creation of a reality that is good to the self that is interactively known and affirmed. She says, "And we will take our time / to make our time / count / clocks / do not intimidate us." She speaks of a collective action, a patient action ("*we* will take *our* time"). It is an act of collective creation ("to *make* our time"). The act of collective creation is performed within another reality, and it is the collective creation of a reality where *we* count.

June Jordan's (1980) understanding of anyone's "life supportive possibilities" is highly interactive. She says:

And it is against such sorrow, and it is against such deliberated strangulation of the possible lives of women, of my sisters, and of powerless peoples—men and children—everywhere, that I work and live, now, as a feminist trusting that I will learn to love myself well enough to love you (whoever you are), well enough so that you will love me well enough so that we will know, exactly, where is the love.

Genny Lim (1981) knows woman as a "house with echoing rooms" only through this knowledge: the knowledge of one's company:

> Sometimes I stare longingly at women who I will never know/ Generous, laughing women with wrinkled cheeks and white teeth/Dragging along chubby, rosy-cheeked babies on fat, wobbly legs/Sometimes I stare at Chinese grandmothers getting on the 30 Stockton with shopping bags/Japanese women tourists in European hats/Middle-aged mothers with laundry carts/Young wives holding hands with their husbands/Lesbian women holding hands in coffee-houses/Smiling debutantes with bouquets of yellow daffodils/Silver-haired matrons with silver rhinestoned poodles/Painted prostitutes posing along MacArthur Boulevard/Giddy teenage girls snapping gum in fast cars/Widows clutching bibles, crucifixes/I look at them and wonder if/they are a part of me/I look in their eyes and wonder if/They share my dreams.

What United States women of color know is something that I want to find in feminist theorizing. To make clearer what it is that we know and what difference it makes in theorizing, I will take us back to Bethel's question "What Chou Mean *We*, White Girl?" I will take you through my understanding of white/anglo feminist theorists' answers to it. In doing so I want to see if I can answer three questions: What is the "problem of difference"? How do we theorize once we recognize "the problem of difference"? And does the "problem of difference" affect only some feminist theorizing? I hope that this essay will make clear that the logic of all theorizing is affected by a recognition of difference. This is one of the lessons uncovered by the knowledge of women of color, the knowledge of one's company. If I am right, it is not just those who theorize about difference who need to worry about it when theorizing. Difference makes the kind of difference that makes inappropriate the theoretical division of labor between those of us who work on difference and those of us who don't.

White women used to simply and straightforwardly ignore difference. In their theorizing, they used to speak as if all women *as women* were the same. Now white women recognize the problem of difference. Whether they *recognize* difference is another matter. As white women are beginning to acknowledge the problem in their theorizing, it is interesting to see that the acknowledgment is a noninteractive one, or at least there is no clear emphasis on interactive acknowledgment. I hope this claim will become clearer. If the acknowledgment is noninteractive, the knowledge that I want to see in feminist theorizing is missing.

The initial claim seems to be that "there are many ways of being, but we can still theorize about women if we acknowledge in some way or other that not everything we say is true of all women." One way of doing this is through the disclaimer. When I read theories about mothering, constructions of the moral domain, constructions of the self, and so on, that are prefaced by disclaimers about the universality of the theoretical claims, I am left at sea as to whether I am to take what I am reading as anthropological or sociological field reports. After the disclaimer, nothing again indicates that difference has been recognized. The logic of the discourse emphasizes ignoring difference and acknowledging a singularity of practice, discipline, or construction. One such disclaimer puts it interestingly and I choose it not because what I have to say applies only to this author, but because the way the author puts the disclaimer captures the situation so well. The author announces that she is working within "the limits of her own particular social and sexual history" (Ruddick, 1984). The disclaimer leaves the reader either within or without these limits. From within these limits everything seems complete and rounded, the discourse gentle and comfortingly safe. From without these limits the theoretical construction appears dangerous. The responsibility for corrections, the author tells us, is left to the reader or interlocutor who is outside these limits, as if the logic of correcting views from outside these limits were clear. So the disclaimer just serves as an announcement that the author will not accept responsibility for the effects of her own particular "social and sexual history" on others.

Most of the time what the theory proposes is not just a description of a particular practice or a particular construction or reconstruction of people. Most of the time a prescription is included. But a prescription *for whom?* How is one who lies outside the limits to correct the prescription? How is one to tell that the discourse that produced this prescription is friendly to oneself? Who is the author in her own eyes with respect to us? Who is the author in our eyes? Who are we in the author's eyes? Why does the author think that all we need to do is to correct the prescription? Why does the author just leave us to write another paper on the subject, but one that is *dependent* on hers even though she does not really acknowledge us? Why does she think she is justified in doing that? Why doesn't she realize that what she is doing is exercising authority and that the authority she would exercise, if we are not careful, is *authority over us?*

I hope it is becoming clearer to you that what I think is significantly missing in much of the work that attempts to acknowledge difference is the *interactive* step. I began by pointing out to you how much difference exists between the work of U.S. women of color and the work of white women in this respect. U.S. women of color know we are different, we have never attempted to tell white women that women are all alike, we have not had the imperialist eye. U.S. women of color have always had an interactive emphasis in our interest in difference: We recognize racism and racism is an *interactive* phenomenon. At the international level, *cultural imperialism* is the interactive phenomenon. I think the two are quite different. Among other things, it is possible not to quite notice cultural imperialism when you are a victim of it, because it is so impersonal. There is no person-to-person mistreatment to make it clear that one is about to be erased from the discourse by being asked to speak in or to listen to a universal voice. There are other interactions where difference plays a significant part. I think they all need to be thought about *in their own right.* These interactions cannot be conflated and confused with each other under the label "difference." What interests many U.S. women of color is the formation of a feminism that overcomes racism, and racism is an emphatically interactive phenomenon. Our interest in theorizing is importantly guided by this concern.

In hearing the "What Chou Mean *We*, White Girl?" question, white/anglo women theorizers did not really hear an interactive demand, a demand for an answer. Looking at the resulting theoretical responses, it seems to me that what they heard was a radical attack on the activity of white women theorizing, an attack that seemed justified to them but that also seemed to them to undermine fundamentally the possibility of any theorizing to the extent that it requires generalization. I think that this interpretation of the question generated the "problem of difference." In hearing the "What Chou Mean We, White Girl?" question and in uttering our many versions of it, U.S. women of color heard and uttered an attack on white racism: Racist feminism does not see the violence done to women of color in denying that we are women or in requiring (what other alternative did their views on women leave us?) that we assimilate if we are to be women at all. I think the difference in emphasis is significant. I think the logic of the difference in emphasis is theoretically significant.

What is the theoretical significance of the difference in understandings of the question? And why did white/anglo feminist theorists hear the demand for an answer in this way? I think that racism played and plays tricks on white women theorists who theorize about difference or who theorize and are aware that they should attempt to overcome the alleged problem of difference in their theorizing. I hope to answer both of these questions by describing these tricks. I have chosen not to exhibit the tricks in particular cases because I want to remain "outside the limits."

In saying that racism plays tricks on white women theorists, I mean not only the contextual racism in which they theorize but also the racism within, the one from which they theorize. So the racism and the theorizer are not separable just as the theorizer and the context of theorizing are not quite separable.

To prepare the ground, I will begin by describing a trick that predates hearing the "What Chou Mean We, White Girl?" question. This trick is easy to describe, and it is very familiar to most women theorizing about women: Women of color always knew that white women and women of color were different; white women all knew that they were different from women of color. But white women never considered the differences important, because they did not really notice us. So they theorized as if all women were the same. One can try to explain away this lack of noticing in many ways related to the received methodologies, but if white women theorists had noticed us, they would have rejected the methodologies. There are, of course, many reasons for this failure to notice us, but they all seem constitutive of racism. Elizabeth Spelman's work is remarkable among white feminist theorists in uncovering the many faces of feminist racism's resilience in this respect. "I look at you," Spelman (1988) says, "and come right back to myself. White children in the U.S. got early training in boomerang perception when they were told by well-meaning white adults that Black people were just like us— never, however, that we were just like Blacks."

The second trick that racism played/plays on white women theorists is conceiving this lack of noticing us as a theoretical problem, which they label the "problem of difference." This is a more complicated trick. Notice that many white women theorizers have heard the "What Chou Mean *We*, White Girl?" loud and clear and are attempting to *interpret* the question and find an answer to it. But white women theorists seem to have worried more passionately about the harm the claim does to theorizing than about the harm the theorizing did to women of color. I say this because even when they heard this claim, they did not notice us. Thus white theorizers interpreting the question saw a problem with the way they were theorizing: The "problem of difference" refers to feminist theories—these theories are the center of concern. Thus the attempted solutions to the "problem of difference" try to rescue feminist theorizing from several possible pitfalls that would render it false, trivial, weak, and so on. The focus of the solutions is on how to generalize without being guilty of false inclusion. The solutions seem incorrect to me because they are addressing the wrong problem.

But the white theorist has been/is also tricked by racism in another way that accompanies the second trick. The white woman theorist did not notice us yet, her interpretation of the question placed the emphasis on theorizing itself, and the generalizing and theorizing impulse led the white theorizer to *think of all differences as the same,* that is, as underminers of the truth, force, or scope of their theories. Here racism has lost its character and particular importance—a clear sign that we have not been noticed. This trick does not allow the theorizer to see, for example, the need to differentiate among racism, colonialism, and imperialism, three very different interactive phenomena.

But what would it be to be noticed? We are noticed when you realize that we are mirrors in which you can see yourselves as no other mirror shows you. When you see us without boomerang perception, to use Spelman's wonderful phrase. It is not that we are the only faithful mirrors, but I think we *are* faithful mirrors. Not that we show you as you *really* are; we just show you as one of the people you are. What we reveal to you is that you are many—something that may in itself be frightening to you. But the self we reveal to you is also one that you are not eager to know for reasons that one may conjecture.

You block identification with that self because it is not quite consistent with your image of yourself. As Marilyn Frye (n.d.) puts it in "Points of Explosion and Ritual Libations: White Feminists Cope with Racism": "Whitely people have a staggering faith in their own rightness and goodness, and that of other whitely people." But you do not expect us to show a self that is good, decent, sensitive, careful in your attending to others. You block identification because remembering that self fractures you into more than one person. You know a self that is decent and good and knowing your self in our mirror frightens you with losing your center, your integrity, your oneness.

You block identification with that self because that person you are is also a mirror for us and that person constructs us as people whose standpoint you find disquieting: angry phantoms or pliable puppets. But whether phantoms or puppets, we are beings whose rules cannot be yours because your rules are used against us.

You block identification with that self we mirror for you because knowing us in the way necessary for you to know that self requires self-conscious interaction. Your fear of duplicity directs you to forget all interaction that we have had because that interaction, when lived and remembered as interaction, reveals yourself to yourself as a duplicitous being. So you are inattentive to our interactions. You are not keenly attentive to what our interactions might reveal.

You block identification with that self because knowing us in the way necessary to know that self would reveal to you that we are also more than one and that not all the selves we are make you important. Some of them are quite independent of you. Being central, being a being in the foreground, is important to your being integrated as one responsible decision maker. Your sense of responsibility and decision-making are tied to being able to say exactly who it is that did what, and that person must be one and have a will in good working order. And you are very keen on seeing yourself as a decision maker, a responsible being: It gives you substance.

You block identification with that self because you are afraid of plurality: Plurality speaks to you of a world whose logic is unknown to you and that you inhabit unwillingly. It is a world inhabited by beings who cannot be understood given your ordinary notions of responsibility, intentionality, voluntariness, precisely because those notions presuppose that each person is one and that each person (unless mad or in a madlike state or under someone's power) can effectively inform her actions with preferred descriptions that include intentionality, and do so all by herself. All other ways of being are outside value, outside worth, outside goodness, outside intelligibility.

In blocking identification with that self, you block identification with us and in blocking identification with us, you block identification with that self. You are in part what we make you up to be and we are in part what you make us up to be. You may not "identify" with that self, but you can't help animating it. You may not want to think about that self, but not thinking about that self leads you not to know what U.S. women of color know:—that self-knowledge is interactive, that self-change is interactive. You cannot shake that self and you cannot infuse that self with the trappings of responsibility. But you can acknowledge her and imbue her fully with ambiguity. We can't shake the selves that we are in your eyes or in your worlds; we do not just animate them *in spite* of ourselves. We are them too: beings with a peculiar lack of substance or lack of credibility or too frightening and intimidating, too dramatic, too predictable, with too much or too little authority:—all out of proportion, not fully real. I can't will not to animate that being. That is not up to me. But I can imbue that being with ambiguity; I can imbue myself with ambiguity. In doing that, I can thereby enact a creative strategy of resistance only when ambiguity is understood and appreciated.

When I do not see plurality stressed in the very structure of a theory, I know that I will have to do lots of acrobatics—like a contortionist or tight-rope walker—to have this theory speak to me without allowing the theory to distort me *in my complexity.*

When I do not see plurality in the very structure of a theory, I see the phantom that I am in your eyes take grotesque forms and mime crudely and heavily your own image. Don't you?

When I do not see plurality in the very structure of a theory, I see the fool that I am mimicking your image for the pleasure of noticing that you know no better. Don't you?

When I do not see plurality in the very structure of a theory, I see the woman of color that I am speaking precisely and seriously in calm anger as if trying to shatter thick layers of deafness accompanied by a clean sense of my own absurdity. Don't you?

When I do not see plurality in the very structure of a theory, I see myself in my all-raza women's group in the church basement in Arroyo Seco, Nuevo Mejico, suddenly struck dumb, the theoretical words asphyxiating me. Don't you?

When you do not see plurality in the very structure of a theory, what do you see?

REFERENCES

Bethel, Lorraine. 1979. "What Chou Mean *We*, White Girl?" In *Conditions: Five* 11, no. 2 (Autumn 1979): 86–92.

Frye, Marilyn. N.d. "Points of Explosion and Ritual Libations: White Feminists Cope with Racism" (unpublished manuscript).

Hernandez Tovar, Ines. 1977. "On Hearing UT Football Fans on the Drag," *Ta Cincho.*

Jordan, June. [1980]. 1990. "Where Is the Love?" In *Making Face, Making Soul—Haciendo Caras: Creative and Critical Perspectives by Women of Color,* ed. Gloria Anzaldúa, 174–176. San Francisco: Aunt Lute.

Lim, Genny. 1981. "Wonder Woman." In *This Bridge Called My Back: Writings by Radical Women of Color,* ed. Cherríe Moraga and Gloria Anzaldúa. New York: Kitchen Table: Women of Color Press.

Lorde, Audre. 1984. "The Master's Tools Will Never Dismantle the Master's House." In *Sister/Outsider: Essays and Speeches,* 110–113 (Trumansburg, N.Y.: Crossing Press.

Ruddick, Sara. 1983. "Maternal Thinking." In *Mothering: Essays in Feminist Theory,* ed. Joyce Trebilcot, 213–230. Totowa, N.J.: Rowman and Allanheld.

Spelman, Elizabeth V. 1988. *Inessential Woman: Problems of Exclusion in Feminist Thought.* Boston: Beacon.

3 / Ethics of Method: Greasing the Machine and Telling Stories

JOYCE TREBILCOT

I remember a dim, paneled office at Bryn Mawr College. It was my first philosophy teaching job and I would often stay late after classes talking with a colleague, an ambitious young male assistant professor. I was struggling to finish my dissertation, so late one winter afternoon he told me about his own, completed several years earlier: "I spent lots of pages," he said, "on motivation." A shock went through me. Motivation! Could this be someone who understood, someone who shared my obsession about which topics were worth studying and why?

But my excitement dissipated as I came to understand that by "motivation" this man meant merely the reasons why his problem was significant for the development of theory, not for him personally. The dissertation pages he referred to as about "motivation" discussed philosophical, not personal, difficulties that gave rise to the problem he studied. In contrast, motivation for me was a matter of how a particular issue was connected with who I am and who I want to be—a matter of why *I* should be working on *this* topic. Motivation for my colleague was just about theories; for me, it was about my relationships to theories. This distinction was based, I think, on the fact that my colleague accepted without question or much consciousness an array of values presupposed by the theoretical framework within which philosophy is done, whereas I was uncomfortable with those values (they were, after all, made to fit him and not me) and needed to articulate and examine them.

I was not able to even begin doing so until a few years later, when feminist ideas were first being developed in academe. Now, in the context of feminist and lesbian feminist thought, I continue to be concerned with values presupposed by doing theory and with motives for working on a particular issue in a partiuclar way. I am interested not only in my own motives but also in those of other writers: Why does a feminist choose some topics and approaches and not others?

THE MACHINE

The ideology of dominant western (white, male, capitalist) culture is like a huge and complex machine that requires continual oiling and fixing, continual attention from hundreds of workers whose job it is to maintain and repair the machine and to keep it adjusted to changes and challenges from within and without. Academics (those academics who are mainly researchers and writers rather than teachers) are trained and supported by society to do the technical work required to keep the machine running.

These maintenance jobs usually provide a moderately good salary, some prestige in mainstream culture, and relatively comfortable working conditions. They also offer the possibility of projecting parts of one's own personality into reality. That is, an academic may develop a bit of theory that actually becomes part of the general ideology, at least for awhile. Although this sort of immortality is rare, its promise, I think, keeps many scholars and researchers at what is often tedious, boring work.

In addition, academics often engage in conventional scholarship because they sense, more or less consciously, that the machine they tinker with, whether or not they actually contribute parts to it, operates in their interest. In the United States, these academics are white, upper- and middle-class men and those who identify with them (including a few women and men of color and white women). Although the academics know that the machine benefits them, and to some extent how it does so, most do not *say* that it does, even to themselves, because to notice would be to admit that there are others whose interests it does not serve.

Thus those who work on the machine tend not to write about motivation in the sense that interests me, that is, by describing their personal, experiential, evaluative connection with the ideology. (But there are exceptions—for example, Descartes.) For most of them, as for my colleague at Bryn Mawr, motivation for studying a particular problem is not a matter of *consciously* making a fit between one's own values and reality.

STORIES

But what about those of us who are mashed to pieces by the big machine? We are inclined to articulate into reality ways of thinking, acting, feeling—ways of being—that make real *our* experiences and benefit *us* or that do the same for others excluded from dominant ideology. Our inspiration comes, it seems to me, from a need for authentic accounts of the selves and worlds that the machine mashes.

The issues we choose to work on often come out of our particular experiences, from our particular places in society, from our sense of relationship with other women. An incest survivor may analyze the family in order to show how it promotes abuse; a Chicana may write about her background to make clear where she comes from; a white woman may examine racism because of what it does to women of color. Sometimes in such writings, the author's motivation is clear even without specific focus on it. Sometimes—and I find these works especially rich—the author gives explicit account of the particular aspects of her life and values that led her to make the theory she presents.

In this sort of writing, there need be no pretense that what is said is "universally" or "objectively" true. An author may present her own story as one of many possible and actual stories—other women are likely to have different accounts, and so is she in different circumstances—and different accounts have different values. Some stories tell a woman that she is not alone; some bring together women with similar experiences or interests; some give directions or clues for making changes; some offer new ideas or information; some make translucent what had been opaque. Some accounts may be of value only to the author, as a stepping-stone; others are valued by several women or many. The idea is not to discover "the truth" and, competitively, to present it more clearly or forcefully or completely than anyone else; it is, rather, to contribute one's own words, insights, speculations, jokes, to feminist realities.

Indeed, in my experience, in writing that includes accounts of an author's motives, questions of truth tend to give way to questions of honesty. Because under the pressures of patriarchy it is a struggle for women to be honest with ourselves, I want to remember when I am writing to ask: Do I contemplate these ideas in feminist consciousness or as I have been taught in patriarchy to do? Do I think the succession of ideas myself or do I follow patriarchal patterns of words drummed into me? Do I remember all that happened or is some of it too painful? Am I trying to prove that I made a choice in order to feel freer when in fact I was forced? Am I giving false reasons for what I *did* choose in order to appear more acceptable to myself or to others? Am I omitting parts of my story because I am embarrassed? And so on.

Of course, even if I am able to relate a story fully and without self-deception, there may be good reasons for not doing so. What if my mother reads this? My partner? My friends? The people I work with? My employer? Sometimes concern about the reactions of others is exaggerated: What I was scared to say may, to my surprise, evoke little or no response or be accepted with understanding and support. In other cases, though, there is danger in honesty. When women tell the truth about ourselves, other people sometimes do withdraw their respect, their love, their money.

One way to avoid such consequences may be to tell one's story as fiction. In fiction, one can work out parts of one's life on paper but then claim that it is "only a story." This approach may succeed to some extent in fooling others—or oneself. I may discover only later that what I have written about a character is in some sense true of me or of someone close to me.

But I am concerned here with "feminist theory"—or, for plurality and process, "feminist theorizings"—not fiction. I am saying that I like theorizings to include accounts of what in the author's experience leads her to her topic and connects with her beliefs about it. There are not many models for such work: bell hooks' *Talking Back: Thinking Feminist, Thinking Black* shows such connections, and so do the writings of Sonia Johnson. Much of what is called feminist theory, however, follows the academic tradition of deliberately impersonal prose. (I myself tend to write in academic style; it is a method trained into me and very hard to eject.) It is no accident, of course, that many beloved feminist theorists are not professional academics and so are not subject to the academy's tendency toward (insistence on) antifeminist methods.

My idea of feminist theory, then, is that it consists of all our stories—contradicting, overlapping, emotional (and, hence, not comprising a "machine"). I believe that each woman, not just those who identify as theorists or writers, have stories of value to others.

But why call storytelling "theorizing"? A theory is supposed to be general or universal; it is supposed to propose or claim something about many individuals, not just one. But this concept of theory belongs to the kind of thought that has us strung out in the first place, to the kind of thought that assigns to the writer the role of God. Atheistic goddess-feminism needs none of it.

Stories, even if "about" only one person, have implications for others as well. A story that makes sense of part of a woman's life includes accounts—"analyses"—of how she is connected to people and practices and institutions around her—and there are lots of general claims in that. So, one might say, feminism reconstructs the concept of theory as an account of reality that does not move either inductively or deductively between the general and the particular but, rather, sites the general in the particular. Someone trained in philosophy might say something like that.

I, however, would not. Indeed, I suspect that the idea of theory repels or attracts on the basis of elitism: One woman likes the idea of "doing theory" because it sounds important (I include myself here); another thinks (usually correctly) that those who claim to do theory are trying to show that they are better than someone else. So I would prefer to abandon the idea of theory/theorizings and speak instead of telling stories. Anyone can tell her story, stories may be true and made up in various proportions; they can be mainly about just one person or about many or about everyone; and they tell more than they say. They include analyses and show motives. They entertain, explain, connect, emancipate. Anyone can take whatever she wants from them in the process of making her own stories/realities/selves, and we can together draw on them in making cultures. Yes, for me it definitely makes more sense to talk about stories than about theories or theorizings.

"ETHICS"

I find writing of the sort I have been discussing here so valuable, so much preferable to academic treatments of ideas, that—if I were to support the concept of "ethics" for lesbian and feminist work (it is too hierarchical for me)—I would be inclined to support an "ethics of method" that includes the idea that it is good when feminists and lesbians write about aspects of reality by telling stories, that is, by saying what they have to say in terms of their lives and the lives of women they care about. But I have decided not to try to persuade other women to adopt my values as their own, so I say only that I do very much value such writing.

If many lesbian and feminist writers were to decide to adopt such a value, one advantage might be that some of the more boring women's studies work would never get written—for example, a scholar thinking about how her subject connects with her own daily life, or with her neighbor's or her sister's, might decide that it doesn't and so shift her energies to a subject closer to her heart, which would surely make for livelier writing. Also, putting the writer in the work helps the reader to understand: If a sociologist writes about right-wing women, I want to know whether she does so because she herself is one, because she is merely curious, because she is a radical who writes out of the pain of having some women so distant from her, or for some other reason. Knowing a writer's motive helps me to make sense of what she says.

Sometimes in their works or in contributors' notes, lesbian and feminist writers explicitly identify themselves in terms of variables such as race, class, age, and region. I want this kind of information when I read, but as I suggest here, I also want more particular information. In a consciousness-raising group I belonged to in the early seventies that consisted of women philosophers (mostly graduate students), I remember discussing a text by a male philosopher and one of the women saying: "If the author were a woman, she would say what is bothering her." I have not forgotten Karen Lucas's remark because it captures for me a precious aspect of feminist and lesbian method. We lesbian and feminist authors often *do* say what is bothering us, which usually has to do with our *particular* thoughts, feelings, and experiences.

As for this essay, I write it to "justify" the kind of work I like best to do. I like working best—at least in this part of my life—when I am making sense of my secrets. When I write out of memory and emotion and make new connections among them and connect them with concepts and values—then the work is most like what I have always wanted to do, and doing it feels good.

Back at Bryn Mawr, it had not occurred to me to include in my dissertation why I chose to write about emotion. It had not occurred to me because, in order to get the Ph.D., I had to write in the voice of one who is simply trying to understand and improve the system of concepts about emotion, in the voice of a maintenance man. Now I try to be free of that constraint so that I can connect philosophizing with everyday life (such a simple idea) and, as I have said, I like it a lot when other writers do, too.

NOTE FOR THOSE CONCERNED
WITH ACADEMIC PHILOSOPHY

In the terms of mainstream academic philosophy as taught in the United States, the approach that I praise here may be taken to involve a fallacy of relevance: a genetic fallacy (taking the origin of an idea to be relevant to its truth) or, more particularly, an *argumentum ad hominem* (an "argument directed to the man," in which something about one's "opponent" or his circumstances is said to show the falsity of his belief). An example from a standard textbook: "To argue that proposals are bad or assertions false because they are proposed or asserted by Communists . . . is to argue fallaciously and to be guilty of committing an *argumentum ad hominem.*"[1] My belief is that it is often better just to try to understand what someone is saying than to judge it as good or bad, true or false, but that insofar as evaluating does occur or is appropriate, it is usually helped by knowing where the author is coming from. What the fallacies of relevance reject, I value.

NOTES

My thanks to Claudia Card for several suggestions on this essay.

1. Irving M. Copi, *Introduction to Logic*, 3d ed. (London: Macmillan, 1968).

4 / A Response to Lesbian Ethics: Why Ethics?

MARILYN FRYE

In conjunction with the publication of her book *Lesbian Ethics*,[1] Sarah Hoagland gave a number of talks to lesbian community audiences around the country. At one of those talks, I was called upon to do the introduction: "We are hungry for ethics"—I began—"We crave moral clarity." This line was well received by the audience it was written for; it seemed to speak the feelings of many of those present. I proceeded, saying that patriarchal fathers feed that hunger with an ethics of rules that works like junk food—temporarily and deceptively soothing the longing without meeting the need. Enjoying my metaphor, I went on to say that what *Lesbian Ethics* offered was the equivalent of delicious bran muffins. Sarah Hoagland's book is indeed tasty and expeditious food for thought. But in suggesting that it provides an ethics that meets our need for ethics, I was very much oversimplifying—indeed, I now think, falsifying both our need and what the book might accomplish.

I spoke of a hunger for ethics. Why the hunger and whose hunger is it? I was speaking of something I recognized in myself and in many of the women in my lesbian community. The first thing that comes to mind to explain why such women are hungry for ethics is that both as feminists and as lesbians, we have in significant ways and degrees rejected and abandoned the values we grew up with, many of the values that are central to the cultures in which, willy-nilly, we live and work. Thus we are trying now to make decisions, choices, and judgments pretty much without the guidance of a system of values we can accept and endorse. We fall back, of course, as Sarah Hoagland points out, into habits of action and interaction that express the values of patriarchy, but we are very displeased when we realize we have done that. We want a new and different ethics to fill the void so we will have a positive alternative and can know what to do and have some confidence when we do act that we have done rightly.

But this does not answer my question. I'm wondering about our need to know what to do and our having confidence that we have acted rightly. Not why we feel we need a *new* ethics, but why we need an ethics at all. I'm wondering if that need itself isn't something that could be given up, indeed, if I dare say so, perhaps *should* be given up.

My intuition is that the need for an ethics is race, class, and history specific, that ethics is a practice and institution that would arise only among people occupying certain positions in certain social orders. That is too grand a theory to argue for here. But at least one need for an ethics is characteristic only of people with an investment of a certain sort in being good and/or in others' being good, in doing the right thing, being right, or being in the right. Not everyone at every time has such an investment. I will briefly discuss here two reasons why a woman, white, christian-cultured, and educated, in our times, in the United States, would tend to have a need for ethics. Both of these reasons are such that exploring them suggests it would be a good idea not to try to satisfy the need but to try to grow out of it.

In an earlier paper, I articulated such a need quite dramatically. It was in the context of a crisis in my effort to respond constructively to criticism of myself and my work as racist. I had come to realize that not only my acts but my capacities for self-criticism and correction were contaminated by racism and that therefore there seemed to be no way to fix what was wrong with me. I wrote:

> It all combined to precipitate me into profound and unnerving distrust of myself. All of my ways of knowing seemed to have failed me—my perception, my common sense, my good will, my anger, honor and affection, my intelligence and insight. Just as walking requires something fairly sturdy and firm underfoot, so being an actor in the world requires a foundation of ordinary moral and intellectual confidence. Without that, we don't know how to be or how to act; we become strangely stupid. . . . If you want to be good, and you don't know good from bad, you can't move.[2]

The phrase that strikes me—even when I first wrote it, it stood out as peculiar—is "don't know how to be or how to act." It suggests that before these developments in my personal and political life, I knew how to be and how to act. How, one might wonder, did I know to be and know to act? And on what had I based my "ordinary moral confidence"?

A description of what might be thought of as being taught moral confidence was given by Minnie Bruce Pratt in her essay in *Yours in Struggle*. Describing the orientation to matters of right and wrong with which she had been raised, she says: "I was taught to be a *judge*, of moral responsibility and of punishment only in relation to *my* ethical system; was taught to be a *martyr*, to take all responsibility for change, *and* the glory, to expect others to do nothing; was taught to be a *peacemaker*, to mediate, negotiate, between opposing sides because *I* knew the right way; was taught to be a *preacher*, to point out wrongs and tell others what to do."[3]

I was taught something like this growing up in a small town south of the mason-dixon line in an upwardly mobile and self-consciously christian and white family. I learned that I and "we" knew right from wrong and had the responsibility to see to it that right was done; that there were others, who did not know what is right and wrong and should be advised, instructed, helped, and directed by us. What I was being taught, in effect, as Carolyn Shafer puts it, is that Right makes Might. Not that Might makes Right. The other way around. I was being taught that *because* one knows what is right, it is morally appropriate to have and exercise what I now would call race privilege and class privilege—to dominate others. Only we did not think of it as "dominating." Knowing right from wrong is what constitutes one as a sort of agent in the world. One *understands* one's agency *as* that of the judge, teacher/preacher, director, administrator, manager, and in this mode, as a decision maker, planner, policymaker, organizer. Such a person knows how to be and how to act. Such a person is self-trusting with respect to moral sensibilities.

This is clearly a cultural context in which individuals would have a vital investment in knowing what is right and wrong, in being right, in being in the right. Knowing this is constitutive of the kind of agency such persons understand and animate.

If one is not simply white/christian/middle-class/"american" but also a woman, there is a nasty twist in the middle of this pretty picture. Judging, preaching, directing, administering, managing, policymaking, are not feminine vocations. In the scheme of the upright, educated, christian gentry, this sort of agency is male. The women of this group have—perhaps since sometime in the last century—tended to divide up into those who accept the feminine parallel vocation of motherhood and community service and those who are ambitious for the "full personhood" held by the males of that social-racial group. Those who are ambitious may become either Athenas or feminists. If one gets a certain sort of male sponsorship, becomes a Daddy's girl, one is allowed to function in these vocations of the righteous—so long, that is, as one is doing things one's sponsors approve of. In this case, one's rightness is not really one's own but is one's sponsors' rightness. One's authority is effective only so long as one identifies wholly with the sponsors.[4] What happens for the feminist is that she somehow discovers her *own* authority and comes to understand herself as authorized by her *own* knowledge of right and wrong to assume the agency of judge, director, instructor, planner, policymaker, administrator.

This feminist—white, christian-cultured, educated, born or assimilated into the middle class—is someone with a doubly determined investment in knowing what is right and wrong. Her knowledge of right and wrong is constitutive of how she conceives her agency, and that it is her *own* knowledge is the key to her conceiving her agency *as her own.*

Well, no wonder she is completely demoralized and petrified by the discovery that she does not, after all, know right from wrong. And no wonder this woman hungers for ethics. She craves clarity and confidence about what are the right ways to act and to be with the whole energy of her passion for Being, for Presence, for Ability.

But only people situated just so in culture, economy, and history ground their understanding of their agency in being right, righteous, and in the right:—namely, those people who must have a foundation for assuming the direction and administration of everything. And Lesbian Nation does not need a class of citizens whose vocation is to run it. And if we can do without such a class of citizens and thus without such a conception of agency, we will not have a need for ethics.

In the quotation I drew from my earlier work coping with the discovery of my racism, there is another phrase that directs us to a second source of the need for ethics. I said, "If you want to be good, and you don't know good from bad, you can't move." At that time, in that context, I very much wanted to be good. I wanted to view myself as good and to be perceived as good; but I also simply wanted to *be* good.

Why should one want to be good? Why, in particular, would a woman want to be good?

We may recall some of the message of Mary Daly's *Gyn/Ecology*.[5] A great deal of the machinery of men's oppression and exploitation of women consists of mechanisms by which women's own energies and resources are turned against us, to suppress our spirits, cloud our judgment, and consume us. And one of the most effective devices for this is the construction and manipulation of good and evil. It is a complex strategy. One part is the identification of certain things as good and others as evil—the naming of vices and virtues and sins. These are falsely and deceptively named. Almost anything that would strengthen or empower us or inspire us with the spirit of rebellion will be named "evil" or "sinful." But this is not enough. We may not avoid the things called "evil," especially since our animal wisdom would generally move us toward them. We must be motivated to heed this naming.

What's needed is *both* the naming of certain things as "good" and "evil" and women's wanting the "good" and shunning the "evil." Ideally, we should learn to care enormously for the "good" and to strenuously dread the "evil." This is accomplished by naming *women* "evil." Eve, Pandora, the Witch, the Stepmother, the Mother-in-Law, the Whore, and so on. Naming women "evil" makes it open season on women—to be "punished," used, scapegoated, ignored, abused. This gives us motivation to attempt to dissociate ourselves from "evil" and associate ourselves with "good." Hence, we are drawn into the contradictory and self-defeating project of trying to distance ourselves from the category of woman by constantly demonstrating, by being good, that we are "exceptional women." Since woman is by definition evil, this project can never be once-and-for-all completed, and we are bound up in it for life, that is, bound up for life in proving that there is nothing of Eve, Pandora, the Witch, the Stepmother, the Mother-in-Law, or the Whore in us—nothing of independence, autonomy, or rebellion. Women are, then, locked into a project of being good that is fundamentally defensive and intrinsically self-defeating and that establishes an urgent need for an ethics to tell us how to be good.

But now I want to modify this picture of woman in patriarchy with another intuition about the race, class, and historical specificity of it. This is suggested to me by many things, but most recently by Elizabeth Spelman's discussion of Aristotle in her new book, *Inessential Woman*. [6] As I understand it, she is saying that everything Aristotle says about women is about, not female human beings, but the wives and potential wives of citizens; in Aristotle, "men and women" means "citizens and their wives." Female slaves and foreigners and wives of artisans and merchants are not "women." Only humans of a certain class have gender. I suspect that the whole scenario Daly uncovered—of the oppressive manipulation of "good" and "evil" and the manipulation of women through it—is a scenario developed by "citizens" for the construction and reduction of their women and only spills over in some ways and at some times into the structures that shape the lives of women and men who do not have the status of citizens. And it seems to me that when a woman (a female with certain kinship relations to a member of the citizen class) is "bad" or "evil," she is *not* a citizen and is reduced to being a mere female. [7] Being "good" is required to retain her precarious status of "citizeness"—a status that by birth she gets a crack at.

In the subculture I grew up in, this distinction between citizenesses and other females was marked semantically by the distinction between "woman" and "lady." As daughters of citizens, our mission was to distinguish ourselves from women (who were "bad") and construct ourselves as ladies (who were "good"). Young women of this subculture who had serious intellectual, political, or economic ambitions recognized that we had to repudiate ladyhood, and we reverted to trying to convince the world (men) that women could be good and hence could deserve or earn the rights, privileges, and safety granted to (male) citizens as a birthright. This is still the project of much of feminist ethics and the lesbian civil rights movement.

Females of many other subcultures in this society (and of many other cultures elsewhere) have no chance of becoming citizenesses and, correspondingly, no such structured-in urgency about being good. I suspect that women who passionately desire to be good are most often women who suppose that by being good they can achieve vicarious citizenship, that is, vicarious participation in the privileges and privileged status of the dominating races and classes. Women with no such hope would not be likely to manifest their ambition for dignity, soundness of character and judgment, and effectiveness in the world as a desire to be good.

If this is so, it seems that it would behoove women who claim to abhor race and class privilege to give up the habit of pursuing them by being and trying to be good. The discovery that one is not good, or doesn't know how to be good, might be welcomed as releasing one from the game of good and evil and thus from the will-bindings that keep us bonded to our oppressors.

I am seeing the need for ethics in lesbian and feminist communities where I reside—understood as a need to know right from wrong, know the good, act rightly, and be good—as a need particular to women trying to earn or maintain a certain status. In my own experience, it seems to me that this is a quite distinctive preoccupation with ethics and that it is more prevalent among white, middle-class-raised or -assimilated, christian-cultured women than among women rooted in other cultural matrices.[8] Thinking on this leads me to wonder if instead of seeking to create a lesbian ethics, many of us who are attracted by a book with the title *Lesbian Ethics* might consider learning to do without ethics entirely.

And I think that it may turn out that this is what Sarah Hoagland's book will help us accomplish.

She is shifting from the language of the modern tradition of ethics: —from knowing what is right or good to deciding what to pay attention to. And her last section is about *meaning,* about the creation of meaning, not about "ethics." Sarah Hoagland's book will *not* meet the need for ethics that may motivate many to purchase it. It is, in fact, quite a frustrating work so long as one clings to that need.

Sarah Hoagland's central thesis is that "agency" can be understood as the creation and maintenance of meaning and value, and what she offers as "ethics" is an open-ended exploration of what kinds of actions and strategies in various situations (in particular, situations of oppression) have created or might create what meanings and values. It is in part empirical, in that it is to some degree a matter of learning and recording what dynamics of interpretation and interaction do arise from the pursuit of certain strategies in certain situations; it is in part creative, in that it generates novel dynamics of interpretation and interaction through novel acts and strategies. Such an "ethics" makes no pretense at all of telling us what is right or how to be good, but I think if it is allowed, it can seduce those of us who feel we need such things into a new space much further from our citizen-fathers' homes, where "right" and "good" no longer trick us into continuing our roles as dutiful daughters.

NOTES

This is a slightly revised version of a talk composed for a panel on *Lesbian Ethics* at the meeting of the Midwest Division of the Society for Women in Philosophy, March 19, 1989, in Indianapolis, which was published as "A Response to *Lesbian Ethics*," *Hypatia* 5, no. 3 (Fall 1990): 132–137.

My thanks to Claudia Card for suggestions which helped me make various points clearer and more accurate.

1. Sarah Lucia Hoagland. *Lesbian Ethics: Toward New Value* (Palo Alto, Calif.: Institute of Lesbian Studies, 1988).

2. Marilyn Frye. "Growing Room" (unpublished, n.d.). Circulated informally under the title "Ritual Libations and Points of Explosion: More Reflections on Being White and Feminist."

3. Minnie Bruce Pratt. "Identity: Skin Blood Heart," in *Yours in Struggle: Three Feminist Perspectives on Anti-Semitism and Racism,* ed. Elly Bulkin, Minnie Bruce Pratt, and Barbara Smith (Brooklyn: Long Haul Press, 1984, 14–15. Emphasis in original.

4. For a useful discussion of the nuclear family dynamics associated with this "Athena," see Miriam M. Johnson, *Strong Mothers, Weak Wives* (Berkeley: University of California Press, 1988), 131–138.

5. Mary Daly. *Gyn/Ecology: The Metaethics of Radical Feminism* (Boston: Beacon Press, 1984).

6. Elizabeth V. Spelman. *Inessential Woman: Problems of Exclusion in Feminist Thought* (Boston: Beacon Press, 1988), 45–57.

7. In the United States, women who are divorced generally suffer a radical reduction in their standard of living, often ending up on welfare, which is a contemporary equivalent of having lost the status of citizen. Good women, of course, keep their husbands and do not cause their children to live in poverty.

8. I am not suggesting that women of other racial, ethnic, and religious cultures and traditions do not care about ethics. Many cultures and traditions place great emphasis on ethics (conceived in a variety of ways), and women of these cultures and traditions clearly care immensely about justice, about doing right by others, about dignity and responsibility, and about being decent human beings. I am talking here about a particular kind of need for ethics and a particular understanding of ethics that is tailored to that need. It seems to me that having that sort of interest in ethics *reduces* a woman's working capacity for a more-than-rhetorical commitment to justice, dignity, and responsibility.

5 / Postmodernism and Other Skepticisms

CHRISTINE PIERCE

Feminist theory, according to some of its practitioners, is a subset of postmodern philosophy.[1] With respect to the possibility of knowledge, Jane Flax, for instance, sets up the choices for feminists as an either/or proposition: postmodernism or the Enlightenment. Feminists, she says, cannot have it both ways: Either what is called "truth" is tainted by history and social practice, as deconstructionist philosophers have shown, or some absolute truth of the whole universe is possible: "We cannot simultaneously claim (1) that the mind, self, and knowledge are socially constituted and that what we can know depends upon our social practices and contexts *and* (2) that feminist theory can uncover the Truth of the Whole once and for all. Such an absolute truth (e.g., the explanation for all gender arrangements at all times is X . . .) would require the existence of an 'Archimedes point' outside of the whole and beyond our embeddedness in it from which we could see (and represent) the whole."[2] Flax's argument follows a recognizable inference schema:

- Postmodern philosophy or Enlightenment philosophy.
- Enlightenment notions are untenable.
- Therefore, "feminist theory . . . belongs in the terrain of postmodern philosophy."[3]

Flax goes on to elaborate this claim: "Feminist notions of the self, knowledge, and truth are too contradictory to those of the Enlightenment to be contained within its categories. The way(s) of feminist future(s) cannot lie in reviving or appropriating Enlightenment concepts of the person or knowledge. . . . [D]espite an understandable attraction to the (apparently) logical, orderly world of the Enlightenment, feminist theory more properly belongs in the terrain of post-modern philosophy."[4]

Without a doubt, Enlightenment philosophers such as Kant were overconfident regarding the powers of reason and promised much more than they could deliver. However, even though both feminists and postmodernists are critical of so-called Enlightenment projects and the universalistic theories associated with those projects, feminist skepticism of the last two decades has been a moderate one compared with the radical skepticism of postmodern philosophy. Moreover, the insight of postmodernism most attractive to recent feminist theory—that advances in knowledge are tentative, limited, constrained by culture, race, class, gender, sexual orientation, and other biases, and applicable only to a fraction of folks—can be salvaged without buying the radical skepticism and relativism of postmodernism.[5]

Flax's own use of the term "contradiction" in her rejection of Enlightenment conceptions indicates that she thinks the notion of contradiction can be employed in some legitimate way despite the dismissal of the principle of noncontradiction by contemporary French feminists Luce Irigaray and and Hélène Cixous as paradigmatically male—penile, to be exact. And since Flax's criticisms of various postmodern thinkers suggest that only some of the conclusions of postmodernism should be saved, it seems equally plausible that some of the ideas of the Enlightenment might be worthwhile as well. If both philosophies can be critiqued for salvageable portions, perhaps feminism ought not to be classified as a subset of either postmodernism or the Enlightenment.

Flax sees feminism and postmodernism as common allies in their criticism of reason—that glory of the Enlightenment—as being ahistoric, transcendental, disembodied, impersonal, and abstract.[6] And in fact, feminists have rightly been concerned with situatedness and the importance of relationships and context in areas such as theories of self. Nevertheless, feminist conceptions of notions in ethical or political theories—justice, for example—can be strengthened by, if not grounded in, certain abstractions. While postmodernists engaged in the unraveling of rational structures cannot take reason as a ground for anything, feminists can appeal to reason unless they choose to abandon it altogether. Which techniques stay and which go can be decided on the basis of relevance. For example, an ahistorical, disembodied concept of the self would be poor psychology; but just such an abstract self in a concept like the "veil of ignorance" might work well to explain justice. The fact that all concrete particular situatedness disappears may be exactly what is needed in order for people to understand what it is like to live in somebody else's shoes.

My preoccupation is with rethinking ethics from a feminist perspective in the midst of the current struggle over which epistemology is more feminist. Reason, I argue, can play a role—albeit a small one compared with Enlightenment hopes—in establishing feminist ethical principles. In particular, I will focus on two concerns: (1) how what has come to be the accepted or politically correct feminist view of affirming differences affects interpretations of a principle of equality, and (2) how the postmodern critique of universal (or universalizing) claims overlooks the difference in the process of universalization between ethical theories and explanatory theories.

Explanatory theories such as those found in psychology, history, and metaphysics are under attack by feminists and postmodernists because the generalizations—sometimes referred to as universal or essentialist statements—they generate inevitably turn out to be false. Explanatory theories are designed to give an account of isolated phenomena, and some theories attempt to account for an extraordinary range of them. Authors Nancy Fraser and Linda Nicholson give as examples the metanarratives of Marx and Enlightenment humanism and the quasi-metanarratives of Nancy Chodorow and Carol Gilligan. Efforts to explain the oppression of women by reference to a single cause, for instance, will unavoidably extrapolate from the experiences of some while leaving out the stories of others. For example, such a theory might single out a domestic life that is typical of white, middle-class, heterosexual women but fails to capture the experiences of lesbians, black women, and working-class women. General claims about gender, in the words of Susan Bordo, create "a false unity out of heterogeneous elements relegating the submerged elements to marginality."[7]

From this enlightened perspective, Gilligan is criticized for ignoring differences in race and class in much the same way as Gilligan criticized Lawrence Kohlberg for ignoring gender differences. Just as Gilligan doubted that Kohlberg's single standard for human moral maturity was really anything of the sort, given that the data for his conclusion included only the moral reasoning of males, so too have some feminists suggested more recently that the type of moral reasoning Gilligan associates with women is better identified with subordinate or minority status.[8] This moderate skepticism regarding universalizing claims is typical of feminist theorizing of the last two decades.

Postmodern skepticism is radical skepticism. Gendered explanations of the kind Gilligan offers are rejected not because she, like Kohlberg, is guilty of false generalization but because of new skepticism about the use of gender as an analytical category.[9] It is not that Gilligan and Kohlberg have the wrong categories; under postmodernism, categories are abolished altogether. Every generalization leaves out something of importance, and our efforts to capture the item left out are endless and lead to a radical particularity. The view is well known: the world as text, subject to endless commentary and particular interpretations, the continual displacement of one text by another. It reminds one of the philosopher Cratylus, who, when convinced of radical skepticism, "did not think it right to say anything but only moved his finger."[10] The feminist celebration of difference that began by discarding false generalizations moves in postmodernism to a radical particularity, what Bordo calls, "the view from everywhere." The feminist worry that some stories are marginalized or not told shifts in postmodernism to the view that there are only particular stories, that no rational standards arbitrate between discourses.

The notion of life as literary criticism—ceaseless textual play—has unsurprisingly prompted some feminists to claim that no (practical) politics can come from postmodernism. When one refuses to order thoughts into concepts, categories, and theories, one eliminates politics. If we have no political theory, we have no practical politics. If we have no feminist theory, we have no women's movement. Some feminists have even been tempted to claim there are no "women," following Michel Foucault's idea that "the homosexual" is an invented classification. Teresa de Lauretis, for example, says the subject of feminism is "not only distinct from Woman with the capital letter, the *representation* of an essence inherent in all women . . . , but also distinct from women, the real, historical beings and social subjects who are . . . actually engendered in social relations. The subject of feminism . . . is a theoretical construct . . . not women."[11] Even if academics can understand perfectly well what is meant, one cannot go into the street and talk about a women's movement if there are no women. One might as well join Cratylus in the bending of a finger. But before we become overly pessimistic regarding the possibility of ethics or political theory, it must be noticed that the postmodern disparagement of universalistic claims applies only to discussions that try to capture truths about the world.

ACTING ON PRINCIPLE

Universalization in ethics is not the same thing as universalization in nonnormative, explanatory principles and theories, such as those found in psychology, history, or metaphysics. Universalization in ethics is a purely formal approach to procedures requiring consistency, insisting that people not make an exception for themselves. As a formal process, universalization in ethics makes statements that do not contain content in the usual narrative sense; that is, universalization in ethics delineates some abstract content such as the notion of equality with some criteria of relevant similarities rather than describing a condition of the external world. Thus the postmodern critique of universalization and generalization in explanatory theories cannot be applied to universalization or generalization in ethics. Universalization in ethics does not fail to tell the stories of some because it tells no stories at all.

Gilligan appeals to ethical universalization in her normative claim that women should be less self-sacrificing and men should be less egoistic.[12] From an empirical standpoint vis-à-vis moral worth, many women are likely to count themselves for less than others, whereas many men tend to count themselves for more than others. To be less inclined to self-sacrifice is to view one's own moral worth on a par with that of other folks. To argue that a woman ought to have such a view is to assume a universalization, that is, a consistency of the standards of moral worth, as the right way to proceed. Without such a view we have only particular stories: the stories of those women who undervalue themselves and the stories of those men who do not. Gilligan's appeal to the principle of universalization arbitrates between these discourses.

Acting on principle, according to Kohlberg, is the highest stage of moral maturity. It makes sense—from a psychological point of view

—that acting on principle would be a late stage in moral development because certain rational capacities must be acquired in order to recognize and apply principles that are not needed, for example, for the authority stage (X is wrong because Mom says so) or even utilitarian stages (X is wrong because doing X raises the level of unwanted suffering in the world). Kant, of course, was not a psychologist and therefore did not use the jargon of "maturity," but he did believe that ethics is a matter of acting on principle. Now part of what is meant by acting on principle is that one must be prepared to ignore the social consequences of one's actions, indeed, if necessary, to ignore the sufferings of others. Acting on principle can be a dangerous thing because people already disposed to do possible social damage might in addition act on the wrong principles. Kant's standards, it must be noted, are even higher than acting on principle; we must first formulate the principles according to formal considerations of reason, such as universalization and not violating the principle of noncontradiction—in other words, the content of principles is determined by abstract, formal rules of reason. Here is where the confidence in reason so typical of the Enlightenment can be seen very clearly in Kant's ethics. Because we are rational beings testing our principles against rational standards, we will come up with the right principles. There is no need to worry about our having the right principles because the rational principles are the right ones, and as rational beings we know what principles have survived the tests of reason.

REJECTING PRINCIPLES: THE DEMISE
OF EQUALITY AND NONCONTRADICTION

In recent feminist scholarship, acceptable projects attend to the recognition of differences among women—in particular, those differences due to race and class. Bordo describes as a feminist dogma the idea that "the only 'correct' perspective on race, class, and gender is the affirmation of difference" revealing itself in "criticisms which attack gender generalizations as *in principle* . . . totalizing."[13] Presumably, to generalize about gender is to intentionally marginalize others. Two lamentable consequences of the celebration of difference for principled ethics is Flax's interpretation of equality as similarity that results in the problematizing and demotion of the principle of equality and the rejection of the principle of noncontradiction by Irigaray and Cixous because of its association with masculine sameness.

Justice, says Flax, is a potentially more useful concept than equality because justice allows for a consideration of differences, whereas equality does not: "Equality as currently understood and practiced is constituted in part . . . by a denial . . . of differences. . . . I cannot imagine equality apart from some measure of sameness."[14] By assuming equality as similarity, Flax creates the following paradox: "If equality requires and reflects sameness, the nature of this sameness itself must be questioned. For it did not escape attention that the concepts different/same were also constituted dualistically and were gendered. The feminine is the 'different' to the masculine 'same.' Hence to attain equality it would appear necessary for women to cease being feminine, at least in the public sphere. . . . Yet if women must cease being feminine to be citizens, to speak of *women*'s political emancipation would be an oxymoron since we must eliminate our 'difference' before entering the public world."[15] The assumption here is that egalitarian arguments are based on similarities between the sexes and that arguments based on sex differences constitute a rejection of egalitarian arguments.[16] It is hard and often unproductive to talk about equality without saying whether one means moral equality, economic equality, equal opportunity, equal representation, and so on. The point of arguments for representation is not to show that differences win out over equality. Rather, the issue here is that whether or not differences are relevant depends on what kind of equality one is talking about. If one is talking about *equal opportunity*, differences should be ignored; however, if one is talking about *equal representation*, differences are important.

For example, I believe there is good reason to suppose that some groups, such as blacks, gays, and women, need representation. One case can be found in Richard Wasserstrom's account of an all-white jury and a black defendant. Police testified that the black defendant, without provocation, threw an empty Coke bottle at their passing car. The defendant said he had been selling copies of the Black Panther newspaper when the police slowed down and said, "Nigger, if we see you on the street with those newspapers again we will kill you." He replied, "You @#$!'s can't scare me." The police insisted they had seen the defendant clearly and that he had thrown the bottle with a pitching motion of the right arm. An eyewitness testified that no bottle was thrown. Moreover, it was demonstrated that the defendant was left-handed. Nonetheless, it took the jury over seven hours to return a verdict of acquittal.

The difficulty the jurors had in reaching the correct decision, says Wasserstrom, requires an explanation. Wasserstrom conjectures that the jurors had a hard time convincing themselves that the police would fabricate a story against the defendant. After all, there is nothing in their white, middle-class experience that would cause them to take seriously the possibility that the police would deliberately and flagrantly lie. However, many black people have had experiences that make them doubt the credibility of the police. On Wasserstrom's analysis, whites bring with them to the jury box a general point of view that affects the way they see the facts. Thus a case can be made for representational juries on the ground that these different points of view should find their way into the jury's deliberations.[17] Since there exists a standard liberal analysis of equality that can accommodate differences, the fleeing to postmodernism in order to escape the paradoxes within Western liberal democracies seems unwarranted in this instance. If we do not interpret equality as similarity, the paradox disappears.

As creator and practitioner respectively of a woman's discourse—*écriture de la femme*—Irigaray and Cixous abandon coherence, consistency, and noncontradiction as reflective of male anatomy. To have a penis is to be the sort of person who would think up such ideas as the principle of identity and the principle of noncontradiction: "Phallic language is based on a sematic economy of 'has' and 'has not,' and endless repetition of the same. . . . The 'one' of the male subject becomes the two of the vaginal lips, constantly in touch with each other in an interaction in which the two are not separated by negation but interact and merge. . . . Instead of the relation of identity, vaginal symbolism suggests contiguity. The law of non-contradiction does not rule because the point is not a repetition of the same. Asked for clarification, a woman cannot answer; she has already moved on, or turned her back on her own thought, in a kind of a vaginal 'fold' within herself."[18] Even as a woman's sexuality is plural, goes the argument, her speech would encompass multiplicity, rejecting rules of grammar, rigid concepts, and boundaries in favor of a language and a philosophy that flow. It is true that the very form of an academic discourse makes ideas such as those of Irigaray and Cixous difficult to describe and comprehend, and so they must turn to metaphor to explain. And metaphor is notoriously easy to laugh at; my love is not *really* like a red, red rose at all. But even within the bounds of metaphor, anatomy is a poor choice to explain the gendering of language; men have two testicles, after all, and the duplication of organs is basic *human* anatomy. If one is going to accept the possibility of rational discourse, as presumably is axiomatic for scholarship to continue, then one must cite some reason for rejecting the principle of noncontradiction other than genitalia.

REASON'S SMALL ROLE

Reason can establish that dominant-subordinate relationships of a carefully specified type are contradictory and a violation of the principle of universalization. A principle opposing the idea that some persons should be dominated because they have less moral worth is a fundamental if limited feminist principle of the sort that is implied by formal rationality. Interestingly enough, Sarah Hoagland, who is very skeptical of principled ethics—although not from a postmodernist perspective—nevertheless articulates the connection between a principle with content regarding dominance and subordination and Kant's formal principle of universalization in a way that immeasurably surpasses Kant's own efforts to bring form and content together. She says:

> Reason . . . can determine moral laws. . . . Now, these laws . . . can't be just any laws. They must be laws that are a matter of pure reason. . . . And to be rational, these laws must be universal (or "categorical"). So Kant offers a formula, what he calls the "categorical imperative": "Act only on that maxim through which you can at the same time will that it should become a universal law.
> The idea of this formula is that every rational being be treated as an end in itself and not merely as a means. For example, by this formula I could not will slavery, for according to the formula I would have to will slavery universally: Always enslave every-

one. But if I willed it universally, then I would be included among those to be enslaved; and as a slave I would not be a being who could will laws. In other words, I would be willing myself to be a being who could not will anything—a contradiction. Thus, it is not possible for me to will such a law morally. It is logic—pure reason, not inclination—which prohibits the willing of such a principle.

More generally, we could not will a universal law that treats everyone merely as a means. Since we are one of that group, it would mean willing a law that treats us as a mere means; and if we were merely a means, we would no longer be the sort of being who could will laws. On the other hand, if we willed such a law for everyone but ourselves, the law would be no longer universal or categorical, hence moral, since it would be excepted in our own case, and thus based on inclination or desire, not reason. It is logically impossible to universally will such laws.[19]

What reason can do is very limited. Moreover, skepticism about principled ethics is justified. Furthermore, what we know about the limitations and pitfalls of principled ethics (sketched in the next section) we certainly did not learn from the Enlightenment.

THE PROBLEMS WITH PRINCIPLES

People Act on Bad Principles

Although acting on bad principles is a problem that does not arise in a Kantian universe, it does in fact happen frequently. Ronald Dworkin, a philosopher of law committed to a principled approach to ethics and law, defends the legal enforcement of morality but only if the conception of morality enforced meets certain rational standards. With these standards in place, he says, laws based on ignorance, hate, fear, and prejudice will be ruled out. However, even though Dworkin's rational standards block laws based on the worst of reasons, laws based on bad reasons are possible in his system because the requirements of reason are so minimal. People have to have a reason—not a good one—for their moral point of view and they must use their reasons consistently. The kinds of things that count as moral reasons (X has a right, X has harmful consequences) must be statable in principled form and attached to a theory. Bad reasons slip easily through Dworkin's net. To condemn homosexuality because it is unnatural is to give a reason that can be expressed in a principled form and is attached to a theory developed by Greek and medieval philosophers. Yet it is a bad reason on many grounds. The biological data do not support it.[20] There is no reason why the purpose of sexuality should be procreation rather than intimacy or pleasure even as there is no reason why the purpose of the mouth should be for eating rather than kissing. "Nature" does not rank purposes for us when something has more than one. So we cannot get very far with minimal rational standards.

Condemning as "sins of omission" the policy of Catholic agencies to refuse even to mention condoms let alone teach safer sex to Hispanic teenagers in New York City at enormous risk for AIDS, a recent *Village Voice* article quotes a Brooklyn priest as saying, "My fear . . . is that we may be sacrificing lives for the sake of a principle."[21] In saying that lives are worth more than principles or at least more than the principle at work here, he hints at the possibility that many have died and more will die for the sake of the wrong principle. The principle (unstated in the article) is that possible people (remember, possible people are not anybody) are worth more than actual people.[22] It is connected to the belief that the sole acceptable purpose of sexuality is procreation.

Consequences Are Ignored

Some take it as a criticism of a principled approach to ethics that social consequences are ignored. As implied above, ignoring consequences can be a good thing or at least unproblematic as long as one is acting on the right principle. Rights, for example, are principles that are designed to specify when even great amounts of social happiness can be ignored or declared illegitimate. For instance, if we take seriously considerations of rights, the many people who might be made happy by denying fundamental rights to gays, women, and blacks would have to forego that happiness. The notion of rights has recently come under much feminist criticism as reflective of Western masculinity in its emphasis on the individual rather than the community. According to Susan Bordo, "Our students still experience this moment of critical and empowering insight when, for example, they

learn from Gilligan (1982) and others that the language of 'rights' is
not the ethical discourse of God or Nature, but the ideological
superstructure of a particular construction of masculinity."[23] The
implication is that the notion of rights can be dismissed because its
foundation is comparatively weak. But if God, Nature, and masculinity are all foundations, they are all equally weak. To say that a
principle should be followed because God says so is not to give a
reason at all but to cite an authority, and unless the authority has
reasons, we have done little more than assert that someone in power
agrees with us. Nature, as we have seen, has little to say on the topic
of evaluation, and it may indeed be that rights reflect masculine
values. But it may also be that certain things, such as autonomy and
liberty, have value independent of the fact that men have prized them
historically.

Principles Can Be Sabotaged

Principles, says Sarah Hoagland, at most "serve as guides for those
who already can act with integrity. Thus, for example, we have fairly
intricate strategies for fair fighting or conflict resolution, and yet we
can use them to sabotage mediation."[24] Illustrations of Hoagland's
point involving academic males using principles to justify their large
share of goodies will spring to the minds of feminists in academe.
Here is one. A former law dean in a discussion of university day care
argued that a lottery is not equitable. (It was assumed that the university could not provide day care for all.) So in the name of equality, the
university did nothing. Instead of trying to do as much as they could,
they justified the status quo without any recognition that the status
quo benefited them.

Hoagland goes on to note that "principles are not something we can
appeal to when all else fails."[25] This is an important point because
many who defend reason have a strong tendency to talk as if pure
reason can save us from bigotry and other irrationalities in the world.

Principles Are Not Applied Correctly

Principles themselves do not tell us how to apply them. Consequently, even the most apparently straightforward translation of
normative principle to actual case can go awry. On an annual basis a

colleague who administers a "survey of beliefs" to students discovers that large numbers who will agree with the principle that "consenting adults have free choice in their sexual activity" will simultaneously argue that homosexuality is not permissible.

Examples in Kant scholarship abound. It is commonplace to admit that at least some of Kant's own examples of how his system is supposed to work fail. For example, although he defended a principle that prohibits suicide, there is no logical contradiction if some or all decide to take their own lives.

In the 1986 Supreme Court case *Bowers v. Hardwick*,[26] the Court held that the Constitution does not confer a fundamental right upon homosexuals to engage in sodomy.[27] Although Michael J. Bowers, attorney general of Georgia, in his petitioner's brief, cited Kant as a philosopher who disapproved of sodomy,[28] legal scholar David Richards finds support in Kant for the opposite point of view. Richards cites Kant as an author of the idea of human rights, as one "who best articulated its radical implications for the significance of respect for moral personality."[29] Extending the Kantian notion of autonomy to sexuality, Richards says: "Sexuality . . . is not a spiritually empty experience that the state may compulsorily legitimize only in the form of rigid, marital procreational sex, but one of the fundamental experiences through which, as an end in itself, people define the meanings in their lives."[30] Rights typically protect certain basic interests or desires even if doing so makes the majority unhappy. Being able to love, according to Richards, is central to human lives. Moreover, "freedom to love means that a mature individual must have autonomy to decide how and whether to love another."[31] Despite Kant's talk about rights as guarantees of proper respect for moral personality or rational autonomy, Kant did not see the implications of his theory for sexual autonomy. In the *Lectures*, he referred to masturbation, same-sex intercourse (male and female), and intercourse with animals as *crimina carnis contra naturam* that "degrade human nature to a level below that of animal nature and make man unworthy of his humanity. He no longer deserves to be a person."[32]

Making Sure You Come Out Right

John Rawls describes and favors a process used in finding answers to ethical and legal questions called "reflective equilibrium" that consists of going back and forth between our rational principles and our intuitions. Intuitions—that stock of beliefs not subjected to rational scrutiny—play some role in the framing of principles. We can find a nice illustration of this in Joel Feinberg's caution regarding the formulation and application of the offense principle. He says: "Bigoted prejudices of a very widespread kind (e.g., against interracial couples strolling hand in hand down the main street of a town in the deep South) can lead onlookers to be disgusted and shocked, even 'morally' repelled, by perfectly innocent activities. . . . For [this reason], the offense principle must be formulated in a very precise way, and supplemented by appropriate standards or mediating maxims, so as not to open the door to wholesale and intuitively unwarranted legal interference."[33] The use of this process of reflective equilibrium assumes that reason is not transcendental, and the reliance on intuition makes the process open to sabotage. Luckily, Feinberg's intuitions tell him that "walking hand in hand down the main street of a town is just as much a right of homosexual as of interracial couples,"[34] although his occasional reference to homosexuality as abnormal shows his intuitions on this topic to be a bit shakier. It never occurs to Feinberg that some interracial couples are also gay couples.

Listen to Feinberg talk about drafting and redrafting the principle that results in protecting the behavior of the interracial couple from legal interference. Clearly, Feinberg is seeking a justification for his liberal intuitions; if one principle fails to do the job, he can find another:

> In my previous writings on this subject, I fell into a trap . . . by forgetting the useful scales analogy, and resorting too quickly to an absolutist mediating maxim which I called, rather grandly, the "standard of universality." If I wanted a reason against *ever* criminalizing interracial hand-holding and the like, all I had to do was cite the reasonableness of the conduct it would forbid. . . . Instead I recommended a stringent standard to be met before the "extent of offense" could be put on the scales at all, namely that "in order for the offense . . . to be sufficient to warrant coercion, it should be the reaction that could reasonably be expected from almost any person chosen at random, taking the nation as a whole. . . ." The chance of these conditions being satisfied, I assumed, should not cost the liberal any sleep.

My own dogmatic slumber, however, was quickly interrupted

by another kind of liberal nightmare, caused by application of the universality standard to examples like . . . public cross-burnings. . . . To prevent this unhappy consequence . . . I proposed an *ad hoc* amendment to the standard of universality itself, so that the special class of offensiveness that consists of abusive, mocking, insulting behavior of a sort bound to upset, alarm, anger, or irritate those it insults, the offense principle could be applied, even though the behavior would *not* offend the entire population. . . . Like most hasty *ad hoc* patch-up jobs, this one put the theory in even worse trouble.[35]

Ultimately, philosophy is no freer than any other discipline from the pulls of larger intellectual currents. The struggles of postmodernism and feminism with the heavy weight of rational structures are continuations of the Romantic movement of the early nineteenth century. Milton told the men of the seventeenth-century Enlightenment that reason was their special gift, a gift specifically *not* granted to women. Adam and Eve in Eden are

> Not equal, as their sex not equal seemed.
> For contemplation he and valor formed,
> For softness she and sweet attractive grace:
> He for God only, she for God in him.[36]

The works of thinkers such as Newton and Kant convinced men that reason was their most godlike tool, the facility that would explain the order of the universe if not today, then certainly tomorrow. When Goethe and Rousseau and Blake began to reject the claims of reason, they seemed compelled to reject also its rampant masculinity. Imagination and inspiration became either feminine or androgynous, and reason became the deity of the mechanistic, obviously patriarchal establishment.

Reason, as we have found, makes a bad deity; but it does make a good tool. Physicists who consider Einsteinian relativity and quantum mechanics to be our current best models of the universe still use Newtonian formulas to plot rocket trajectories. Feminist attorneys who understand the origins of civil rights in property protection invented in the capitalistic Renaissance can still use those rights in court to empower minorities.

Where postmodernism will go in its deconstruction of the philosophies of the Enlightenment has yet to be seen. It is easy to understand how the postmodern repudiation of the one true universal
story dovetails with much of feminist thought. After all, most of the
one true universal stories in Western history, psychology, and so on
have been about white, heterosexual men. Patriarchal resistance to
multidimensional accounts is at least as big a problem as relativism
(some feminists would say greater) in terms of damage to women.[37]
Moreover, multidimensional accounts do not entail relativism. To
deny that there is a single right view of history, for example, is not to
agree that any view of history is as good as any other. But if there are
only discourses and no rational way to arbitrate between or among
them, then relativism seems to be an obvious consequence. Feminism as a force in the world must keep a balance: understanding
the skepticism toward reason as a masculinist, historically weighted
method of organizing knowledge while recognizing that not all of the
laboriously created works of the past are useless for our own liberation. Certainly you can destroy the master's house with the master's
tools.[38]

NOTES

My thanks to Beth Timson, Claudia Card, and Sandy Bartky for their ideas
and suggestions for this essay.

1. A brief description of postmodern philosophy follows: "Within the last
decade, there have emerged . . . radical arguments against claims of objectivity in the academy which have been tied to broad analyses of the limitations
of modern Western scholarship. The proponents of such analyses, linked
under the label of 'postmodernists,' have argued that the academy's ideal of 'a
God's eye view' must be situated within the context of modernity, a period
whose organizing principles they claim are on the decline. The postmodernist critique of modernity is wideranging; it focuses on such diverse elements
as the modern sense of the self and subjectivity, the idea of history as linear
and evolutionary, and the modernist separation of art and mass culture. I will
focus, for the moment, on the postmodernist critique of the idea of a transcendent reason.
"Postmodernists have gone beyond earlier historicist claims about the inevitable 'situatedness' of human thought within culture to focus on the very
criteria by which claims to knowledge are legitimized. The traditional historicist claim that all inquiry is inevitably influenced by the values of the

inquirer provides a very weak counter to the norm of objectivity. The response can be made that while values and culture might affect the choice of questions the scholar brings to her or his inquiry, they cannot affect the truth or falsity of the answers the scholar gives to such questions. This is because the criteria which determine the truth or falsity of such answers are themselves independent of the specific perspective of the inquirer. But the more radical move in the postmodern turn was to claim that the very criteria demarcating the true and the false, as well as such related distinctions as science and myth or fact and superstition, were internal to the traditions of modernity and could not be legitimized outside of these traditions. . . . Therefore, the postmodern critique has come to focus on philosophy and the very idea of a possible theory of knowledge, justice, or beauty." (Linda J. Nicholson, Introduction, *Feminism/Postmodernism* [New York: Routledge, 1990], 3–4).

2. Jane Flax, "Postmodernism and Gender Relations in Feminist Theory," *Signs: Journal of Women in Culture and Society,* 12, no. 4 (Summer 1987), 633.

3. Ibid., 625.

4. Ibid.

5. Robert Paul Wolff makes a similar point about limitations on advances in knowledge, but his remarks are not directed at postmodernists. See "Social Philosophy: The Agenda for the Nineties," *Journal of Social Philosophy* 20, nos. 1, 2 (Spring/Fall 1989): 5.

6. Jane Flax, "Beyond Equality: Gender, Justice, and Difference," lecture at Duke University, February 12, 1990.

7. Susan Bordo, "Feminism, Postmodernism, and Gender-Scepticism," in Nicholson, ed., *Feminism/Postmodernism,* 139.

8. Joan C. Tronto, "Beyond Gender Difference to a Theory of Care," *Signs: Journal of Women in Culture and Society* 12, no. 4 (Summer 1987): 649.

9. See Bordo, "Feminism, Postmodernism, and Gender-Scepticism," 135.

10. Aristotle, *Metaphysics,* 1010a 12, 13; see also 1010a 1–15. Richard McKeon, ed., *The Basic Works of Aristotle* (New York: Random House, 1941), 745–746.

11. Teresa de Lauretis, *Technologies of Gender: Essays on Theory, Film, and Fiction* (Bloomington: Indiana University Press, 1987), 9–10. See also Denise Riley's discussion of the problem in *"Am I That Name?" Feminism and the Category of "Woman" in History* (Minneapolis: University of Minnesota, 1988), chaps. 1 and 5.

12. Carol Gilligan, keynote speaker, Women and Moral Theory Conference, SUNY, Stony Brook, March 22–24, 1985.

13. Bordo, "Feminism, Postmodernism, and Gender-Scepticism," 139.

14. Flax, "Beyond Equality," 1–3.

15. Ibid., 3–4. Emphasis in original.

16. I discuss the idea of equality as similarity in my review of Elizabeth Wolgast's *Equality and the Rights of Women* (Ithaca, N.Y.: Cornell University Press, 1980), in *Philosophical Review* 93, no. 1 (January 1984): 93–97.

17. Richard Wasserstrom, "The University and the Case for Preferential Treatment," *American Philosophical Quarterly* 13, no. 2 (April 1976): 165–170.

18. Andrea Nye, *Feminist Theory and the Philosophies of Man* (New York: Routledge, 1989), 194–195.

19. Sarah Lucia Hoagland, *Lesbian Ethics: Toward New Value* (Palo Alto, Calif.: Institute of Lesbian Studies, 1988), 257.

20. Michael Ruse, *Homosexuality: A Philosophical Inquiry* (New York: Basil Blackwell, 1988), 188–192.

21. *Village Voice*, February 20, 1990, 28.

22. The stated principle, I think, is not what is in fact motivating Catholic policymakers. My point here is about what principle would justify the reasoning if it were true rather than about what principle is motivating them.

23. Bordo, "Feminism, Postmodernism, and Gender-Scepticism," 137.

24. Hoagland, *Lesbian Ethics*, 10.

25. Ibid., 11.

26. *Bowers v. Hardwick*, 106 S. Ct. 2841 (1986).

27. I have discussed this case at length in the introduction to chapter 4 ("Sexual Autonomy and the Constitution") of *AIDS: Ethics and Public Policy*, ed. Pierce and Donald VanDeVeer (Belmont, Calif.: Wadsworth Publishing Company, 1988), 173–182, and in "AIDS and *Bowers v. Hardwick*," *Journal of Social Philosophy* 20, no. 3 (Winter 1989): 21–32.

28. Petitioner's Brief, 20.

29. David A. J. Richards, *Sex, Drugs, Death, and the Law: An Essay on Human Rights and Overcriminalization* (Totowa, N.J.: Rowman and Littlefield, 1982), 31.

30. Ibid., 52.

31. Ibid., 55.

32. Immanuel Kant, *Lectures on Ethics*, trans. Louis Infield (New York: Harper Torchbook, 1963), 170.

33. Joel Feinberg, *Offense to Others* (New York: Oxford University Press, 1985), 25–26.

34. Ibid., 43.

35. Ibid., 27–29.

36. *Paradise Lost*, bk. 4, in *John Milton's Complete Poems and Major Prose*, ed. Merritt Y. Hughes (New York: Odyssey, 1957), 285.

37. Charlene Haddock Seigfried holds this view. See her "Why Isn't There a Pragmatic Feminism or Feminist Pragmatism?" paper presented at Midwest SWIP, Michigan State University, East Lansing, February 17, 1990.

38. I take issue here with Audre Lorde's often quoted advice to feminists that "the master's tools will never dismantle the master's house." Of course, Lorde did not anticipate in her remarks a deconstructionism that would undercut assertion altogether. See Audre Lorde, *Sister/Outsider: Essays and Speeches* (Trumansburg, N.Y.: Crossing Press, 1984), 112.

6 / Feminist Ethics:
Projects, Problems, Prospects

ALISON M. JAGGAR

Presently in the United States, there is much talk about and interest in so-called feminist ethics. In September 1988, for instance, what was planned as a small, one-day conference at an out-of-the-way branch campus of the University of Minnesota lasted two full days with concurrent sessions and attracted several hundred participants from the United States, Canada, and even Britain. Evident at that conference, however, as well as in other conferences and publications on this topic, were both a remarkable lack of consensus about future directions for feminist ethics and an even more remarkable lack of self-conscious reflection as to just what feminist ethics was. Generally assuming that the project of feminist ethics was self-evident, conference participants offered a wide variety of philosophical models for pursuing it. In the course of the sessions, contributors proposed as leads for feminists to follow both canonical (and male) philosophers, such as Aristotle, Hume, Kant, Hegel, Bentham, Mill, Sartre, and Camus, as well as noncanonical (and female) figures, such as Edith Stein, Simone Weil, and Iris Murdoch. The keynote speakers at the conference, by contrast, were more willing to depart from the philosophical canon: One urged the need for "global" feminism; the other suggested finding at least some of our moral inspiration in "maternal thinking."[1]

Given this bewildering plethora of suggestions, how can we determine which of these, or other, proposals provides the best model for feminist ethics? Indeed, how can we be sure which of them is even an instance of feminist ethics? In this chapter, I wish to address these questions. I shall begin by describing the emergence of the term "feminist ethics" in the United States, and then discuss several distinct enterprises in feminist ethics. My discussion will be simultaneously sympathetic and critical and is designed to be productive in several ways. First, it will help to clarify what feminist ethics is and, perhaps more significant, what it is not. This will both enable the formulation of certain conditions of adequacy for any feminist approach to ethics and provide grounds for rejecting some misconstruals of feminist ethics, misconstruals that presently are not uncommon. In addition, identifying the problems encountered in the course of undertaking various feminist projects will help to locate traps that those working in feminist ethics should avoid and point toward an agenda for contemporary feminist ethics. Finally, I shall suggest, though I shall not have time to argue, that feminist concerns bring certain deep problems in moral epistemology into sharp focus, problems that I do not think have been adequately addressed by contemporary nonfeminist theorists.

THE EMERGENCE OF CONTEMPORARY
FEMINIST ETHICS

The history of Western philosophy includes a considerable amount of philosophical reflection on women and their situation, much of it overtly misogynist and arguing that women should be subordinate to men because they are inferior to them in some way. Frequently, women's inferiority to men has been explained in terms of women's allegedly defective capacity to reason, a defect that was elaborated with imaginative virulence by canonical philosophers such as Aristotle, Aquinas, Kant, and Hegel (Mahowald 1978; Bell 1983). In opposition to this misogynist tradition, however, there exists a small but distinguished minority of philosophers who have opposed women's subordination and the historically dominant belief in women's inherent inferiority. Plato, Mill, and Marx are in this minority and, although certain features of their views have now become targets of feminist criticism (for example, Coole 1988), they may be viewed as pioneers in feminist ethics insofar as they used the philosophical resources of their times to challenge at least some aspects of women's subordination to men.

For much of the twentieth century, philosophers in the Anglo-American tradition paid little explicit attention to the agelong debate over women's place in society. When I received my philosophical training in the 1960s, for instance, I encountered virtually no mention of sex or gender and if I had thought about this omission at all, I would have assumed it indicated that sex and gender were nonessential human attributes and therefore irrelevant to philosophical concern with the supposedly ultimate issues of truth, beauty, and goodness.[2]

In the late 1960s, however, as part of a general resurgence of feminist activism, an unprecedented explosion of feminist ethical debate occurred. It erupted first among the general public but soon filtered into academic philosophical discourse. Actions and practices whose gendered dimensions hitherto had been either unnoticed or unchallenged now became foci of public and philosophical attention as feminists subjected them to outspoken moral critique, developed sometimes dramatic strategies for opposing them, and proposed alternatives that nonfeminists often perceived as dangerously radical. First grass-roots and soon academic feminist perspectives were articulated on what philosophers called "applied" ethical topics, which included abortion, equality of opportunity, domestic labor, portrayals of women in the media, and a variety of issues concerning sexuality, such as compulsory heterosexuality and rape. In the following decade, feminists displayed increasing ethical concern about pornography, reproductive technology, so-called surrogate motherhood, militarism, the environment, and the situation of women in developing nations.

While some feminist philosophers addressed the practical moral issues raised by contemporary social life, others turned their attention to traditional ethical theory. There they discovered numerous examples of male bias. Conspicuous among these examples, as noted already, were denials that women were capable of being full moral agents, a claim made originally by Aristotle but elaborated and refined by modern theorists such as Rousseau, Kant, and Hegel. For theorists such as these, the virtues of which women were capable were of a lesser kind than the virtues proper to men. Moreover, the supposedly feminine virtues prescribed conduct—such as silence, obedience, and faithfulness—whose moral value (if any) seemed to lie in its tendency to promote specifically masculine interests, indicating that the moral weight assigned to women in much traditional ethical theory was considerably less than that assigned to men.[3]

A somewhat less obvious form of male bias in traditional ethical theory was the way that the domestic realm was conceptualized.

Nineteenth- and twentieth-century philosophers especially tended to portray it as an arena outside the economy and beyond justice, private in the sense of being beyond the scope of legitimate political regulation. Even philosophers such as Aristotle or Hegel, who viewed the home as the location for a certain kind of ethical life, typically described it as a realm in which the most fully human excellences were incapable of being realized.[4] Feminist philosophers began early to criticize this conceptual bifurcation of social life. They pointed out that the home was precisely that realm to which women had historically been confined and that it had become symbolically associated with the feminine, despite the fact that heads of households were paradigmatically male. These feminists argued that the philosophical devaluation of the domestic realm made it impossible to raise questions about the justice of the domestic division of labor (Okin 1989), obscured the far-reaching social significance and creativity of women's work in the home (Jaggar and McBride 1985), and concealed, even legitimated, the domestic abuse of women (as well as children, especially girls) (Jaggar 1983; MacKinnon 1987).

The two parallel strands of feminist ethical work—the attention to contemporary ethical issues on the one hand and the criticism of traditional ethical theory on the other—together gave rise to the term "feminist ethics," which came into general use in the late 1970s and early 1980s. At this time, a number of feminist philosophers began expressing doubts about the possibility of fruitfully addressing so-called women's issues in terms of the conceptual apparatus supplied by traditional ethical theory. For instance, a rights framework was alleged by some to distort discussions of abortion insofar as it constructed pregnancy and motherhood as adversarial situations.

Another feminist criticism of the tradition was that some of its assumptions were incompatible with what was now beginning to be claimed as a distinctively feminine moral experience or sensibility. Contract theory, for instance, was criticized for postulating a conception of human beings as free, equal, independent, and mutually disinterested, a conception claimed by some to be contrary to the experience of most women (Held 1987; Baier 1984). Even the requirement of impartiality, usually taken as a defining feature of morality, became the object of feminist criticism insofar as it was alleged to generate prescriptions counter to the moral intuitions of many women (Noddings 1984; Sherwin 1987).

These sorts of concerns about some of the basic assumptions of traditional ethical theory led some feminists to assert that the problem with "malestream" ethics was not just that it had derogated women's moral competence and neglected issues of special concern to women but that its fundamental understanding of moral competence was masculine; therefore, it formulated and resolved moral issues in ways that were claimed to be distinctively masculine. Feminist ethics, then, in the newly emerging view, was no longer a matter of simply applying traditional ethical theory to contemporary issues, much less of seeking to show that women were as capable as men of moral agency. In other words, feminist ethics was not simply a matter of adding women and stirring them into existing theory. Instead, the new view held that feminist ethics must be dedicated to rethinking the deepest issues in ethical theory—what counted as moral issues and by what means they might properly be resolved—in light of a moral sensibility perceived as distinctively feminine.

This radical conception of the feminist ethical enterprise was encouraged by the much publicized work of developmental psychologist Carol Gilligan (1982), whose book *In a Different Voice: Psychological Theory and Women's Development* seemed to demonstrate empirically that the moral development of women was significantly different from that of men. Claiming that females tend to fear separation or abandonment, whereas males tend to perceive closeness as dangerous, Gilligan reported that girls and women often construed moral dilemmas as conflicts of responsibilities rather than of rights and sought to resolve those dilemmas in ways that would repair and strengthen webs of relationships. Furthermore, Gilligan described females as supposedly less likely than males to make or justify moral decisions by appeal to abstract rules; instead she claimed girls and women were more likely to act on their feelings of love and compassion for particular individuals. Gilligan concluded that whereas men typically adhered to a morality of justice whose primary values she identified as fairness and equality, women often adhered to a morality of care whose primarily values she identified as inclusion and protection from harm. For this reason, Gilligan claimed, studies of moral development based exclusively on a morality of justice did not provide an appropriate standard for measuring female moral development and in this respect should be recognized as male biased.

Many feminists seized on Gilligan's work as offering evidence for the existence of a characteristically feminine approach to morality, an approach assumed to provide the basis for a distinctively feminist ethics. For some, indeed, feminist ethics became and remains synonymous with an ethics of care. Just how an ethics of care should be delineated, however, was far from evident; nor was it clear whether it should supplement or supplant an ethics of justice. Gilligan spoke of a marriage between the two perspectives, but the compatability of the partners was far from evident. Even the empirical connection between women and care was soon challenged by other psychologists, who alleged Gilligan's samples to be nonrepresentative, her methods of interpreting her data suspect, and her claims impossible to substantiate, especially when the studies were controlled for occupation and class.

Despite its problems, Gilligan's work exerted an influence that can hardly be overstated. Writing on the so-called ethics of care has become a small industry within academia and outside the academy Giligan has received many honors. In moral philosophy specifically, at least two distinct consequences of Gilligan's work may be discerned. On the one hand, her claims have encouraged the current revival of neo-Aristotelian approaches to ethics, approaches that seek to broaden the Englightenment tradition's perceived focus on individuality, impartiality, and reason so as to include an appreciation of the moral significance of community, particularity, and emotion. On the other hand, Gilligan has inspired further philosophical attempts to develop theoretical approaches to ethics grounded in a distinctively feminine experience.

Prominent examples of this sort of enterprise are Nel Noddings's *Caring: A Feminine Approach to Ethics and Moral Education* (1984) and Sara Ruddick's *Maternal Thinking: Toward a Politics of Peace* (1989). These books contrast with each other in various ways. Ruddick is interested primarily in the issue of conflict resolution, whereas Noddings sketches an approach to a more comprehensive ethics; Noddings sees women as "natural" carers, in a sense at least partially biological, whereas Ruddick is clear that men, too, can mother; and Ruddick is explicitly concerned to develop a feminist ethics, whereas Noddings, as the subtitle of her book shows, makes no such claims. Nevertheless, in spite of these contrasts, the books invite comparison insofar as both suggest that child-rearing encourages the development of a distinctive moral sensibility, a sensibility that, at least in present circumstances, is predominantly feminine.

To understand feminist ethics as it is practiced today in the United States requires recognizing that much academic philosophical work in feminist ethics exists in continuity with work outside academic philosophy. Many feminist philosophers derive moral inspiration from feminist communities outside the academy and theoretical inspiration from disciplines outside philosophy, such as history, psychology, and especially literature; conversely, some feminist activists and many feminist scholars in disciplines other than philosophy read the work of feminist philosophers. Popular feminist books and journals frequently engage in ethical consideration of moral or public policy issues and sometimes offer more general discussions of supposedly "masculine" and "feminine" value systems. There are even grass-roots journals of feminist ethics—for example, *Lesbian Ethics* (United States), *Feminist Ethics* (Canada), and *Gossip: A Journal of Lesbian Feminist Ethics* (Britain). One may note striking parallels between the claims made by feminist academics and those made by feminist nonacademics.

While some philosophers direct their work in feminist ethics primarily toward an academic audience, others are more concerned with addressing nonacademic feminist communities. Included in the latter group are Marilyn Frye (1983), Sarah Lucia Hoagland (1989), María C. Lugones (1983; 1987b), and Joyce Trebilcot (forthcoming). Hoagland's *Lesbian Ethics: Toward New Value,* for instance, seeks to articulate and systematize the moral wisdom she finds in lesbian feminist practice and writing and to recommend a "moral revolution" specifically for the lesbian community. Heterosexual women, Hoagland says, can also fit into her schema—though not as heterosexual women—but she refrains, presumably deliberately, from addressing the question of how, if at all, men can utilize her work.

In concluding this brief survey of the development of contemporary feminist ethics in the United States, it should be noted that those in the United States who currently describe themselves as contributing to the development of feminist ethics are mainly, though not exclusively, white women. It is predictable that women are more likely than men to be feminists and that people of color are less likely than whites to be either philosophers or, because of feminism's racist history, feminists. Nevertheless, a few male philosophers, such as

Lawrence Blum, are doing significant work in feminist ethics, and there does exist a considerable amount of writing by people of color, both fiction and nonfiction, that seems compatible with the moral and theoretical inspiration of feminist ethics.

THE PROJECTS OF FEMINIST ETHICS

Attention to So-Called Women's Issues

We have seen already that one major criticism feminists have made of traditional Western ethics is that it has either devalued or ignored issues or spheres of life that are associated with women, whether the association be empirical, normative, or symbolic. Feminists have argued convincingly that this devaluation or neglect has been deleterious to women's interests in a variety of ways: women's virtues have been seen as less significant than those associated with men; women's work has gone unrecognized or its creativity has been unappreciated; and the abuse of women and children, especially girls, has been ignored. For all these reasons, then, it is essential that feminist ethics should address certain hitherto neglected issues or areas of life.

In turning philosophical attention to these issues or areas, however, one must be cautious in identifying them as "women's" issues or in "women's" sphere. There are several reasons why this caution is necessary. One is that such language may be taken to imply that there is something natural or inevitable about women's concern for these issues. In order to counter such still-prevalent sexual determinism, it is important to be continually explicit that if women indeed show more concern than men for so-called personal relationships and less for international politics, this difference is less likely to be the consequence of some innate predisposition than to be the result of women's culturally assigned confinement to and/or responsibility for the one area of life and their relative exclusion from the other.

In addition to reinforcing stereotypes about men's and women's predispositions, the language of women's issues may also be taken to suggest that moral or public policy issues can be divided cleanly into those that are and those that are not of special concern to women. This is mistaken for several reasons. On the one hand, since men's and women's lives are inextricably intertwined, there are no women's issues that are not also men's issues; the availability or otherwise of child care and abortion, for instance, has significant consequences for the lives of men as well as women. Typically, both men and women are involved in all areas of life (though usually in different ways), even those areas that have come to be coded culturally as masculine or feminine. Men are involved in domestic, sexual, and "personal" relations, just as women are involved in the economy, science, and even the military, despite the symbolic casting of the former as feminine concerns and the latter as masculine enterprises.

On the other hand, since men and women typically are not what lawyers call "similarly situated" relative to each other, it is difficult to think of any moral or public policy ("human") issue in which women do not have a gender-specific interest. For instance, such issues as war, peace, and world starvation, though they are certainly human issues in the sense of affecting entire populations, nevertheless have special significance for women because the world's hungry are disproportionately women (and children), because women are primarily those in need of the social services neglected to fund military spending, and because women benefit relatively little from militarism and the weapons industries.

For these reasons, it would be a mistake to identify feminist ethics with attention to some explicitly gendered subset of ethical issues. On the contrary, rather than being limited to a restricted ethical domain, feminist ethics has *enlarged* the traditional concerns of ethics. Approaching social life with an explicitly feminist consciousness has enabled it both to identify previously unrecognized ethical issues and to introduce fresh perspectives on issues already acknowledged as having an ethical dimension.

Feminist Evaluations of the Philosophical Canon

Feminist critiques of the philosophical canon are obviously an indispensable part of feminist ethics. The specific history of ethics in the West sets the intellectual context for Western ethics today. Thus any contemporary project in philosophical ethics must engage with our tradition—even if it is in reaction to it.

Feminist evaluations of Western ethical tradition require familiarity with canonical texts and contemporary work in feminist ethics. Indeed, since evaluation can be done only from a point of view, evaluating the canon requires taking a stand on certain contemporary feminist claims. For instance, evaluating allegations of male bias in philosophical treatments of women or criticisms of philosophical exclusions of women or supposedly women's issues presupposes taking philosophical positions on women's "nature" or the relevance of women's experience or the moral status of certain issues. Feminist claims about the possibility of appropriating parts of the canon for gender-neutral or even explicitly feminine approaches to ethics draw even more evidently on contemporary philosophical arguments addressed directly to issues of gender. Obviously, in order to determine how feminism may utilize existing ethical texts, those who evaluate the canon must have in mind a certain conception of the projects of feminist ethics and how they should be accomplished. Thus feminist work in the history of ethics is inseparable from engagement in contemporary feminist theorizing.

Reading some work in feminist ethics, it would be easy to infer that feminism requires a wholesale repudiation of the canon. Such authors are not limited to "gynocentric" French feminists such as Helen Cixous and Luce Irigaray (though not Julia Kristeva), for whom the development of *écriture feminine* is fundamentally subversive of the "phallogocentrism" of the Western tradition. Kathryn Morgan (n.d.) describes Anglophone feminist ethics as "an epistemological, metaphysical, ethical, and political paradigm shift so profound that often its practitioners are viewed as operating completely outside the bounds of anything recognizably philosophical." Marilyn Frye questions whether feminists really need ethics at all (Frye, 1991).

Before dismissing Western ethics entirely, however, feminists should take into account some other considerations. It is undeniable that we have inherited specific ethical discourses and even if these are sometimes inadequate for feminist purposes, it would hardly be conceivable, let alone prudent, for feminists (or anyone else) to resolve to start from scratch and reinvent everything. And contrary to the stereotypes that prevail in some quarters, the preceding brief survey has demonstrated that contemporary feminist ethics, like contemporary ethics in general, is characterized by variety, experimentation, and disagreement. Thus though some feminists indeed speak dismissively of almost the entire Western ethical tradition, others believe that the only parts of the tradition requiring feminist critique are its overtly misogynist elements. Many more, probably most, feminist philosophers argue for appropriating certain aspects of the canon and turning them to feminist purposes. Just as feminist political theory includes liberals, Marxists, and anarchists as well as those who claim to be simply feminists "unmodified" (MacKinnon 1987), so ethics includes feminist Aristotelians, Humeans, utilitarians, existential-ists, and contract theorists as well as "carers," "maternal thinkers," "womanists," and "spinsters." Given this variety in feminist ethics, and the ongoing nature of feminist evaluations of the canon, it would be presumptuous and sectarian to attempt to specify which aspects of Western ethical tradition are or are not suitable for feminist appropri-ation.

At this point, I'd like to address feminist claims that the Western tradition, or some parts of it, are distinctively masculine. Though such claims are often made, (indeed, I have made them myself), and though they can sometimes be suggestive or illuminating (for exam-ple, Di Stefano's analysis of Hobbes [1983]), there are many concep-tual and methodological difficulties in the way of establishing them. Among the most obvious of these difficulties is that the canonical texts of our tradition, like all texts, are open to competing interpreta-tions. Thus one feminist reads Diotima's speech in Plato's *Sym-posium* as contributing to the construction of a symbolic order that banishes femininity, whereas another reads it as celebrating the feminine (Fraser 1989). A second obvious difficulty is that since Western ethical tradition is immensely rich and varied, almost any generalization that one might make about it is open to immediate challenge by counter examples. It may be possible to argue that certain themes, such as a preference for permanence over change or for reason over emotion, have historically been dominant, but the existence of counter themes must also be recognized.

More difficult problems are raised by the variety and multidimen-sionality of the meanings of "masculinity" and "femininity." These terms may refer to empirical characteristics of men and women (empirical association), to social ideals for men and women (norma-tive association), or to things or attributes culturally associated with maleness and femaleness (symbolic association). Note that some-thing may be masculine or feminine in one or more of these senses but not in the others. For instance, chastity may be a social ideal for women regardless of women's actual sexual practice and even when women are culturally associated with sexual license. Rationality may be both normatively and culturally associated with masculinity even when actual men are often quite irrational.

The meanings of masculinity and femininity may be unclear in other ways. Not only do the characteristics considered masculine and feminine vary widely across cultures and history, but in complex societies they are also typically associated with other, seemingly nongendered, attributes such as class or race. For example, rationality and property owning may have been viewed as distinctively masculine attributes or ideals during certain periods in Western history, but obviously they were attributes or ideals only for men of a certain class and, perhaps, race. Similarly, the ideal of feminine chastity is not only culture-specific but also restricted by class and race. Thus those attributes viewed currently in Western societies as characteristically masculine in fact are often ideals only for bourgeois men. Consequently, the individualism allegedly characteristic of much Enlightenment ethical theory may be described plausibly either as masculine or as bourgeois. In this context, it is interesting to note that a number of the attributes currently seen as characteristically feminine have also been associated with negritude, with colonial Indians, and with indigenous Africans.[5] These considerations do not rule out in principle the possibility of characterizing certain features of Western ethics as masculine or feminine, but they do demonstrate the urgent need for precision in the use of these terms.

Even when relatively precise meanings for masculinity and femininity have been stipulated, it is not easy to justify their attribution to philosophical themes. If claims that Western tradition is masculine mean no more than that it has been constructed primarily by men rather than women, this is neither entirely true (Waithe 1987) nor, in itself, very interesting philosophically. If it means that certain assumptions or themes can be identified as empirically characteristic of men's thinking, then feminists have to account for those men whose views have been historically anomalous—though of course they can always assert that some men may think like women, just as some women are supposed to think like men. But claims about masculine and feminine ways of thinking, understood as claims about how men and women actually do think, are not easy to establish empirically, as we shall see in the next section. Nor is it much easier, given the symbolic complexity of our culture, to establish certain philosophical themes as symbolically masculine or feminine.

Finally, even if some philosophical assumptions or themes could be persuasively established as masculine or feminine in some relatively precise and well-established sense, it is not clear what the implications would be for feminist ethics. Whether the feminine is construed as empirical characteristic, social ideal, or symbolic association, it has been constructed inevitably in circumstances of male domination, and its value for feminism is likely, therefore, to be very questionable. In some cases, it is arguable that feminists would do better to appropriate what may have been constructed as the masculine aspects of Western ethics rather than the feminine ones.

For all these reasons, I believe that it is often more to the point for feminists to evaluate the philosophical canon in terms of whether or not it is male-biased rather than in terms of its supposed masculinity or femininity. Such bias can be demonstrated only through detailed arguments showing that specific claims or assumptions, evident in specific texts, function ideologically to delegitimate women's interests or subordinate them to men's. I believe that if feminist ethics focuses on male bias rather than on masculinity and femininity, it will be more likely to produce results that are not only textually defensible but also philosophically interesting and politically significant.

Feminist Ethics as Feminine Ethics

Philosophical attention to people's actual moral experience is part of what might be called the naturalist turn in contemporary moral epistemology—indeed, in contemporary epistemology generally. A focus on the moral experience of women specifically, however, is typically a feminist reaction to the canonical neglect or devaluation of women's moral experience. In principle, there is no reason why the experience of women could not simply be included as one element in a human moral experience undifferentiated by gender. We shall see later that a few contemporary ethical texts, through their use of gender-neutral language, create the impression of doing precisely this. In the context of explicitly feminist approaches to ethics, however, emphasis on women's moral experience is more typically part of the project to develop a distinctively feminine view of ethics.

From a feminist point of view, the call to reflect on women's moral experience is politically and methodologically indispensable. Cer-

tainly, there is a political point in revalorizing what has been conceptualized as the feminine. Moreover, a basic respect for women's
moral experience is necessary to acknowledging women's capacities
as moralists and to countering traditional stereotypes of women as
less than full moral agents, as childlike or close to nature.

Methodologically, empirical claims about differences in the moral
sensibility of women and men make it impossible to assume that any
approach to ethics will be unanimously accepted if it fails to consult
the moral experience of women. It is even plausible that women's
distinctive social experience may make them especially perceptive
regarding the male bias that feminists believe has pervaded so much
of male-authored Western moral theory.[6]

Like feminist attention to so-called women's issues, however,
feminist attention to women's moral experience may be misinterpreted. For instance, it may be taken as presuming that women's
moral experience is indeed substantially different from men's rather
than simply as investigating the question. In addition, the enterprise
of discovering women's moral experience is fraught with methodological difficulties. An obvious one is that the term "moral experience" is extremely broad, often used to cover such items as intuitions
about the resolution of specific moral problems, perceptions of what
is or is not moral, moral priorities, methodological commitments,
even emotional responses and actual behavior. Studying women's
moral experience, then, requires a careful analysis of the precise
object and method of our investigation.

There is also the question of which women we choose as the
subjects of our investigation. Just as feminists have complained that
traditional claims about "our" moral experience have excluded
women, so certain groups of women, such as women of color, lesbians, or nonmothers, have complained that the claims made by
feminists about "women's" moral experience have excluded them.
Gilligan's early work was criticized for making claims about women
on the basis of a study of female students at Harvard, clearly an elite
and extremely nonrepresentative sample. And women without children, especially those opposed to having children, have complained
that the emphasis on mothering in current feminist ethics does not
resonate with their own moral experience. It may well be that wom-
en's moral sensibilities vary so much, not only from culture to culture but even within cultures, that it is impossible to identify a single

distinctively feminine approach to ethics, even within a given culture.

Yet another methodological (and moral) problem in investigating women's moral experience is that it does not come prepackaged in familiar philosophical language. We have already encountered Gilligan's claims that the language of traditional ethical theory distorts the actual process of (some) women's moral thinking. Sara Ruddick has asserted that to articulate women's moral experience, we need a new language. But who is to develop this language and who is to confirm that it is appropriate? Who is authorized to speak for women? How can philosophers (or anyone) appropriate the experience of other women? Perhaps what is needed is the opportunity for women to speak for themselves. But even when women speak for themselves, there remains the potential for confusion, ideological manipulation, even self-deception.

These possibilities point to a final problem that confronts attempts to derive feminist ethics from women's moral experience: the problem that the feminine is not the feminist. This is true both on the empirical level where actual women are often strongly opposed to feminism, on the normative level where feminine ideals are often subversive of feminist aspirations, and on the symbolic level where what has been constructed as feminine in circumstances of male domination is often associated with values that are conspicuously nonfeminist and may even tend to promote women's subordination (Lloyd 1984).

Thus even though the project of feminist ethics must include a reevaluation of what has been constructed as feminine, and possibly even a rehabilitation of some aspects of it, this cannot be done in an uncritical way. Although *feminist* ethics may begin with *feminine* ethics, it cannot end with it.

Ethics for Feminists Only?

Some recent work in feminist ethics seems to abandon the Enlightenment injunction to prescribe universally as if for the rational subjects of a kingdom of ends. Instead, some feminists seem to believe they are prescribing for only a limited community, whether this is understood as a community of black women, of Western feminists or lesbians, or of women generally. Those feminist philosophers who address their work explicitly to limited communities may be seen as aligning themselves with the historicist tendency in contemporary moral philosophy. In Anglophone moral philosophy, this tendency is most evident in the so-called communitarianism of Michael Walzer (1983), Michael Sandel (1982), and Alasdair MacIntyre (1981), but it is also apparent in the recent work of John Rawls (1985), who, in spite of his announced Kantian loyalties, has now explicitly disavowed any pretensions to articulating a universal theory of justice and has limited the claims of his theory to those who share the traditions of liberal democracy.

Several philosophical and political factors have combined to discredit the idea of a universal morality. On the political side, they include concerns to avoid ethnocentrism and postcolonial domination. On the philosophical side, they include concerns about the indeterminacy of moral principles and doubts about the possibility of a universal or transcendent moral reason. Regarding the indeterminacy of moral principles, it is argued that even if universal normative principles could be identified, they would have to be given a highly abstract formulation and therefore would necessarily remain vague or indeterminate until they were interpreted in specific contexts. It is then pointed out that different contexts, different cultural institutions, and different moral and political practices inevitably would generate different interpretations of the principles and therefore different conclusions about right and wrong in specific instances. Unless some universal reason can be identified, there is no way of choosing some of these interpretations as "correct." But now the idea of a universal reason is increasingly doubted. Instead, it is increasingly accepted that reason is culturally constituted, consisting primarily of sets of traditional practices that take various forms. On such a view, the rules of inference taken to define rational argument cannot be justified independently of social agreements about what kinds of inferential moves are acceptable—and those agreements are inherently incomplete, open to contestation and regnegotiation. There is no essence of rationality against which they can be measured. These considerations point not only toward a naturalistic as opposed to a rationalistic moral epistemology—that is, toward an ethics grounded in actual moral experience—but also toward an understanding of ethics as plural and local rather than singular and universal, grounded not in transcendent reason but rather in historically specific moral practices and traditions.

The specter that haunts this regional understanding of ethics is, of course, the specter of relativism. Although the term "relativism" may be interpreted in a number of different ways, one of its central meanings is expressed by Gilbert Harman, whose naturalism "denies that there are universal basic moral demands and says different people are subject to different basic moral demands depending on the social customs, practices, conventions, values and principles that they accept" (1984). Such a view would seem to preclude feminist moral criticism of the domination of women where this is an accepted social practice and even to entail that only feminists are bound by feminist ethics.

Some tendencies in contemporary feminist ethics do seem to point toward this conclusion. One is the contemporary flirtation with postmodernism and another is claims that men are incapable in principle of the kind of moral sensibility that women are alleged to share. Nel Noddings (1984), Mary Daly (1978), Nancy Hartsock (1983), Susan Griffin (1980), and Adrienne Rich (1976) are sometimes interpreted, perhaps misinterpreted, as making such claims because they emphasize the epistemological and moral significance of the distinctively female experiences of menstruation, sexual intercourse, pregnancy, birth, and lactation. If such claims could be substantiated, they would seem to entail that a feminist ethics must be limited to women. Standing in opposition to such claims, however, is the work of many other feminist theorists, including me, who have argued the ultimate incoherence of biological determinism and pointed out that even those experiences that are biologically inaccessible to men gain meaning only in specific cultural contexts (Jaggar 1984). Indeed, even many of those who assert that it is possible to identify certain distinctively feminine forms of moral experience view these forms as resulting from women's characteristic social situation and state explicitly that they are open, at least in principle, to men (Ruddick 1989). In this context, it seems worth re-emphasizing that all women are not feminists and that some men are.

Against the relativist tendency in feminist ethics should be set feminism's concern that its moral critique of the practices (and theory) of the larger society—and perhaps even the practices (and theory) of other societies—should be objectively justified. Feminist ethics recognizes that we inhabit a painfully prefeminist world and takes itself to be contributing to the transformation of this world into one in which the basic moral commitments of feminism have become universally accepted—and in which, consequently, feminism has become otiose. From a feminist perspective, therefore, feminist ethics is necessarily transitional. Because of feminism's essential interest in social transformation, it is hard to see how feminists could be content with the parochial conventionalism or conservatism often associated at least with the communitarian tradition of contemporary moral relativism.

Given all this, it is probably best to view the restriction on ethical domain made by some contemporary feminist authors as a methodological strategy for developing distinctively feminist approaches to ethics. Alternative worldviews, whether scientific or moral, typically are projects best pursued in communities—but communities that share certain assumptions. Although feminists differ widely on a range of normative and theoretical issues, they do constitute a community in the sense that all share a few common assumptions. These include the view that the subordination of women is morally wrong and that the moral experience of women is worthy of respect. Feminist ethics may seek to explain or justify these claims, but it never seriously questions them. Indeed, it may be viewed as a collective commitment to working out the practical and theoretical consequences of these assumptions, a commitment perhaps analogous to the projects of those who develop so-called Christian or Marxist ethics, seeking to develop distinctive ways of living and thinking that reflect fundamental normative commitments currently shared by only a limited community.[7]

The feminist commitment is incompatible with any form of moral relativism that condones the subordination of women or the devaluation of their moral experience. It is neutral, however, between the plural and local understanding of ethics on the one hand and the ideal of a universal morality on the other. Feminists are committed to ethical theories that do not rationalize women's subordination or devalue their moral experience—but there may be many such theories.

Feminist Ethics as Gender-Blind

The idea that feminist ethics is only transitional, a temporary adaptation to a prefeminist world, lends credence to claims that the most advanced forms of feminist ethics today are gender-blind, addressing issues no longer identified as men's or women's issues in terms of categories that do not recognize distinctions of gender. Although such theories may appeal to moral sensibilities that feminists have often supposed to be distinctively feminine, they themselves do not identify these sensibilities as gendered. Is it possible that approaches to ethics that eschew references to gender might be more thoroughly feminist than approaches that claim explicit allegiance to feminism? While certainly paradoxical, such claims are not prima facie absurd.

Even though they should not be dismissed a priori, I contend that feminists should look on such claims with great suspicion. We should not forget that much of the achievement of feminist scholarship in a number of disciplines over the past twenty years has consisted precisely in identifying various forms of male bias concealed within apparently gender-blind assumptions or conceptual frameworks. Failing to recognize distinctions of gender at a time when gender operates as a set of socially instituted expectations that regulate every aspect of our lives, mostly to the advantage of men, is equivalent to refusing to acknowledge a pervasive system of domination. Pretending that social distinctions and privileges do not exist usually is equivalent to perpetuating them, as has become clear in legal contexts in the United States, where gender-blind and thus supposedly nondiscriminatory applications of law have often resulted in worsening women's situation (MacKinnon 1987; Jaggar 1990).

Examination of specific texts shows that male bias in philosophical writing did not end with the current wave of feminist scholarship. Susan Okin identifies a number of examples of what she calls "false gender-neutrality" in recent political and ethical theory, ranging from discussions of the issue of abortion in terms of fetuses and their "parents" to recommendations that we draw our moral inspiration from traditions such as Thomism that, Okin notes, "synthesize the Aristotelian view that women are a deformity in nature with the Christian view that women's sexuality is to blame for men's sinful lust" (1989:59). One author's discussion of Aristotle's views in gender-neutral language is so "patently absurd," Okin writes, that "one is left with the impression that it is his conscious intention to make the reader forget about the exclusionary nature of Aristotle's views about who could lead 'the good life for a human being' " (1989:45).

In our present social and intellectual circumstances, it is more than likely that ethics that is not done with an explicitly feminist consciousness will embody at best unintentional forms of male bias. For the time being, it is prudent to begin from the assumption that every ethical issue, practical or theoretical, is also a feminist issue. When our present situation is still so conspicuously prefeminist, it is premature to talk about a humanist rather than an explicitly feminist ethics. Silence about women's subordination may often mean witting or unwitting consent to it. Although feminist ethics does indeed look forward to a world in which explicit feminist commitments have become otiose, that world is still far in the future.

FEMINIST ETHICS AND THE FUTURE

The preceding analysis of several contemporary projects in feminist ethics makes it possible to draw some conclusions about feminist ethics in general. First of all, feminist ethics may be identified by its explicit commitment to challenging perceived male bias in ethics. Approaches that do not express such a commitment should be characterized as nonfeminist, a characterization that does not entail they are thereby necessarily antifeminist or male-biased. Nonfeminist ethics may or may not be male-biased; specific texts must be analyzed on a case-by-case basis.

Although feminist approaches to ethics are united by the shared project of eliminating male bias in ethics, they diverge widely in their views of how this project may be accomplished, divergences that result from a variety of philosophical differences, including differing conceptions of feminism, a perennially contested concept. Since such differences are likely to persist for the foreseeable future, feminist ethics cannot be identified in terms of a specific range of topics, methods, or orthodoxies. It cannot be restricted, for instance, to an examination of a few "women's issues" or to any allegedly feminine approach to ethics. There is no feminist ethics "unmodified."

The unifying feminist commitment to eliminating male bias in ethics is grounded, however, on at least two assumptions shared by all feminist approaches to ethics. The first of these is that the subordination of women is morally wrong; the second is that the moral experience of women should be treated as respectfully as the moral experience of men. These assumptions generate a certain practical and theoretical agenda for feminist ethics. On the practical level, these are, first, to articulate moral critiques of actions and practices that perpetuate women's subordination; second, to prescribe morally justifiable ways of resisting such actions and practices; and, third, to envision morally desirable alternatives that will promote women's emancipation. These goals are extremely general, but reflection on existing feminist criticisms of nonfeminist moral theory permits the specification of certain necessary conditions of their fulfilment.

First of all, feminist ethics can never begin by assuming that women and men are similarly situated—although it may discover that this is the case in certain respects in specific contexts. However, feminist ethics needs not only constant vigilance about the all-pervasiveness of gender privilege; it must also be sensitive to the ways in which gendered norms are different for different groups of women—or in which the same norms affect different groups differently. Ultimately, feminism's concern for *all* women means that feminist ethics must address not only "domestic" issues of racism or homophobia or class privilege but also such international issues as environmental destruction, war, and the current grotesque inequality in access to world resources.

In order to offer guides to action that will tend to subvert rather than reinforce women's present systematic subordination, feminist approaches to ethics must understand individual actions in the context of broader social practices, evaluating the symbolic and cumulative implications of any action as well as its immediately observable consequences. They must be equipped to recognize covert as well as overt manifestations of domination, subtle as well as blatant forms of control, and they must develop sophisticated accounts of coercion and consent. Similarly, they must provide the conceptual resources for identifying and evaluating the varieties of resistance and struggle in which women, particularly, have engaged. They must recognize the often unnoticed ways in which women and other members of the underclass have refused cooperation and opposed domination while acknowledging the inevitability of collusion and the impossibility of totally clean hands. In short, since feminist approaches to ethics are transitional, they must also be nonutopian, extensions of rather than alternatives to feminist political theory and exercises in nonideal theory rather than in what Rawls calls ideal theory.

Furthermore, since most of women's lives have been excluded from that domain conceptualized as public, an additional requirement for feminist approaches to ethics is that they should be able to provide guidance on issues of so-called private life: intimate relations, sexuality, and child-rearing. Thus they must articulate the moral dimensions of issues that may not hitherto have been recognized as moral. In addition, we have seen that feminist approaches to ethics must provide appropriate guidance for dealing with national and international issues, strangers and foreigners. In developing the conceptual tools for undertaking these tasks, feminist ethics cannot assume that moral concepts developed originally for application to the "public" realm—concepts such as impartiality or exploitation—are appropriate for use in the "private" realm; neither can it assume that concepts such as care, developed in intimate relationships, will necessarily be helpful in the larger world. Indeed, the whole distinction between public and private life must be examined critically by feminist ethics, with no prior assumptions as to whether the distinctions should be retained, redrawn, or rejected.

On the metaethical level, the goal of feminist ethics is to develop theoretical understandings of the nature of morality that treat women's moral experience respectfully but not uncritically. Although the abandonment of transcendental approaches to ethics leaves moral philosophers with no alternative to starting from actual moral experience, it is obvious that no critical ethical theory can be satisifed with convention and must find a way of moving from description to prescritption. Attempts to do this, of course, face some of the deepest problems in moral epistemology. I have identified some of these problems in the preceding section, but they are not, in principle, specific to feminst ethics.

Certain features of feminist ethics, however, illuminate these epistemological problems with special clarity. Most notably, the feminist insistence on the need for ethics to theoretically address both "actually existing" difference and "actually existing" domination displays the deficiencies and dangers inherent in the notion of idealized hypothetical consensus, a theoretical device that purports to bridge the gap between actual and rational moral belief by constructions of what people would, hypothetically, accept morally if only they were, contrary to fact, fully informed, rational, and uncoerced. The feminist recognition that difference and domination are pervasive features of our ethical situation leads, I would argue, to prioritizing actual over hypothetical consensus—and so actual over hypothetical dialogue. Such a view is foreign to most Anglo-American ethics. Bruce Ackerman, for instance, recently stated that "a morally reflective person *can* permissibly cut herself off from real-world dialogue" (1989:6):—and even Jürgen Habermas, one of the very few philosophers who has asserted the necessity for actual rather than hypothetical dialogue, to my knowledge has not addressed the practical question of how we should carry on our moral lives in the face of the apparently overwhelming difficulties in the way of achieving real-life moral consensus. It is my own view, though I cannot argue for it here, that the search for a feminist moral epistemology must confront these difficulties directly—a confrontation that will illustrate yet again the inseparability of feminist ethics from feminist politics. However, this is a topic for another time (Jaggar, forthcoming).

NOTES

This essay was first published in Herta Nagl-Docekal and Herlinde Pauer-Studer, eds., *Denken der Geschlechterdifferenz: Neue Fragen und Perspecktiven der Feministischen Philosophie* (Vienna: Wiener Frauenverlag, 1990).

I gratefully acknowledge helpful comments on an earlier draft of this paper from Claudia Card, Virginia Held, Marcia Lind, and Linda Nicholson. Perhaps unwisely, I have sometimes failed to follow their advice.

1. The conference was "Feminist Explorations in Feminist Ethics: Theory and Practice," organized by Eve Browning Cole and Susan Coultrap-McQuin in Duluth, Minnesota, October 7–8, 1988. The keynote speakers for the conference were Charlotte Bunch, who spoke on "A Global Perspective on Feminist Ethics and Diversity," and Sara Ruddick, whose paper was entitled "Maternal Thinking and Peace Politics."

2. In retrospect, one may speculate that one reason for my teachers' silence about issues of sex and gender was an assumption that "the woman question" had been largely resolved with the granting to women of such formally equal rights as the right to hold property and the right to vote. In addition, philosophers who thought about questions of sexual difference may have assumed that these had now become issues for psychology and physiology rather than philosophy. Finally, twentieth-century philosophers generally seem to have supposed that an author's views about women were philosophical asides, not integral to the central philosophical doctrines and therefore safely omitted

from a study of his/her work. For instance, a 1961 edition of the works of John Stuart Mill included his relatively minor essays "Nature" and "Utility of Religion" but excluded his classic "On the Subjection of Women" (Lerner 1961).

3. Aristotle asserted that virtue for women consisted in obedience, silence, and modesty, and Rousseau prescribed obedience and faithfulness for women. Kant thought that although the morally admirable person was characterized by rationality, self-control, strength of will, consistency, action based on universal principles, and adherence to duty and obligation, women were "generally incapable of deep thought and of sustained mental activity against obstacles. . . . Women [were] essentially incapable of acting otherwise than in accordance with their immediate inclinations and feelings. They [were] unable to adhere to moral principles of action and [could not] acknowledge any moral constraint on doing what pleases them" (Blum 1982:290). For Kant, women's virtues included charm, docility, complaisance, a feeling for beauty, and concern with a pleasing appearance.

4. Hegel believed that the ethical stage of family and marriage does involve rationality and universality but only at a lesser or incomplete level. Men, through their participation in labor, civil society, and (the highest level) the public life of the state, are able to transcend this stage, but women, confined to the home, are not. (Blum 1982; Pateman 1988). Unlike Hegel, Marx denied explicitly that women should be confined to the home, but he held a similarly derogatory view of the activities of the home. Although recognizing that the procreative labor assigned to women was socially necessary, Marx regarded it as less than fully human and believed that women could develop their truly human capacities only through labor outside the home. He even described the activities of the home, including "eating, drinking and procreating," as mere "animal functions" (Jaggar 1983:131).

5. Elizabeth V. Spelman has shown how the failure of much feminist theory to be sufficiently specific in using the terms "masculinity" and "femininity" has often resulted in the implicit equation of "women's" condition with the condition of white, middle-class, heterosexual, Christian women in Western industrialized countries (Spelman 1988).

6. Claims that women's distinctive social experience gives women a kind of epistemic privilege are characteristic of the "feminist standpoint" epistemology developed by, among others, Nancy Hartsock (1983), Alison Jaggar (1983; 1989), and Dorothy Smith (1987).

7. The reminder that feminist ethics is necessarily transitional suggests a new interpretation of Susan Sherwin's previously mentioned challenge to impartiality—though it does not illuminate Nel Noddings's challenge to this norm. If feminist ethics is viewed as a transitional ethics, then Sherwin's claim that women should have moral priority may be interpreted as a piece of moral strategy rather than a long-term moral ideal. In a prefeminist world, distinctions of gender are almost always relevant in assessing rights and responsibilities. The feminist commitment to women may seem biased or partial to nonfeminists, but for feminists it may not necessarily constitute a fundamental challenge to the ideal of impartiality.

REFERENCES

Ackerman, Bruce. 1989. "Why Dialogue?" *Journal of Philosophy* 86, no. 1 (January): 5–22.

Baier, Annette. 1985. "What Do Women Want in a Moral Theory?" *Nous* (March): 53–63.

Bell, Linda A. 1983. *Visions of Women.* Clifton, N.J.: Humana.

Blum, Lawrence. 1982. "Kant's and Hegel's Moral Rationalism: A Feminist Perspective," *Canadian Journal of Philosophy* 12, no. 2 (June): 287–302.

Coole, Diana. 1988. *Women in Political Theory: From Ancient Misogyny to Contemporary Feminism.* Boulder, Colo.: Lynne Rienner.

Daly, Mary. 1978. *Gyn/Ecology: The Metaethics of Radical Feminism.* Boston: Beacon Press.

Di Stefano, Christine. 1990. "Masculinity as Ideology in Political Theory: Hobbesian Man Considered," *Hypatia Reborn: Essays in Feminist Philosophy,* ed. Azizah Y. al-Hibri and Margaret A. Simons, 90–109. Bloomington: Indiana University Press.

Fraser, Nancy. 1989. "Introduction," *Hypatia* (special issue on French feminist philosophy) 3, no. 3 (Winter): 1–10.

Frye, Marilyn. 1983. *The Politics of Reality: Essays in Feminist Theory.* Trumansburg, N.Y.: Crossing Press.

———. 1991. "A Response to *Lesbian Ethics:* Why *Ethics?*" In *Feminist Ethics,* ed. Claudia Card, chap. 4. Lawrence: University Press of Kansas.

Gilligan, Carol. 1982. *In a Different Voice: Psychological Theory and Women's Development.* Cambridge, Mass.: Harvard University Press.

Griffin, Susan. 1980. *Women and Nature.* New York: Harper Colophon.

Harman, Gilbert. 1984. "Is There a Single True Morality?" In *Morality, Reason, and Truth: New Essays on the Foundations of Ethics,* ed. David Copp and David Zimmerman, 27–48. Totowa, N.J.: Rowman and Allanheld.

Hartsock, Nancy. 1983. *Money, Sex, and Power: Toward a Feminist Historical Materialism.* New York: Longman.

Held, Virginia. 1987. "Non-Contractual Society." In *Science, Morality, and Feminist Theory,* ed. Marsha Hanen and Kai Nielsen, 111–37. Calgary: University of Calgary Press.

Hoagland, Sarah Lucia. 1988. *Lesbian Ethics: Toward New Value.* Palo Alto, Calif.: Institute of Lesbian Studies.

Jaggar, Alison M. 1983. *Feminist Politics and Human Nature.* Totowa, N.J.: Rowman and Allanheld.

———. 1984. "Human Biology in Feminist Theory: Sexual Equality Reconsidered." In *Beyond Domination: New Perspectives on Women and Philosophy,* ed. Carol C. Gould, 21–42. Totowa, N.J.: Rowman and Allanheld.

———. 1989. "Love and Knowledge: Emotion in Feminist Epistemology," *Inquiry: An Interdisciplinary Journal of Philosophy* 32, no. 2 (June): 151–76.

————. 1990. "Sexual Difference and Sexual Equality." In *Theoretical Perspectives on Sexual Difference*, ed. Deborah L. Rhode, 239–254. New Haven and London: Yale University Press.

————. 1990. "Taking Consent Seriously: Feminist Practical Ethics and Actual Moral Dialogue." Paper presented at Midwest SWIP, Madison, November 11.

Jaggar, Alison M., and William L. McBride. 1990. " 'Reproduction' as Male Ideology." In *Hypatia Reborn: Essays in Feminist Philosophy*, ed. Azizah Y. al-Hibri and Margaret A. Simons, 249–269. Bloomington: Indiana University Press.

Lerner, Max. 1961. *The Essential Works of John Stuart Mill*. New York: Basic Books.

Lloyd, Genevieve. 1984. *The Man of Reason: 'Male' and 'Female' in Western Philosophy*. Minneapolis: University of Minnesota Press.

Lugones, María C., with Elizabeth V. Spelman. 1990. "Have We Got a Theory for You! Feminist Theory, Cultural Imperialism, and the Demand for 'The Woman's Voice.' " In *Hypatia Reborn: Essays in Feminist Philosophy*, ed. Azizah Y. al-Hibri and Margaret A. Simons, 18–33. Bloomington: Indiana University Press.

————, with Elizabeth V. Spelman. 1987a. "Competition, Compassion, and Community." In *Competition: A Feminist Taboo?* ed. Helen Longino and Valerie Miner, 234–247. New York: Feminist Press.

————. 1987b. "Playfulness, 'World'-Traveling, and Loving Perception," *Hypatia* 2, no. 2 (Summer): 3–19.

————. 1991. "On the Logic of Pluralist Feminism." In *Feminist Ethics*, ed. Claudia Card, chap. 2. Lawrence: University Press of Kansas.

MacIntyre, Alasdair. 1981. *After Virtue: A Study in Moral Theory*. London: Duckworth.

MacKinnon, Catharine A. 1987. *Feminism Unmodified: Discourses on Life and Law*. Cambridge, Mass.: Harvard University Press.

Mahowald, Mary Briody. 1978. *Philosophy of Woman: Classical to Current Concepts*. Indianapolis: Hackett Publishing Company.

Morgan, Kathryn Pauly. N.d. "Strangers in a Strange Land: Feminists Visit Relativists" (unpublished paper).

Noddings, Nel. 1984. *Caring: A Feminine Approach to Ethics and Moral Education*. Berkeley: University of California Press.

Okin, Susan Moller. 1989. *Justice, Gender, and the Family*. New York: Basic Books.

Pateman, Carole. 1988. *The Sexual Contract*. Stanford, Calif.: Stanford University Press.

Rawls, John. 1985. "Justice as Fairness: Political Not Metaphysical," *Philosophy and Public Affairs* 14, no. 3 (Summer): 223–51.

Rich, Adrienne. 1976. *Of Woman Born*. New York: W. W. Norton.

Ruddick, Sara. 1989. *Maternal Thinking: Toward a Politics of Peace*. Boston: Beacon Press.

Sandel, Michael J. 1982. *Liberalism and the Limits of Justice.* Cambridge: Cambridge University Press.

Sherwin, Susan. 1987. "A Feminist Approach to Ethics," *Resources for Feminist Research* 16, no. 3 (September): 25–28.

Smith, Dorothy. 1987. *The Everyday World as Problematic: A Feminist Sociology.* Boston: Northeastern University Press.

Spelman, Elizabeth V. 1988. *Inessential Woman: Problems of Exclusion in Feminist Thought.* Boston: Beacon Press.

Trebilcot, Joyce. Forthcoming. *In Process: Radical Lesbian Essays.* Albany: SUNY.

Waithe, Mary Ellen. 1987. *A History of Women Philosophers: Ancient Women Philosophers,* 600 B.C.–500 A.D. Vol. 1. Dordrecht: Martinus Nijhoff.

Walzer, Michael. 1983. *Spheres of Justice: A Defense of Pluralism and Equality.* New York: Basic Books.

Part Two
Character and Moral Agency

7 / Why Terrorism
Is Morally Problematic

BAT-AMI BAR ON

In my life and in the lives of members of my family, terrorism has been a formative force. In this essay I will examine how terrorism forms the terrorized. I will argue that what is morally problematic about terrorism is that it produces people who are psychologically and morally diminished and it is, therefore, cruel. This brute fact is not addressed by the standard moral arguments offered by contemporary philosophers about terrorism. Those arguments appeal to the "just war" tradition and thus to abstract principles. Looking at the way in which terrorism forms the terrorized reveals that such appeals are insufficient to condemn and especially to condone terrorism.

That terrorism operates psychologically in certain ways became clearest for me just after the *intifada*[1] started. I was in Israel and talking with one of my cousins about the situation. I argued that the formation of an independent Palestinian state was the only realistic compromise solution to the Jewish-Israeli[2]–Palestinian conflict. I was told in response that the formation of an independent Palestinian state would endanger the state of Israel with a war. When I claimed that the *intifada* together with the militarily enforced official Israeli repression constitute a war, I was told that at least this war is not happening within Israel's borders and thus does not endanger the majority of the Jewish-Israeli population.

I realized as the discussion developed that my cousin genuinely believed that for the Palestinians an independent state would be first and foremost a means to assert a destructive power against her and her family and against the Jewish-Israeli population. Motivating this belief was a deep-seated fear that also motivated a clinging to the Israeli military as the only shield against the expected destruction and a commitment to the deployment and use, including inhumane use, of the military against the Palestinians.

Since Jewish-Israeli life within the 1948 disengagement lines, which delineate what is popularly believed to form the pre-1967 Israeli borders, seemed undisturbed by the *intifada,* my cousin's fear can make sense only given the history of the Jewish-Israeli–Palestinian relationship. Looked at from the Jewish-Israeli perspective, this relationship has been colored by Palestinian terrorism ever since the beginning of Jewish settlement in the area at the end of the nineteenth century. My cousin's fear, a fear I recognize in myself, is a product of growing up under and living with the constant threat of terrorism. Although this threat was magnified by the Israeli government's official pronouncements and the official history of Israel,[3] it was nonetheless real.

For the purpose of this essay the only salient fact about terrorism is that it is a practice of terrorization in which terror is a means to an end other than itself.[4] The means used to terrorize, the possible distinctions among the ends, and the practitioners of terrorism are all insignificant insofar as this essay is concerned. Knowing the means, ends, and practitioners may help one to list the different kinds of terrorism, to chart it historically and culturally, to understand the relation between it and technology, or to see its place in local or global social, political, or economic structures or power relations.[5] But knowledge of the means, ends, and practitioners of terrorism does not shed light on terrorism as a formative process.

Letting terrorism be understood as a practice of terrorization in which terror is a means to an end other than itself does not permit one to categorize as terroristic a random attack on a school by a psychotic person, no matter how violent and terrifying, since it is not a means to a further end. On the other hand, such a conception of terrorism does permit one to categorize as terroristic certain practices of nation-states—for example, the repressive actions of the Argentinian junta during the "dirty war," the nuclear strategies of the United States and the USSR, the actions of criminal organizations such as the Colombian drug cartel, and the U.S. government's tactics of intimidation against organized crime—since they do have ends other than terrorization.

The inclusive conception of terrorism that I have adopted here would trouble anyone committed to a distinction between terrorism and freedom fighting, be the source of the commitment politically on the left or on the right—hence, a commitment to the work of groups such as the El Salvadoran Farabundo Marti National Liberation Front (FMLN), or the Afghan Mujahadin, respectively. Conor Cruise O'Brien, who believes that a distinction between freedom fighters and terrorists is viable, says:

> We reserve the use [of the words "terrorism" and "terrorist"] in practice for politically motivated violence *of which we disapprove.* The words imply a judgement about the political context in which those whom we decide to call terrorists operate, and above all about the nature of the regime under which and against which they operate. We imply that the regime itself is *legitimate.* If we call them "freedom fighters" we imply that the regime is illegitimate.[6]

O'Brien's claims, which focus on what he calls "politically motivated violence," first suggest that in ordinary usage "terrorism" and "freedom fighting" are terms used not merely to describe but also to morally condemn and commend. His analysis then points out that the basis for the moral condemnation or commendation is the end of the "politically motivated violence" and that it is the ends with the moral meanings attached to them that are used to distinguish between terrorism and freedom fighting.

Although O'Brien's analysis of the ordinary usage of terrorism and freedom fighting is not wrong, the ordinary-language distinction between the two terms is not strong enough to be able to claim that the two are conceptually distinct. They are not. The ordinary-usage distinction between terrorism and freedom fighting presupposes that the ends of a practice are the necessary and sufficient criteria to distinguish among practices, and this is just not so. Furthermore, according to the ordinary usage, the terms "terrorism" and "freedom fighting" have certain normative connotations that are important for the distinction between them. Yet these connotations are simply the products of Western politics.

"Terrorism" as a negative term was coined in 1795 by the French Directory to refer specifically to the repressive measures practiced by Robespierre's government. It later was used to describe the activities of nineteenth-century clandestine oppositional groups in Russia. Not surprisingly, because these groups were considered revolutionary, "terrorism" retained its negative connotations in the dictionaries of the time even though these groups were different from the French revolutionaries, and their ends differed also. Furthermore, these groups did not necessarily consider themselves terroristic, and if they did, they viewed terrorism positively. As they saw it, they were freedom fighters.[7]

I think this brief discussion shows that terrorism and freedom fighting are not conceptually distinct and thus that terrorists can be freedom fighters and freedom fighters can be terrorists. One could similarly show that other distinctions people attempt to make to save some action from being classified as terroristic will not work. If terrorism is a practice, then, as uncomfortable as it may be to think so, the Allies' strategic use of air raids against the German civilian population during the Second World War was as terroristic as the Germans' bombardment of London with V rockets. The Irish Republican Army relies on terrorism in its war of liberation, as did the Palestine Liberation Organization. And the South African and Salvadoran death squads, even if only covertly supported by their governments, are also terroristic.

Suppose, then, that terrorism is a practice of terrorization in which terror is a means to an end other than itself. What can be said about it as a process through which the terrorized are formed?

In *The Demon Lover: On the Sexuality of Terrorism*,[8] Robin Morgan claims that terrorism democratizes violence and brings men to experience the world in relation to each other similarly, though not identically, to how women experience the world in relation to men. She begins with the description of the woman.

> Look closely at her. She crosses a city street, juggling her briefcase and her sack of groceries. Or she walks down the dirt road, balancing a basket on her head. Or she hurries toward her locked car, pulling a small child along with her. Or she trudges home from the fields, the baby strapped to her back. Suddenly there are footsteps behind her. Heavy, rapid. A man's footsteps. She knows this immediately, just as she knows that she must not look around. She quickens her pace in time to the quickening of her

pulse. She is afraid. He could be a rapist. He could be a soldier, a harasser, a robber, a killer. He could be none of these. He could be a man in a hurry. He could be a man merely walking at his normal pace. But she fears him. She fears him because he is a man. She has reason to fear. She does not feel the same way—on a city street or dirt road, in parking lot or field—if she hears a woman's footsteps behind her.[9]

Morgan later adds the comparable description of the man:

Now look closely at him. He hurries through the airport to catch his plane. Or he pedals his bicycle, basket laden with books to the university. Or he mounts the steps to his embassy on official business. Or he snaps a fresh roll of film into his camera and starts out on an assignment. Suddenly, there are footsteps behind him. Heavy, rapid. A man's footsteps. In the split second before he turns around, he knows he's afraid. He tells himself he has no reason to fear. But he fears. *He does not feel the same way if he hears a woman's footsteps behind him.*[10]

Morgan's descriptions make it vividly clear that as a formative process, terrorism produces people who are afraid. Terrorized people's fear is deep and easily triggered by the slightest indication of possible danger. Yet the fear is triggered by things and movements that are not extraordinary within an ordinary day-to-day context. And the day-to-day ordinariness of the terrorized circumstances does not dissipate the fear.

Morgan does not talk about the consequences of living a life in which fear is triggered so easily under what should be ordinary circumstances. Some of the consequences are described by Leo Lowenthal in his "Terror's Atomization of Man,"[11] an essay written in 1946 about fascist state terrorism. According to Lowenthal, terrorism interrupts the causal relation between what people do and what happens to them. As a result, the terrorized's sense of a continuous experience and memory weakens and even breaks down. This in turn leads to a shrinking or breakdown of personality.

How this happens can be clarified somewhat by a comparison of terrorism with seasoning, the process used by pimps to form prostitutes. Kathleen Barry discusses the process in *Female Sexual Slavery*,[12] and Marilyn Frye elaborates on it in *The Politics of Reality*.[13] Frye writes:

> While he holds her in captivity and isolation he brutalizes the victim in as many ways as there are to brutalize.... The abductor's brutality functions in several ways. By placing the victim in a life-threatening and absolutely aversive situation, he maximizes the urgency of the victim's taking action in her own behalf while making it utterly impossible for her to do so. This puts maximum force into the process of alienating her from herself through total helplessness. The result is radical loss of self-esteem, self-respect and any sense of capacity or agency.... After having been in a situation where her presence as agent has been reduced to nothing, she now has the opportunity to try to act in support of her physical survival. She can try to discover what pleases and what displeases the man, and try to please him and avoid displeasing him.[14]

Like seasoning, terrorism places its victims in a life-threatening situation in which one feels both a need to do something to save oneself and a helplessness. The terrorized too will experience an alienation from self and a loss of the sense of oneself as an agent capable of acting on her or his own behalf and deserving of respect. The sense of alienation from self together with the lack of a sense of agency and dignity constitute a dissolution of the individual self. What is left is a will to survive, as evidenced in the case of the victim of seasoning, who attempts to live through satisfying the pimp.

Another way to understand terrorism as a formative process is by comparing it with torture, which, like seasoning, is also a practice in which brutalization is used as a means to break a person down. In *The Body in Pain*,[15] Elaine Scarry analyzes several aspects of torture. Like Morgan, Scarry begins with the transformation of the ordinary. Like Lowenthal, she emphasizes the consequences of torture, which also constitute the dissolution of the ordinary world. Scarry describes the transformation of a room:

> In torture the world is reduced to a single room or set of rooms. Called "guest rooms" in Greece and "safe houses" in the Philippines, the torture rooms are often given names that acknowledge

and call attention to the generous, civilizing impulse normally present in the human shelter. They call attention to the impulse only as a prelude to announcing its annihilation. The torture room is not just the setting in which the torture occurs. . . . It is itself literally converted into another weapon, into an agent of pain. All aspects of the basic structure—walls, ceiling, window, doors—undergo this conversion.[16]

Scarry proceeds from here to focus on the interrogation and its end—the confession—and calls attention to elements that Frye focuses on in her discussion of seasoning. Scarry writes: "Torture systematically prevents the prisoner from being the agent of anything and simultaneously pretends that he is the agent of some things. Despite the fact that in reality he has been deprived of all control over, and therefore all responsibility for, his world, his words, his body, he is to understand his confession as it will be understood by others, as an act of self-betrayal."[17]

It is not only confession that will be experienced as self-betrayal. The torturer controls the tortured body and voice and can make the tortured act or stop acting, speak, sing, or scream or stop speaking, singing, or screaming.[18] The torturer's control is a function of the ability to cause pain, and it is through the experience of pain that the tortured is formed into a self-betrayer because this experience dissolves the distinction between outside and inside the body, conflates the private and the public, destroys language, and obliterates the contents of consciousness.[19]

Like the tortured, the terrorized may come to experience themselves as self-betrayers, and the possibility of self-betrayal is one of the things they fear most, because the terrorized, like the tortured, realize very quickly once their terrorization begins that what is at issue for their tormentors is the length of time it may take for them to break down and betray themselves by accepting the terrorists' demands. Indeed, from the point of view of the terrorist, as from the point of view of the torturer, terrorization consists of a series of tests of strength that are designed to reveal the weakness of their victims to the terrorist and to the victims.

When the victims feel tested, they know that what is being tested is the strength of their will. As they become aware of their weakness, they also become aware of the erosion of their will. This is accompanied by a diminishing sense of self, since under these conditions the self becomes the will. Everything else is stripped away. When the will erodes totally or when it feels as if it has been broken, nothing is left of the self.

One may want to claim that although a comparison of terrorism with seasoning or torture may provide some insight, terrorism actually differs significantly from both because it does not occur in circumstances that allow for the kind of intensity that takes place in seasoning or torture. After all, in the case of terrorism, the terrorized are not totally at the mercy of the terrorists. In fact, only some terrorized are not at the mercy of the terrorists, usually those living under the threat of some form of political terrorism, especially when it is an oppositional practice. When, for example, a state is in the business of terrorizing its citizenry and has in place the organizations necessary for carrying out the terrorizing—such as the Nicaraguan national guard during Somoza's rule—the people are very much at the mercy of their state. Under these conditions, people can usually find refuge from their government only by becoming exiles. Resistance is a viable alternative to exile only when the resistance movement has succeeded in occupying and maintaining a territory in which its members are relatively safe, as the Sandinistas did in Nicaragua.

Still, most torture happens within Goffmanian total institutions[20] such as jails, prisons, concentration camps, and special torture camps. Seasoning has in common with torture the confinement and isolation of its victims. Being and feeling at the mercy of torturers and pimps is the function of the confinement and isolation. Terrorists, on the other hand, do not confine and isolate the terrorized.

Again, much too much is claimed about terrorism in general. But even in the case of those terrorized by oppositional political terrorism—the kind of terrorism that at the outset seems just not to take place in circumstances resembling the confinement and isolation of the tortured—the situation is much more complicated. This fact is testified to by the practices states institute to control terrorism (such as careful inspection of people and luggage in airports) and the general fear that terrorism endangers the liberal democratic state.[21]

This general fear, noted by many contemporary experts on international oppositional political terrorism, causes liberal democratic states to risk violating civil liberties because of the practices they have to institute to prevent terrorism within their borders. To be effective they have to work like a screen that does not permit infiltration by terrorists into the state. They must also facilitate tracing an infiltration if and when it occurs.

Thus in Israel, for example, roads at certain intervals have checkpoints staffed by military personnel, who stop and inspect all cars. For buses, the armed soldiers get in and inspect the luggage racks, making sure that every item has an owner among the people on the bus. To maximize security on its campus, the University of Tel-Aviv is surrounded by a fence, and at the gates, security personnel check every bag that is brought in. Security personnel check every bag brought into every public building in Israel, including movie theaters. Helicopters patrol the seashores on the hour, and a civilian militia patrols them on foot. It also patrols the streets of every town twenty-four hours a day. Children at summer camps and at schools are always accompanied by armed guards on their field trips. Everyone in Israel is expected to carry officially issued identity papers and produce them upon the demand of the police, militia, or army. Everywhere in Israel there are posters that remind the public of terrorism and of the people's obligation to be alert and vigilant, to always survey their environment for suspicious items, movement, or individuals.

These various practices instituted by states to combat terrorism confine and isolate the citizenry and put it under constant surveillance. Surveillance makes one feel simultaneously safer and more vulnerable. One feels safer because one feels protected by it. But at the same time, one feels more exposed and not only to one's own government, especially if terrorists have been successful in their attempts, because this means that they are even better at surveillance than the government. The consequences of this state of affairs are best captured by Foucault's explanation of the workings of Bentham's panopticon in *Discipline and Punish*.[22] According to him the panoptic mechanism arranges things so that it is possible to see everyone constantly and recognize everyone immediately, and anyone can use it at anytime. The effect is to induce in those who are observed a state of conscious and permanent visibility that assures the automatic functioning of power.

Thus even in the case of terrorists who do not confine and isolate their victims, circumstances are altered in response to their terrorism. The new situation has within it the elements needed to create for the terrorized an intense experience of feeling totally at the mercy of the terrorists. This suffices to start the process of the formation of the self as the self of a terrorized person, a fearful self that contracts and is organized more and more around its experience as a certain level of strength of will.

My description of terrorism can tempt one to argue that what is morally problematic with terrorism is that it is a coercive practice, a practice whose structure Marilyn Frye describes as follows: "The structure of coercion, then, is this: to coerce someone into doing something, one has to manipulate the situation so that the world as perceived by the victim presents the victim with a range of options the least unattractive of which (or the most attractive of which) in the judgement of the victim is the act one wants the victim to do."[23] But to argue this, though formally correct, requires the conceptual classification of terrorism with practices that do not involve the intentional erosion of selves and the intentional breaking of wills, such as a state's paternalistic imposition of seatbelts, helmets, or a 55-mile-per-hour speed limit. Conceiving terrorism as a practice of terrorization through which a self is intentionally eroded and a will is intentionally broken implies, I believe, that *what morally problematizes terrorism is that it is cruel.*

That cruelty is the crux of what is morally problematic with terrorism becomes clearer when one thinks about the things terrorists do when they terrorize: bombing a city, shooting indiscriminately in an airport, abducting and killing people. Such events provide the occasion for a variety of possible attitudes and moral dispositions toward those who suffer as a result of these terroristic acts. Some people are motivated to help the victims of terrorism. Others are motivated to increase their suffering. The latter disposition is cruelty. One expects people who intentionally induce and increase suffering either to take pleasure in other people's pain or to be indifferent to it. Tom Regan notes these two kinds of cruelty in "Cruelty, Kindness, and Unnecessary Suffering."[24]

The central case of cruelty appears to be the case where, in Locke's apt phase, one takes "a seeming kind of pleasure" in causing another to suffer. . . . Not all cruel people are cruel in this sense. Some cruel people do not take pleasure in making others suffer. Indeed, they seem not to feel anything. Their cruelty is manifested by a lack of what is judged as appropriate feeling . . . for the plight of the individual whose suffering they cause. . . . [T]hey are . . . insensitive to the suffering they inflict, unmoved by it, as if they were unaware of it or failed to appreciate it as suffering.[25]

Terrorists intentionally intensify the suffering of people whom they intentionally victimize. And although they may not take pleasure in this, in some important sense they have to be indifferent to the pain they cause. Sergey Nechaev and Mikhail Bakunin express this clearly in their *Revolutionary Catechism*, written in 1869 for clandestine Russian oppositional groups. In this booklet, they say:

1. The revolutionary is a lost man; he has no interests of his own, no cause of his own, no feelings, no habits, no belongings; he does not even have a name. . . .

2. In the very depths of his being, not just in words but in deed, he has broken every tie with the civil order, with the educated world and all laws, conventions, and generally accepted conditions and with the ethics of this world. . . .

. . .

6. Hard with himself, he must be hard toward others. All the tender feelings of family life, of friendship, love, gratitude, and even honour must be stifled in him by a single cold passion for the revolutionary cause. . . .

. . .

13. . . . He is not a revolutionary if he feels pity for anything in this world. If he is able to, he must face the annihilation of a situation, of a relationship, or of any person who is part of this world—everything and everyone must be equally odious to him.[26]

Terrorists are cruel, therefore, not only because they create and worsen in an obvious way the suffering that comes through the body but also because they create the anguish that the terrorized experience as they feel their selves erode and fear they will break.

So, if cruelty morally problematizes terrorism, what, then, is morally wrong with cruelty? It is not easy to capture what is morally wrong with cruelty. But cruelty horrifies, and Steven G. Smith suggests that the repugnance felt is a "protesting recoil from a violation" of normative, value-laden "shoulds" and "should nots."[27] Given Smith's analysis, in the case of a terrorist's cruelty, the violated "should not" seems to be the Kantian categorical imperative prohibiting the use of people as means only. Yet there are also "shoulds" that seem to be violated by cruelty: the "shoulds" of compassion, kindness, and hospitality.

Lawrence Blum believes compassion is directed at "a person in a negative condition, suffering from harm, difficulty, or danger (past, present or future)."[28] He points out that it characteristically involves "imaginative dwelling on the condition of another person, an active regard for his good, a view of him as a fellow human being, and emotional responses of a certain degree of intensity."[29] Tom Regan contrasts cruelty with kindness: "A kind person is one who is inclined (disposed) to act with the intention of forwarding the interest of others, not for reasons of self-gain, but out of love, affection or compassion for the individuals whose interests are forwarded."[30]

Philip Hallie contrasts cruelty with hospitality. In "From Cruelty to Goodness,"[31] he says that he learned that the two were opposites after reading about the Huguenot French village of Le Chambon de Ligon, which saved about six thousand people, many of them Jewish children, from the Nazis. The village, whose population was poor, had about thirty-five hundred people. Beginning in 1940, the villagers sheltered the refugees, taking many of them across the mountains to neutral Geneva. What was so special about the villagers of La Chambon was that they sincerely welcomed the refugees, shared everything they had with them and were surprised when asked why they did it. According to them, even though this endangered them as individuals and as a community, this is what they should have done if they were to manifest their belief in a love for humanity.

Neither cruelty nor compassion, kindness nor hospitality, enters the standard moral discussions of terrorism with their limited focus on political and especially oppositional terrorism. These discussions are usually framed by the Western "just war" tradition.[32] According to this tradition, one has to distinguish between the general question of whether some resort to force is morally justified and the particular question of whether this or that specific form of force is morally justified. The answers to these two questions, which are presumed to be independent of each other, can be found by following certain guidelines. These guidelines define the "just war" tradition.

To assess whether some resort to force is morally justified one needs to decide (1) whether there is a just cause for the use of force, that is, some wrong to be redressed through it; (2) whether there is a legitimate authority seeking to use it, popular support for it, and ways of controlling it; (3) whether force is being used as the last resort; and (4) whether the overall damage that will result from the use of force is at least balanced by the good that will be attained by it. On the other hand, to assess whether a specific form of the use of force is morally justified, one needs to decide (1) what is the balance of proximate good and bad that would result from using a specific form of force, and (2) whether this specific form of force discriminates between combatants and noncombatants.

Michael Walzer frames his discussion of political oppositional terrorism very strictly within the "just war" tradition. He argues that it is morally unjustifiable because it fails to discriminate between combatants and noncombatants.[33] R. M. Hare argues that political oppositional terrorism, which he distinguishes from revolutionary violence, is morally unjustifiable because it leads to more destruction than good.[34] Among the latest variations on both arguments is that of C. A. J. Coady. He argues that no form of political terrorism could be morally justified because it fails to discriminate between combatants and noncombatants and because it is ineffective.[35]

Those who morally object to terrorism are not the only ones who rely on the "just war" tradition. Robert Young appeals to this tradition by arguing that revolutionary terrorism is morally justifiable because of its just cause, because it is a tactic of last resort, and because it is more economical than a war, achieving the same results with less destruction.[36] According to Young, even if revolutionary terrorism involves harming noncombatants, it is not ultimately morally unjustifiable. It just requires a more complex justification.

Though the "just war" tradition has provided a framework for the standard discussions of terrorism, most of the arguments either for or against terrorism do not use all of the criteria or guidelines for assessment that the tradition provides. In addition, they do not clearly distinguish between the assessment of use of force in general and the assessment of a specific use of force. Thus, for example, both Hare and Young, while treating terrorism as a specific use of force, discuss it primarily in terms designed for assessing the use of force in general. And no one seems to bother to assess whether terrorism has a legitimate authority behind it.

For me, this problem of legitimate authority is not as important as the fact that from the beginning of its construction by Augustine, the "just war" tradition was designed to legitimate certain wars. A war's just cause was given priority to make this possible. Limitations on the legitimate use of force were put in place to mitigate its destructiveness. In using the "just war" framework to discuss terrorism, the issue becomes the possibility of its legitimation. Just cause is made the most important criterion of assessment. Destructiveness is a concern only in relation to the possible need to limit it.

I do not know why just cause was given priority over other criteria. I think that concern only about the physical destructiveness of certain forms of force—about the extent of injury, death, and rubble—is much too limited a moral worry, at least in the case of terrorism. The most important issue is not the balance between advantages gained and material destruction. The most important issue is the formation of persons through terrorization and the fact that terrorism requires terrorists to be cruel rather than compassionate, kind, and hospitable.

It could be said that my issue is addressed by concerns about destruction typical of the "just war" tradition because what I worry about is psychic injury, a worry that need not be restricted to the terrorized but can be extended to the terrorist. In the process of terrorization, terrorists also form themselves as psychically injured persons.

Further, if my concerns are seen as belonging to an "ethics of care," which gives precedence to empathy, their conflict with the standard moral discussions of terrorism, insofar as they are framed by the "just war" tradition, can be viewed as a conflict with justice. An "ethics of justice" gives precedence to abstract moral principles concerned with justice, and the "just war" tradition seems to be motivated by concerns situated within this kind of ethics.[37]

However, my concern with how individuals are formed through terrorization, be it the terrorized or the terrorists, is not merely a

concern with the physical damage inflicted, and I am not uncon-
cerned with justice. Like others who have tried to argue that an ethics
of care and an ethics of justice, though different, are not really in
conflict,[38] I am interested in challenging the prioritization of justice
and not in its substitution by empathy. Both empathy and justice
have to be accorded a serious place in moral thinking.

I am not certain how to accord both empathy and justice a serious
place in moral thinking. Yet when I reflect on terrorism, I find that
responses to the terrorism of organized crime or perhaps to covert
right-wing state terrorism (for example, that practiced in Guatemala)
are helpful in clarifying the relation between empathy and justice in
the moral assessment of terrorism. As I see it, the difference between
the responses to these two forms of terrorism is that though both
horrify because both are cruel, the horror in the case of organized
crime is not accompanied by surprise at or disillusionment with the
cruelty of the criminals, whereas the horror in state terrorism is
accompanied by surprise at and disillusionment with the cruelty of
politicians. Unlike the terrorism of organized crime, the terrorism of
a state against its citizens leaves the victims with a deep sense of
betrayal.

I believe this difference in response can be accounted for by expectations from the relation between the ends and the means used to
achieve them. The ends of organized crime—the accumulation of
wealth and power—do not limit the means that can be used to obtain
them. On the other hand, unless one is already disillusioned and
corrupted by cynicism, one cannot view the means to the ends that
politicians ought to have—the service and maintenance of communities for the good of their members—as independent of these
ends. Organized crime can achieve its ends by all means necessary.
Criminals need not be just or decent. However, politicians must be
just and decent and so cannot use all means necessary to achieve their
ends.

Moreover, there are means that would not fit organized crime's
ends but would undermine them just as there are means that would
not fit the ends that politicians ought to have but would undermine
them. Terrorism is not a means that would undermine the ends of
organized crime. Yet even if one could show, as the Guatemalan
right-wing politicians try to, that terrorism may serve a greater com-
munal good in the future (for example, increase the wealth available

for distribution to all the members of the community, thereby making the community better and more just), it is very hard to see how this should count for more than what happens to the people who are terrorized and who terrorize. Terrorism produces fearful people with diminished selves organized around the experience of the fear of the loss of their strength of will. It also produces cruel people, people who feel no compassion or kindness and are inhospitable. Could such people enjoy the promised future goods?

If there is a promised future good whose value seems overwhelming, it is freedom from conditions in which people are formed as they are by terrorism. Contrary to Fanon and Sartre,[39] I doubt very much that such a future can be brought about by terrorism. Fanon's patients are much more resilient than I think people really are, especially given the growing evidence on post-traumatic stress disorder.[40] Post-traumatic stress shapes the lives not only of individuals whose experiences resulted in the stress but the young people who grow up with them as well. The children of Holocaust survivors have Holocaust nightmares.[41]

So in the case of terrorism, it seems that one cannot fail to give precedence to empathy, to concern about what happens to people who are terrorized and to people who terrorize. Yet this concern has its foundation not merely in care for people as individuals and the possibility that they may be harmed but also in care for them as members of communities. As producers and distributors of wealth and power, communities can continue for a long time independently of the kind of people who populate them. But good communities—communities that are fairly just, that get along not only contractually but generously, that take each other concretely into consideration, and whose members are free of daily fears for their survival and physical well-being—these communities need people who care. Neither the terrorized nor the terrorists can care well enough—for themselves or for others.[42]

NOTES

Versions of this chapter were read at the SUNY College at Oswego and at Le Moyne College. I would like to thank the Central New York Feminist Philosophers Study Group, Sandra Bartky, and Claudia Card for their insightful comments.

1. The *intifada* is the Palestinian uprising in the areas that were occupied by the state of Israel in the 1967 Six Days War. Following the Israeli War of Independence in 1948, these areas were held by Jordan (the West Bank, or Judaea and Samaria) and Egypt (the Gaza Strip), respectively. The *intifada* began in December 1988. Its declared end is the formation of an independent Palestinian state.

2. I am using the term "Jewish-Israeli" in order both to emphasize the multinational character of the Israeli population in which the Jews form the majority, and to locate the conflict more accurately.

3. Recent revisionist historical work is very suggestive. See, for example, Bernard Avishai, *The Tragedy of Zionism: Revolution and Democracy in the Land of Israel* (New York: Farrar, Straus, Giroux, 1985); Simha Flapan, *The Birth of Israel: Myths and Realities* (New York: Pantheon, 1987); Yosef Gorny, *The Arab Question and the Jewish Problem* (Tel-Aviv: Am Oved, 1985); and Michael Janson, *Dissonance in Zion* (London: Zed, 1987).

4. There are many discussions of the definition of terrorism and a consensus on the use of terrorization as a means to an end in terrorism. The following are a few examples of analyses of the concept of terrorism: Eugene Victor Walter, "Violence and the Process of Terror," *American Sociological Review* 29, no. 2 (April 1964): 248–257; Grant Wardlaw, "The Problem of Defining Terrorism," in Wardlaw, *Political Terrorism: Theory, Tactics, and Counter-Measures* (Cambridge: Cambridge University Press, 1982), 3–17; and Carl Wellman, "On Terrorism Itself," *Journal of Value Inquiry* 13 (1979): 250–258.

5. For attempts to list, chart, and understand the history, culture, and social, economic, and political place of terrorism, see H. Edward Price, Jr., "The Strategy and Tactics of Revolutionary Terrorism," *Comparative Studies in Society and History* 19 (1977): 52–66; Luigi Bonanate, "Some Unanticipated Consequences of Terrorism," *Journal of Peace Research* 16 (1979): 192–212; William Gutteridge (editor for the Institute for the Study of Conflict), *Contemporary Terrorism* (New York: Facts on File, 1986); Alberto Melucci, "New Movements, Terrorism, and the Political System: Reflections on the Italian Case," *Socialist Review* 11, no. 2 (March-April 1981): 97–136; Christopher Dobson and Ronald Payne, *The Terrorists: Their Weapons, Leaders, and Tactics* (New York: Facts on File, 1982); and Noel O'Sullivan, ed., *Terrorism, Ideology, and Revolution: The Origins of Modern Political Violence* (Brighton, England: Wheatsheaf Books, 1986).

6. Conor Cruise O'Brien, "Terrorism under Democratic Conditions: The Case of the IRA," in *Terrorism, Legitimacy, and Power: The Consequences of Political Violence*, ed. Martha Creshnaw (Middletown, Conn.: Wesleyan University Press, 1983), 91.

7. Walter Laqueur, *Terrorism: A Study of National and International Political Violence* (Boston: Little, Brown, 1977), 6; and Ze'ev Ivianski, "Individual Terror: Concept and Typology," *Journal of Contemporary History* 12, no. 1 (Jan. 1977): 43–46.

8. Robin Morgan, *The Demon Lover: On the Sexuality of Terrorism* (New York: W. W. Norton, 1989).

9. Ibid., 23–24.

10. Ibid., 49–50.

11. Leo Lowenthal, "Terror's Atomization of Man," *Commentary* 1, no. 3 (January 1946): 1–8.

12. Kathleen Barry, *Female Sexual Slavery* (Englewood Cliffs, N.J.: Prentice-Hall, 1979).

13. Marilyn Frye, *The Politics of Reality: Essays in Feminist Theory* (Trumansburg, N.Y.: Crossing, 1983).

14. Ibid., 62–63.

15. Elaine Scarry, *The Body in Pain: The Making and Unmaking of the World* (New York: Oxford University Press, 1985).

16. Ibid., 40.

17. Ibid., 47.

18. Ibid., 52–54.

19. For two moving testimonies, see Jacobo Timerman, *Prisoner without a Name, Cell without a Number* (New York: Alfred A. Knopf, 1981), and Alicia Partnoy, *The Little School: Tales of Disappearance and Survival in Argentina* (San Francisco: Cleis, 1986).

20. See Erving Goffman, "On the Characteristics of Total Institutions," in Goffman, *Asylums: Essays on the Social Situation of Mental Patients and Other Inmates* (Garden City, N.Y.: Anchor Books, 1962), 1–124.

21. See, for example, Paul Wilkinson, *Terrorism and the Liberal State* (New York: New York University Press, 1977).

22. Michel Foucault, *Discipline and Punish: The Birth of the Prison* (New York: Pantheon, 1978), 195–230.

23. Frye, *Politics of Reality*, 56–57.

24. Tom Regan, "Cruelty, Kindness, and Unnecessary Suffering," *Philosophy* 55 (October 1980): 532–541.

25. Ibid., 533–534.

26. Cited in Franco Venturi, *Roots of Revolution: A History of the Populist and Socialist Movements in Nineteenth-Century Russia* (New York: Grosset's Universal Library, 1966), 365–367, and in Walter Laqueur and Yonah Alexander, eds., *The Terrorism Reader: A Historical Anthology*, rev. ed. (New York: New American Library, 1987), 68–72.

27. Steven J. Smith, "Rational Horror," *Philosophy Today* 27 (1983): 307–316.

28. Lawrence Blum, "Compassion," in *Explaining Emotions*, ed. Amelie Rorty (Berkeley: University of California Press, 1980), 507–518.

29. Ibid., 513.

30. Regan, "Cruelty, Kindness, and Unnecessary Suffering," 536.

31. Philip Hallie, "From Cruelty to Goodness," *Hastings Center Report* 11, no. 3 (June 1981): 23–28.

32. This tradition is sometimes referred to as a theory. I follow the usage and general description employed by James Turner Johnson, who has written extensively on the subject. See his *Ideology, Reason, and the Limitation of War: Religious and Secular Concepts, 1200–1740* (Princeton, N.J.: Princeton

University Press, 1975), *Just War Tradition and the Restraints of War: A Moral and Historical Inquiry* (Princeton, N.J.: Princeton University Press, 1981), and *Can Modern War Be Just?* (New Haven, Conn.: Yale University Press, 1984). Virginia Held calls attention to the reliance on the "just war" tradition in her "Violence, Terrorism, and Moral Inquiry," *Monist* 67, no. 4 (October 1984): 605–624, but does not develop the point.

33. Michael Walzer, *Just and Unjust Wars: A Moral Argument with Historical Illustrations* (New York: Basic Books, 1977).

34. R. M. Hare, "On Terrorism," *Journal of Value Inquiry* 13 (1979): 241–249.

35. C. A. J. Coady, "On the Morality of Terrorism," *Philosophy* 60 (1985): 47–69.

36. Robert Young, "Revolutionary Terrorism, Crime, and Morality," *Social Theory and Practice* 4, no. 3 (Fall 1977): 287–302.

37. The distinction between an ethics of justice and an ethics of care and a discussion of the conflict between them were elaborated by Carol Gilligan, *In a Different Voice: Psychological Theory and Women's Development* (Cambridge, Mass.: Harvard University Press, 1982).

38. See, for example, Michael Stocker, "Duty and Friendship: Toward a Synthesis of Gilligan's Contrastive Moral Concepts," and Marilyn Friedman, "Care and Context in Moral Reasoning," in *Women and Moral Theory,* ed. Eva Feder Kittay and Diana T. Meyers (Totowa, N.J.: Rowman and Littlefield, 1987), 56–68 and 190–204, respectively; and Marilyn Friedman, "Beyond Caring: The De-Moralization of Gender," in *Science, Morality, and Feminist Theory,* ed. Marsha Hanen and Kai Nielson (Calgary: University of Calgary Press, 1987), 87–110.

39. Franz Fanon, *The Wretched of the Earth* (New York: Grove, 1968); preface by Jean-Paul Sartre.

40. See, for example, Amia Lieblich, *Tin Soldiers on Jerusalem Beach* (Tel-Aviv: Schocken, 1979); Keith Walker, ed., *A Piece of My Heart* (New York: Ballantine, 1985); and Esther D. Rothenblum and Ellen Cole, eds., *Another Silenced Trauma: Twelve Feminist Therapists and Activists Respond to One Woman's Recovery from War* (New York: Harrington Park, 1986).

41. See, for example, Helen Epstein, *Children of the Holocaust* (New York: Penguin Books, 1979).

42. For ideas about noncontractual communities, see Virginia Held, "Non-Contractual Society," in *Science, Morality, and Feminist Theory,* ed. Marsha Hanen and Kai Nielson (Calgary: University of Calgary Press, 1987), 111–138; Iris Marion Young, "Impartiality and the Civic Public: Some Implications of Feminist Critiques of Moral and Political Theory," in *Feminism as Critique,* ed. Seyla Benhabib and Drucilla Cornell (Minneapolis: University of Minnesota Press, 1987), 56–76; and Marilyn Friedman, "Feminism and Modern Friendship: Dislocating the Community," *Ethics* 99 (1989): 275–290.

8 / Philosophy Is Not a Luxury

RUTH GINZBERG

SURVIVAL

Western androcentric philosophy has positioned itself as a hallmark of civilization: It is conceived as culture, an enrichment of human life that has the opportunity to flourish only after basic survival needs are met. For women in an androcentric and misogynistic world, the option of embellishing a life in which basic survival already is assured has not been available. This is because our basic survival is not assured in the ways construed as preconditions for culture, civilization, philosophy, and—presumably—ethics.

Androcentric culture—including philosophy, we are told—arises within the context of a hierarchy of needs. Of these, the bodily needs come first: air, water, food, shelter, physical integrity. On the next level are needs for interaction with others: communication, cooperation, mutual assistance, reproduction. Without reasonable assurance of those in the first tier, questions about needs arising in the second tier are presumed to be moot. Societies in which virtually all efforts are directed toward meeting these first two tiers of basic needs commonly have been characterized as "primitive." Further up in the hierarchy come things that are seen as enhancements but not fundamentally necessary, the things that constitute human flourishing, which typically has been contrasted with survival: happiness, intimacy, leisure, freedom, reflection, comfort, recreation. The pinnacle of flourishing is posited to be civilization: science, history, art, politics, literature, philosophy. The ordering of this hierarchy is roughly (1) individual bodily well-being, (2) community well-being, (3) psychological and spiritual well-being, and (4) intellectual and aesthetic well-being, each level depending on the attainment of those preceding it before it can emerge as a "need."

The nature of oppression is such that no form of survival is assured to those who are oppressed. Indeed, *total* oppression occurs when those who are oppressed are dead; they do not survive on any level of the survival hierarchy, including the most basic level—that of individual bodily well-being. In other forms of less totalizing oppression, other levels of the hierarchy of survival are denied. What the various sorts of oppression have in common is that to some extent or another, each compromises some type of well-being, including individual bodily well-being, community well-being, psychological and spiritual well-being, and intellectual and aesthetic well-being. What it means for such well-being to be compromised is that there are coercive circumstances in which one or more types of well-being are "allowed," insofar as they occur at all, contingent on the benevolence or convenience of oppressors.

Given the hierarchy of needs, it would seem to follow that those groups who are oppressed do not and cannot have civilization. Women are oppressed. We lack the basic conditions of cultural agency; often we lack even the basic conditions for individual survival. Thus it would follow that women are unable to reach the highest level of this hierarchy, to concern ourselves with the ideas and artifacts that constitute civilization—that is, science, history, art, politics, literature, philosophy, ethics.

Indeed, under this description of civilization we are especially unable to reach these higher levels of civilization qua women. That is, to whatever extent we manage to concern ourselves with the ideas and artifacts that constitute civilization, it is, at very least, because of our identification as "humans" rather than as women and thus as participants in the civilizations of man (*sic*). On more sinister readings women are seen as co-opted, captured, enslaved by, or artifacts of, rather than participants in, such civilizations.[1]

Women, as many have pointed out, historically have been associated with the body, the lowest level of this hierarchy. More than one philosopher has noticed that the "mind/body" split actually is a gender split as well. That which is "of the mind"[2] gets assigned to masculinity and thus to men, whereas that which is "of the body"[3] gets assigned to femininity and thus to women.

It is interesting to note that, collectively, as women have worked to liberate ourselves by "developing" beyond "mere" bodily concerns, we became interested in community. The notion of women as the caretakers of community and its concerns is now similarly well-entrenched in feminist as well as in nonfeminist theory. Indeed, recent conceptions of ethics that have been associated with women or with feminism have been noticeably community-oriented in flavor, in part because researchers and theorists find that women "think" or "speak" in terms of community once we move beyond conceptions of ourselves as "mere" bodies. This is not surprising when we still see our project as that of struggling to climb the ladder of needs.

Theorists who want to move "beyond" questions about women and community often find themselves focusing on the next level of this hierarchy: psychological or emotional well-being, posited as a sort of mental life that sits atop an already-jelled structure of body and community. Out of this notion is born the so-called "postfeminist" gender scholarship, which erroneously assumes that women's survival is already assured and which claims to concern itself with questions about women's flourishing instead. One feature of this postfeminist view is that it is no longer desirable, necessary, or even acceptable to define women in terms of oppression. This is thought to contribute to the perpetuation of the oppression. While some theorists work at constructing "positive" accounts of what it means to be a woman on the one hand, postmodern theorists work at deconstructing concepts, notions, terms, and ideas that serve as anchors for meaning on the other. Essentialism seems to move to the foreground of the philosophical scenery, appearing now as a critically important philosophical mistake.

In this milieu, relatively comfortable white, middle-class academic women attend to this philosophical mistake with renewed passion, working to deconstruct the ontology of the social and political "worlds" in which we struggle, refocusing attention toward the role of identity in creating meaning. The result is a renewed attention toward personal happiness, intimacy, leisure, freedom, reflection, comfort, and recreation—the part of the hierarchy thought to encompass "flourishing" rather than "survival"—much to the disappointment of those women who feel unprivileged enough not to be able to concern our/themselves with this level of the hierarchy yet. Fights break out between and among those who ought to be allies. We align ourselves in more and more fragmented groups, accusing one another of unself-consciously enjoying too much of some privilege: white privilege, heterosexual privilege, academic privilege, middle-class privilege, ableist privilege, postrevolutionary privilege ("Well, when *I* was growing up [going to school, looking for a job, coming out, having children, being battered, writing a book, and so on], *I* didn't *have.* . . .") We even suspect each other of having (or granting) "marginalist" privilege, of attributing more credibility to those who can claim "many" and "severe" forms of oppression rather than "just a few minor ones."

At times it looks as though, collectively, we must continually find or claim or create additional forms of oppression just for the purpose of interrupting the endless tug "beyond" strategies for survival toward strategies for flourishing (where "flourishing" is applicable only to those who've moved beyond "mere" survival). Many times it is true that we, or those around us, genuinely don't appreciate or acknowledge the privilege we and/or they enjoy. Sadly, we find ourselves struggling for epistemic and moral authority—*philosophical* authority, as it were—through the destructive process of repeatedly "calling" one another on newly detected moral inconsistencies or unacknowledged epistemic privileges.

However, there is a problem here. By construing the philosophical enterprise as an artifact of culture that emerges only at the "highest" stage of civilization, and by construing civilization as that which occurs when the highest stages in a hierarchy of needs are attained, the very definition of the conditions under which philosophy occurs precludes the possibility of a prerevolutionary gynocentric philosophy. We wind up believing that we must choose from a smorgasbord of unsatisfactory choices.

Some attempts to create gynocentric philosophy give us moral theory for a utopian sort of postrevolutionary gynocentric world.[4] Other attempts offer what some feminist critics call "victimologies," theories that describe us wholly in terms of our predictable responses to conditions of oppression.[5] Some supposedly gynocentric ontologies look suspiciously as though they embed dubious, quasi-biologistic assumptions about women (not to mention lesbians, feminism, the world, knowledge, truth, and so on).[6] The suggestion is afoot that theory is itself androcentric and that anthropology is the best we can do.[7] Many of us feel positioned precariously at the edge of

some postmodern abyss where "construction crews" and "deconstruction crews" alternately build and tear town every imaginable
conception of meaning. Such weirdness serves not only to divide us
against one another. It also suggests that the fault lies with the
conception of philosophy as part of "flourishing" *as opposed to* part of
"survival."

GYNOCENTRISM, SURVIVAL, AND PHILOSOPHY

For women, survival is a fundamental issue. Until we put survival at
the center of our philosophical thinking, we are constantly at risk of
having our theory-creation process lose sight of how fundamental is
survival, rendering our theory irrelevant to our survival.

Women must constantly concern ourselves with how to survive
batterings, rapes, wars and other violence, racism, homophobia, de-
pression, mother-blaming, poverty, hatred, isolation, silencing, rup-
turing of our communities, exhaustion, spiritual co-optation, conceptions of health that view us as diseased in ways that we are not and
that do not address or even acknowledge our actual suffering, indoctrination in patriarchal thinking in the place of genuine education,
demands on us to do more than our share of the work of the world,
trivialization of our knowledge, and destruction of those things that
are beautiful and that nourish our souls. None of these things is of our
own doing. They are the results, and the evidence, of our oppression.
In one way or another, we often find ourselves not knowing whether,
or how, we will survive. When we do survive, we often suffer survivors' guilt. No level of the posited survival hierarchy is assured: not
our individual bodily well-being, or our community well-being, or
our psychological well-being, or our intellectual or aesthetic well-
being.

Yet we struggle to formulate conceptions of gynocentric morality
under these conditions of oppression without questioning the androcentric conception of philosophy as a part of culture, where
"culture" emerges only after survival is assured. We must conceive
ethics—indeed, I suspect, all of philosophy—as a part of our survival.
We have no choice. For so long as we don't take that step, we are still
doing androcentric philosophy with a "feminist twist."

Of course there is a way in which survival seems as though it ought to be assured. There is something very disquieting about thinking of survival as eternally intertwined with the summum bonum; it is seductively appealing to be able to hope to transcend the sort of life in which survival is constantly at issue. Nevertheless, history shows us repeatedly that survival cannot be taken for granted. It *is* an accomplishment "just" to survive. No woman is exempt, despite our apparent abilities to more-or-less "pass" or otherwise "make it" in a still mostly hostile patriarchal environment. That we are taught to see our mere survival as a personal *failing* of some kind is an insidious aspect of the very social and political arrangements that endanger our survival. We might otherwise see it as an accomplishment, as a piece of political action. Instead, we find ourselves thinking that we want or need to assure our survival first and that then we can embellish our lives with culture, philosophy, or civilization later. We see ourselves as still at the "lowest level" when we notice that we are still struggling to survive. Yet survival is neither an underachievement nor an embarrassment. It is an act of political resistance (not just a personal strategy) to survive, and it is another act of political resistance to refuse to see "mere" survival as failing. Both of these are important acts of political resistance.

ETHICS AND FEMINIST EROS

Audre Lorde identifies the erotic as "a considered source of power and information within [women's] lives" that "rises from our deepest and non-rational knowledge."[8] The erotic, she claims, provides "the power which comes from sharing deeply any pursuit with another person," as well as "the open and fearless understanding of . . . [the] capacity for joy." This is important because "the sharing of joy, whether physical, emotional, psychic, or intellectual, forms a bridge between the sharers which can be the basis for understanding much of what is not shared between them, and lessens the threat of their difference."[9]

This is a political claim, not a claim about hedonism or "rights" to pleasure. When Lorde asks the question, "Why would the erotic be a good thing?" she answers it quite differently from those who would claim the main benefit to be some sort of pleasure. She sees the erotic as an epistemic force that tempers the individualistic sense of self; it is the source of both power and information, which encourages resistance to atomism and unchecked individualism and which leads to understanding.[10] Thus the suppression of the erotic constitutes a primary interpersonal harm. Lorde further claims that this is one of the major social arrangements that has perpetuated the oppression of women.

I suggest that there is a conception of moral philosophy emerging from the writings of Audre Lorde and other lesbian feminist theorists that is based in the very acts of surviving rather than in culture. This is not accidental. That a philosophical system be based in the very acts of surviving is, I claim, one of the inevitable features of a gynocentric philosophical framework. This is also what links gynocentrism with a radical refusal of other forms of oppression: racism, class oppression, imperialism, heterosexism, species-chauvinism, even "man-hating," for example. Rather than separating survival from "flourishing" or "culture" in order to position philosophy as part of either "flourishing" or "culture" (or both), philosophy is conceived as *part* of survival in a conceptualization in which all forms of well-being are taken to be part of survival. Audre Lorde is explicit about this when she writes that "For women—poetry is not a luxury. It is a vital necessity of our existence. It forms the quality of the light within which we predicate our hopes and dreams toward survival and change."[11]

Survival, so positioned, is central to any conceptualization in which the summum bonum (if there is such a thing) is not taken to be something that transcends physically, psychologically, and socially embedded life but rather that is taken to be just exactly that. The sketch that emerges is that of an immanent rather than a transcendent philosophical theory, in which survival is not transcended but embraced.

KNOWLEDGE, EROS, AND SURVIVAL

In such an immanent philosophical theory, survival occupies a niche similar to that which is occupied by knowledge in androcentric philosophy. Because of this, it makes sense to claim that gynocentric philosophical theories are based in ethics rather than in epistemology. Survival is arguably a moral concept. It is surely not merely an epistemic one.

The gynocentric framework unfolding in the work of lesbian feminist theorists finds its roots in a fundamental assertion of the importance of nondomination rather than in a foundational assumption of the importance of distinguishing knowledge from nonknowledge. This nondomination, I claim, emerges from the centrality of survival. What remains yet to be shown, but which seems intuitively obvious, is that when survival is reconceived as *not* "that which is a precondition for the emergence of culture" but rather as "that which infuses every aspect of well-being," it is going to turn out that any form of domination inhibits some sort of well-being and therefore is antithetical to survival in its fullest meaning. Thus a philosophical system in which survival is central necessarily will be one in which domination holds the position of an inconsistency.

Although the details of such a scheme remain yet to be fully articulated, the nature and position of the erotic within the androcentric and gynocentric frameworks give us a clue to understanding their different groundings. Audre Lorde's sense of the erotic is a subjective, affective sense of yearning to join that which seems subjectively separate. This, it is important to note, is *not* the much-maligned "urge to merge." Ontologically, "merging" makes two things become one, and for eros to exist, there must continue to be more than one. For example, if my erotic enjoyment of you actually causes me to lose track of the fact that you and I are separate, then it is not really erotic enjoyment, at least not in Lorde's lesbian feminist sense of erotic, but rather it is some other form of self-centered hedonism.

This sort of self-centered hedonism is what continually crops up in the position of the erotic in androcentric frameworks. But this is because androcentric frameworks define the erotic in terms of knowledge, where knowledge is conceived to be fundamentally a property or attribute of, or somehow attached only to, single, clearly individuated "knowers." Thus within androcentric frameworks, the erotic turns out to be some kind of intentional state (as it were) that relates a single mind to some particular intentional object (the erotic object). This turns out to be a domination relation (or a quasi-domination relation) because of the relation of mind to intentional object: They are not equals. The mind "targets" or "penetrates" the thing-to-be-known in ways that are not even plausibly symmetrical.

But there is no such claim about the erotic within the gynocentric framework; indeed, one of the things about the lesbian-feminist conception of the erotic is that it cannot be a property or attribute of a single thing held or perceived or encountered by another single thing (for example, a single mind). When the erotic, like everything else, is defined with respect to survival rather than with respect to knowledge, it emerges as the "glue" that brings seemingly separate things to a shared commonality. Indeed, the paradigmatic erotic connection within such a gynocentric framework is that of being as committed to your survival as I am to my own.

This is not the same as *conflating* your survival with mine (or vice versa), or *conditioning* your survival on mine (or vice versa), or being unable to distinguish your survival from mine. These conflations arise when the relation of the erotic to survival is defined in terms of knowledge, as occurs in the androcentric framework. Thus the erotic—rather than political necessity, coercion of some sort, contractual arrangements between negotiating parties, or the like—becomes the primary source of moral community.

SURVIVAL AND MORAL COMMUNITY

In survival-centered ethics, grand theory seems out of place. This is not to say that we want, or ought to want, to abandon theory. But the majority of our moral judgments are contextual, involving a pretty small group of folks, most of whom we already know: Should I call my friend or leave her alone? Should I picket with my union? Should I let my neighbor with repulsive politics use my extra parking space? Should I hassle my teenager about doing her homework? Should I go to the trouble to recycle this odd piece of plastic?

In androcentric ethical theories, as a member of "the" community of moral agents in good standing, I am presumed to be able to exercise my own judgment about most of these things without needing to consult all those who might be affected, and—for the most part—whatever decisions I make will be accepted by others as being my business or my decision. Indeed, if I do not have the agency necessary to make or act on such decisions, then I am presumed not to be a member of "the" community of moral agents in good standing. Folks may disagree with my moral judgments on such issues but usually not on the basis that I'm not a qualified moral agent. They also don't usually disagree with my judgments on the basis that I haven't properly consulted a large enough moral community.

But when someone does call into question the size and scope of the moral community affected by, or owed accountability for, my decision or act, it turns out to be a devastating sort of challenge. This is because in andocentric theories, it is exactly in calling into question the size and scope of the moral community to which I owe accountability for my decision to act that the key to claiming a sufficient stake to complain about my moral decisions lies. A common way to claim a moral right to influence a decision or act is to claim to be a relevant member of the moral community affected by, or owed accountability for, that decision or act.[12] For example, anti-abortion proponents claim the right to influence a woman's decision about the fetus in her uterus by contending that the morally relevant community is larger than just the woman and her doctor: They claim that the rest of the world has a stake in whether the fetus is born or not and that the fetus has a stake in it as well. Thus they seek to expand the relevant moral community to include themselves and the fetus, and this is what purports to give them a right to participate in the decision. Indeed, this claim is not wholly false—thus its appeal. The rest of the world does have some stake in how populous a world we inhabit and with which particular people or potential people we share our talents or skills, troubles, toils, joys, and resources. The argument is similar to that which claims that the rest of the world has a stake in whether or not I commit suicide. Or wear a seatbelt.[13] To move a question from the realm of "personal choice" to the realm of "accountable moral choice," androcentric philosophy argues that the decision is political or has a political impact on a broader moral community.

For feminist philosophers who have come to believe that the personal *is* political, this renders communitarian sorts of moral theories simultaneously and paradoxically appealing and problematic, for "moral community" is, among other things, conceived as those to whom we hold ourselves to be accountable. We come to wonder what decisions if any are truly "personal"; indeed, *every* decision becomes political by virtue of its being connected (through ourselves and our connections) to some moral community greater than ourselves. A paradigm example of this is radical lesbian separatists' challenge to all women to rethink heterosexuality; the challenge itself is to the notion that with whom I sleep is not a "personal" *as opposed to* a "political" choice. That is, I am responsible and accountable to a larger community than just myself and my partners for the decisions I make about with whom I am sexually involved, and the scope of my accountability is greater than just a question of to whom I might transmit any germs I may carry.

This sort of move is particularly compelling to those of us trying to conceive a gynocentric ethics without first divesting ourselves of the notion of philosophy as transcendence of survival issues. The reason it is so compelling is that it rightfully challenges the idea that community survival has been "taken care of" already.

Survival of lesbian or gynocentric communities is not assured. In the hierarchy of needs, I would not yet be in a position to move "beyond" survival issues unless I were willing to abandon my responsibilities or accountability to those lesbian or gynocentric communities whose survival is not yet assured. This sets up a dichotomy between evincing disloyalty to my still-oppressed sisters or joining them in their moral community. But this dichotomy is only apparent, because it results from the ways in which relatively gynocentric moral community has been conceived by feminists still within a hierarchy of survival and needs relations.

DISSENT AND MORAL COURAGE

The dichotomy becomes more salient when we ask what constitutes moral courage under conditions in which the personal is political. The type of moral courage on which I want to focus is the courage to dissent. The line between moral courage and moral irresponsibility is blurred by the positioning of ethics as the transcendence of survival issues.

For those who have come to believe that the personal is political, it is easier to make moral judgments that are in accord with one's moral community than to dissent. Androcentric individualistic moral theories provide an easy outlet for dissent: Many moral judgments can be chalked up to the "personal" and taken out from under the scrutiny of the moral community. Indeed, a final and sufficient reason for a moral judgment might well be, "I just did what I had to: I was true to my own conscience." If a liberal individualist with similar-minded friends constituting her moral community decides to leave or join or start a church, love a man or a woman or both or neither, gestate or abort or prevent or use donor sperm to induce a pregnancy, work for a university or teach on street corners, marry or divorce or remain single or lesbian, join the army or join the demonstration, smoke marijuana or abstain, vote Republican or Democrat or Communist or Peace and Freedom or not vote at all—these conveniently can be written off as "personal" decisions, ones in which her moral community has considerably less stake than she. This is because among liberal individualists, it is understood that she had to transcend issues of community survival in order to get to be a bona fide moral agent in the first place. If her survival or her moral community's survival actually is at stake, then she "regresses" back to survival issues. To the extent to which this is so, she is not yet "civilized." The preconditions for moral agency haven't been met. Thus she is not a moral agent accountable to a moral community for those decisions. She is accountable only to herself, perhaps including her own sense of personal integrity, "and" (as it were) her individual survival "instincts."

But under conditions in which the personal is political, liberal individualism falters. Any decision, by virtue of being political, is fair game for being held accountable by and to my moral community. It is also fair game for becoming grounds for my exclusion from a moral community. This is where the conditions differ markedly from those of liberal individualism.

This milieu, for example, is illustrated by the positions of some separatists. What under liberal individualism is counted as "guilt by association" (a bad thing to be avoided) becomes valued as the legitimate concept of attending to access (to one's energy, ideas, and so on). For example, the black separatist moral community does not want me as a member if I am not a black separatist, no matter how sympathetic I might be. It objects to shoring me up with its information, ideas, energy, enthusiasm, care, concern, and attention just so that I can be replenished enough to survive as a white person under conditions of white racism.

As we rethink the ontology of persons and of communities, moral courage takes on new dimensions. For example, in the lesbian feminist reading of "the personal is political," membership in one's moral community turns out always to be at issue. This often has been experienced and expressed as pressure on members of such communities to behave in ways that are "politically correct." The pressure to be "politically correct" is especially strong for those who construe moral decision-making in this connected, contextual, particular way. For if one is expelled or shunned by one's moral community, what context is there in which to make moral judgments? I risk genuine "demoralization" when my moral judgments differ enough from those of my moral community for me to be excommunicated, for if I am expelled from my moral community, some piece of my moral agency itself is at stake.

I say "some piece of" my moral agency is at stake because most of us are simultaneously members of a number of moral communities. One rarely loses one's membership in all of one's moral communities at once. For example, my household might be one moral community; my five or ten closest friends might be another; my religion might be another; my AA group another; my union, neighborhood, town, or indeed my country might be others. When I am expelled from one moral community, I am rarely expelled from *all* moral communities of which I am a member. (Even if I am deported, my friends are still my friends. They may even try to help me return.)

But many times those moral communities serve different functions in my life; they serve to facilitate different kinds of, or just different, moral judgments. Perhaps I joined my AA group because my friends and my office coworkers did not or could not provide a moral community in which I could be satisfied with my moral judgments and actions surrounding alcohol. If my AA group expels me and I now have to look toward my family, my friends, and my office coworkers (and "the world") for a particular context in which to make judgments about drinking, I may make different decisions than I would if I were still in AA. The pressure to avoid rejection, expulsion, or excommunication from one's moral communities is high. Groups such as AA use this as a compelling force; I may not remain in AA if I continue to drink and encourage others in the group to get sauced with me. So in virtue of wanting to remain part of that moral community, I abstain. The pressure of the community "helps" me to do that.

This sort of pressure occurs in other moral communities surrounding other issues as well and is the phenomenon reported as pressure to be "politically correct." For example, it is difficult to be both a deeply concerned member of a feminist moral community and a believer in fetuses' rights to be born. One is strongly urged to change one's views or to leave that moral community. It is, thus, true—but doesn't quite capture the force of it—to say that it takes moral courage to resist doing or not doing something that is "politically correct" just because that is so under such circumstances. Furthermore, obviously not all such resistance is appropriately seen as moral courage.

It could hardly be called "moral courage," for example, except by stretching the definition beyond recognition, for a fourteen-year-old to become hooked on cocaine despite the disapproval of her moral community.[14] On the other hand, one might want to say that many other sorts of instances of refusing to be bullied by pressure from one's moral community are indeed acts of moral courage. Under conditions of contextualized moral decision-making though, in which the personal is the political and the moral community is the context, those very acts of moral courage may jeopardize membership in one's moral community, thus putting one's moral agency at stake when one disagrees with that community. When "moral agency" means, at least in part, maintaining and attending to one's embeddedness in a moral community, then acts of both moral courage and moral irresponsibility are equally alienating; indeed, in some ways the two begin to look quite indistinguishable. Both are instances of ignoring community context.

This scheme embraces a conservatism and a pressure toward maintaining the status quo while at the same time encouraging the splintering and factionalization of moral communities. For when I dissent in a way that risks my membership in my moral community, one thing that helps me decide if I am being morally irresponsible or morally courageous is whether I can find or create a new moral community in which to find context. If I am in solidarity with only myself, my moral community is so small that I may be forced to change my views, for I cannot create enough of a moral context to function in a community of only one. On the other hand, if others join me in my dissent, we may form a new moral community. Under this description, politics becomes not the creation and shaping of ideas and beliefs through interaction but the creation and shaping of moral communities themselves.[15]

DISSENT AND ALIENATION

To avoid the problem of continually having the shape of moral communities to be at stake rather than the moral issues for which community provides the context, consensus-making has been an important part of feminist (and other relatively communitarian) theories of contextualized moral agency and judgment. Dissent is problematic within a context in which consensus is constitutive. In theory, when members of the community aren't in agreement they remain in dialogue with one another until consensus is reached. There is a commitment all the way around to remain in open communication on the points of disagreement until agreement is reached through nonadversarial interaction. Most folks agree that this sometimes may take a very long time. But that's acceptable; process is as important as product.

This may be true and even workable in some situations. But in situations in which disagreement is too fundamental, the dissentient risks excommunication rather than simply an added time commitment to reach consensus. What she risks is alienation, not being late for dinner. Separatist theories have made this point explicit. Zionist separatists, for example, do not welcome non-Zionists into Zionist moral communities and indeed tend to excommunicate folks who become non-Zionists. What comes to be at issue, then, is who a "Zionist" might be, and, in fact, separatist moral communities spend much time debating such things: Who is a *real* feminist? A *real* lesbian? A *real* Jewish Zionist? My merely calling myself a feminist does not make it so; I need to be in agreement with certain principles if the rest of the feminist community is to agree that I am a feminist. This is the old problem of "who counts" in a moral community. It is not a new but rather a very old question— the question of what, minimally, one must have in common with others in a moral community in order to be a full participant.[16]

The problem is not unique to feminist attempts to conceive moral community. Vigorous dissent in moral communities posited by androcentric theory also has the possibility of putting membership at stake. If one dissents too vigorously in a moral community in which "rationality" is the basis for membership, for example, one eventually risks being labeled "irrational," in which case one's membership expires. But that is different because it is not for one's *views* that one loses membership in one's moral community but rather for one's *capacities* (or perceived capacities). If one can follow the rules for reasoning and communication, then one can stay and continue the dialogue no matter how divergent one's views are from those that prevail.

One's membership in feminist moral communities is determined not by what one knows or by what capacities one has but by what moral judgments one shares. This is one feature that makes dissent particularly problematic, for what one dissents *about* within a moral community is, in fact, moral judgments. If moral communities were merely monolithic single-issue political organizations, this might not be too bad (that is, I could just leave the pro-X community when my views change and join the anti-X community or even the no-opinion-about-X community; no peripheral loss here, because the only thing at issue in the context of such a community is X), but they are not. For example, it might be difficult to articulate the constellation of moral principles and judgments and support that I share with my family of origin, a typical moral community. But my dissent about, for example, acceptable choices of "lifestyle" could easily cause my family to disown me. If this happens, I lose not only my family's conversation, debate, and general moral community surrounding matters of lifestyle; I also lose those things with respect to patriotism, religion, money, sex, promise-keeping, work, friendship, and a whole host of other moral axes, many of which are probably pretty central to my survival.

MORAL CONFLICT

In feminist conceptions of morality, it seems we have various moral communities to which we are responsible for our judgments and actions. The acknowledgment of this is already a step away from most androcentric moral theories, which postulate "the" universal moral community. Conceptions of moral theory as part of civilization invoke at this point concerns about relativism. The same insights from which pluralistic notions of civilization or "culture" or moral community emerge also yield worries about moral relativism. The problem experienced by those actually trying to live this way, though, is not that of relativism between distinctly different moral communities but that some of one's own moral communities overlap and—creating moral dilemma—conflict.

For example, if "the world" is the relevant moral community, then many would agree that Karl Marx did the right thing in devoting his life to his work. The world and many folks in it are certainly better off for having his writings in it. But three of his children died of poverty-related conditions, and his wife quite literally went crazy. To what moral community was Marx responsible? Workers of the world? His family? Both? What happened when those conflicted? He was unable to be true to both communities at once. Did Marx make the right choice? Would we think that he had made the right choice had his talents been less, had his work not been read, had he remained another obscure, unemployed writer whose family suffered tremendously from the poverty brought on by his stubbornness? Should he have chosen between the workers of the world and his family, forgoing membership in one moral community so that he could be part of the other? If so, how should he have chosen?

One possible description of moral conflict is that which occurs when overlapping moral communities require incompatible moral principles or judgments for sustaining one's membership or solidarity. One might think this situation to be the mark of inconsistency or hypocrisy in one's life, but it is not so simple. There are so many possible scenarios in which this might occur; I rather believe it is the norm. Indeed, this sort of situation seems to be constitutive of moral dilemma in contextualized moral decision-making.

It is the parallel of moral dilemma brought on by "conflicting rules" in rule-based moral systems. The difference, though, is that the dilemma of conflicting rules is thought to be resolvable, at least theoretically. This is a problem of inconsistency; if the rules are just evaluated and revised carefully enough, with particular attention toward eliminating inconsistency, then eventually there will be a system of rules that has no conflicts.[17]

But what possible parallel solution could there be for the problem of overlapping and conflicting moral communities? The analogy with the expectation of consistency in rule-based systems is the utopian hope for a single moral community in context-based systems. But how can there be a single moral community when one's moral community is based in actual particular connections and interactions with others? We do not have such actual particular connections and interactions with *all* others. To whatever extent connections with *all* others exist, they are largely abstract, not particular.

MORAL ANGUISH AND SURVIVAL

The question of whether a single moral community can actually exist is too important to leave unaddressed. It is a strength of gynocentric moral theory that we consider such "practical" problems right along with "theoretical" problems. We have made no progress if we still imagine "the" moral community and don't address the fact that there could be no single moral community in a contextual conception of ethics.[18] Much of our moral anguish arises out of our conflicting senses of responsibility and accountability to multiple moral communities. We do not worry about the theoretical problems associated with relativism. We worry about de-moralization. We worry about staying sane or getting sane. We worry about survival.

But this, I would like to suggest, is a clue to how we might proceed, not an occasion for pessimism. These worries need not be considered prephilosophical. This approach takes our moral anguish to be full-fledged philosophy. It provokes and energizes work on at least such philosophical themes as the erotic, knowledge, community, courage, dissent, conflict, and alienation—and this philosophical work can emerge from the actual experiences of our everyday lives.

For feminists, philosophy is not a luxury.

NOTES

My thanks to Terry Winant, without whose friendship and collegial support this essay would not have been written. She posed just exactly the right philosophical questions at the right times, commented on numerous prior drafts without ever making me feel embarrassed, and prevented me from littering this paper with sentences as long and unwieldy as this one. Thanks also to Claudia Card, Elise Springer, Naomi Scheman, and members of the summer 1990 feminist reading group at Wesleyan University, and a grateful nod in the direction of Audre Lorde for the title.

1. This, for example, was the argument made by Susan Griffin in *Woman and Nature: The Roaring Inside Her* (New York: Harper and Row, 1978).

2. That is, "culture": religion, intellectual life, problem-solving, inquiry.

3. That is, "survival": birth, death, food, cleanliness.

4. For example, Sarah Lucia Hoagland, *Lesbian Ethics: Toward New Value* (Palo Alto, Calif.: Institute of Lesbian Studies, 1988).

5. For example, Sara Ruddick, *Maternal Thinking: Toward a Politics of Peace* (Boston: Beacon, 1989); and Carol Gilligan, *In a Different Voice: Psychological Theory and Women's Development* (Cambridge, Mass.: Harvard University Press, 1982).

6. For example, ecofeminist theories about what women are "really" like outside of patriarchy. See Judith Plant, ed., *Healing the Wounds: The Promise*

of Ecofeminism (Philadelphia: New Society Publishers, 1989); and Irene Diamond and Gloria Feman Arenstein, eds., *Re-Weaving the World: The Emergence of Ecofeminism* (San Francisco: Sierra Club Books, 1990).

7. For example, Joyce Trebilcot, "Dyke Methods," *Hypatia* 3, no. 2 (Summer 1988): 1–13.

8. Audre Lorde, "Uses of the Erotic: The Erotic as Power," in Lorde, *Sister/Outsider: Essays and Speeches* (Trumansburg, N.Y.: Crossing Press, 1984), 53. First presented at the Fourth Berkshire Conference on the History of Women, Mount Holyoke College, August 25, 1978. Also published as a pamphlet by Out & Out Books (available from Crossing Press).

9. Ibid., 56.

10. This sort of understanding appears to be what Mary Field Belenky, Blythe McVicker Clinchy, Nancy Rule Goldberger, and Jill Mattuck Tarule refer to as "connected Knowing," in *Women's Ways of Knowing: The Development of Self, Voice, and Mind*, ed. Belenky, Clinchy, Goldberger, and Tarule (New York: Basic Books, 1986). Belenky et al. found that "connected knowers seek to understand people's ideas in the other people's terms rather than in their own terms" and that these connected knowers "were attached to the objects they sought to understand: they *cared* about them" (124).

11. Audre Lorde, "Poetry Is Not a Luxury" in *Sister/Outsider*, 37.

12. For example, the United States claimed (finally) that it needed to become involved in World War II by contending that the morally relevant community was "the world." But before it became involved, it justified its noninvolvement by contending that the relevant moral community was "Europe." Similarly, this is how the world gets to claim that individual (minor) Nazis "shouldn't have done that." The claim is that their relevant moral community was not merely their elected government and its official decisions and policies.

13. Note that these are two conclusions of the sort that have gained favor recently as political sentiments favoring liberal individualism have lost ground to conservative, paternalistic attitudes. Note too that although radical lesbian feminist moral, political, and epistemic theories *also* oppose liberal individualism, it is vastly different from conservative, paternalistic opposition to liberal individualism. Unfortunately, on too many occasions these two very differing perspectives have tried to foster political coalitions (for example, the antipornography movements) by blurring this distinction—not, in my view, a good strategy for the long run.

14. However, there certainly is a way of construing drug experimentation by teenagers under these conditions as inexperienced attempts to experiment with moral courage in the form of resistance. After all, fourteen-year-olds are not exactly experienced moral agents; they are still learning, indeed just beginning to experiment, with the concept of moral agency itself.

15. I first proposed this idea in a paper (unpublished) I wrote in 1985 entitled "Art and Morality: A Feminist Perspective." In that paper, I argued that art (by defining or identifying moral communities) served the parallel function to that of law, except that law functions within rule-based moral systems and art functions within nonrule-based moral systems.

16. John Stuart Mill tried to solve this problem with respect to utilitarianism in a way that relied on ethics' being based in culture. This is where gynocentric ethics departs from utilitarianism. Mill claimed that one only became a full participant in the moral community by being educated—which, of course, presumes a culture. Survival is not subject to the problems of cultural relativism in the same way that knowledge or education is.

17. This is the somewhat naive hope behind some conceptions of what a codified legal system can provide.

18. This, for example, is one of the serious shortcomings of Sarah Hoagland's *Lesbian Ethics*. Despite her brilliant and creative efforts to develop a new moral sensibility, she steadfastly refuses to address the question of multiple moral communities. In her world, the lesbian moral communiuty is "the" moral community.

9 / What's Wrong with Bitterness?

LYNNE McFALL

Bitterness is a refusal to forgive and forget. It is to maintain a vivid sense of the wrongs one has been done, to recite one's angry litany of loss, long past the time others may care to listen or sympathize. Those who repeat the minor or even major injustices of their unhappy lives ("My mother never loved me"; "My husband didn't even come to the hospital when Johnny was born") bore us. At best, they lack decorum. Like laughter in church, the bitter draw attention to themselves in a way that upsets our sense of propriety with regard to suffering. This is not the place, we may think wherever the complaining occurs. "You're so bitter" is condemnation, never praise (except perhaps by one who shares the malign gift), designed to silence the sufferer. We are tempted to back away from it, saying, "Live or die but don't poison everything."[1]

My aim in this essay is to show that bitterness may be justified; further, that we might have reason to resist the suggestion of silence. Still, I shall claim, there is also reason, finally, to let go.

One argument for the first claim is this: If you're not bitter, you're either (1) cynical or (2) you haven't been paying attention. And it is better to be bitter, which includes hope, than cynical, which does not. (There are also the options of extreme good fortune and saintly unconcern with one's mean fate. But since both are, for humans, rare, the real choice is between bitterness and cynicism.)

There are two questions we can ask about an emotional attitude. What are the facts to which it is a response? Is this attitude a rational response to those facts? Fear, for example, would be a rational response to the fact that an assailant has put a knife to your throat and said, "your money or your life." It would not be a rational response to the delivery of flowers (without special explanation).

The disagreement between those who are bitter and those who are cynical may be over the factual rather than the evaluative claim—the way the world is, not just the proper response to it. On the cynical view, bitterness is a form of emotional stupidity based on false hope.[2] Those who continually wail, "But it's not fair!" are properly met with the response, "Life is not fair."

Bitterness is a response to suffering of a particular sort: the disappointment of one's important hopes. That hope is necessary is shown by the fact that you can't betray someone's hopes who has none. That the hopes must be important ones is shown by any case of trivial hope, unrealized. We may hope the beer will be cold, but if it is not, we ordinarily do not become bitter on that account.

If this is right, then bitterness would seem to be justified where one's important hopes were themselves legitimate. Thus the question of whether and under what conditions bitterness may be justified is connected with what Kant called one of the three main questions of philosophy: What may I hope?[3] If bitterness is a consequence of disappointed hope, and such hope is demonstrably false hope, then bitterness will not be a justified response to it. If, on the other hand, one's hope is legitimate but nonetheless disappointed, then bitterness may be justified.

What is bitterness, beyond disappointed hope?

In the *Oxford English Dictionary*, bitterness is defined as "deep sorrow or anguish of heart" and as "animosity, acrimony of temper, action, or words." The definition of the adjective "bitter" also shows both the more active, vocal, and vengeful form and the more passive, silently sorrowing form. "Bitter" means (1) injurious, baleful, cruel, severe; characterized by intense animosity or virulence of feeling or action; and (2) attended by severe pain or suffering; sore to be borne; grievous, painful, full of affliction; expressing or betokening intense grief, misery, or affliction of spirit.[4]

So we can distinguish between *active* bitterness and *passive* bitterness. What justifies one may not justify the other. At the extremes, the difference is between mute grief and cruelty.

Another distinction worth making is between *partial, object-directed* bitterness and bitterness that characterizes the *person*. Consider, for example, bitterness about losing a job due to discrimination. In this case, bitterness has an object and is partial rather than complete (one may be bitter *about* isolated instances of discrimination without becoming a bitter *person*). But where there is a pattern of discrimination, and this affects many important aspects of a person's life (job prospects, housing opportunities, the conditions of self-respect), then bitterness may characterize the person and be complete. What justifies partial and object-directed bitterness may not justify complete bitterness or bitterness that characterizes the person. Bitterness is like happiness in this respect. We may be justifiably happy *about* winning the lottery without being a happy person or having grounds for believing that ours is a happy life.

Without attempting a catalog of evil, human or natural, we can note that by the time a person reaches the age where senility becomes a real threat, she has generally lost a loved one through death, been betrayed by a friend or lover (or both together), failed miserably to attain some important goal (if you've got everything you want, you're not asking for enough), been the object of physical violence or other remarkable acts of injustice, in short, lost several things she thought she couldn't live without. Which is not to mention natural catastrophes such as fires, floods, earthquakes, volcanoes, and the not-less-difficult-to-bear-because-inevitable betrayal of the body: death.

Is bitterness as a response to the inevitable justified? I don't think it is, for reasons given below, and in spite of the moving advice of Dylan Thomas to his father:

And you, my father, there on the sad height,
Curse, bless, me now with your fierce tears, I pray.
Do not go gentle into that good night.
Rage, rage, against the dying of the light.[5]

But the question that interests me more is whether bitterness may be a justified response to harms and losses that are a consequence of human agency (wickedness, moral stupidity, weakness, or indifference)—what we think of as *avoidable* harms and losses, and which are, for that reason, more "bitter," harder to take.

Let's begin with the least problematic case: partial, passive bitterness that is a response to an avoidable harm or loss.

Consider a common tale of heartbreak and desire: sexual betrayal. Here, aside from the pain of jealousy and forced abstinence, the wrong done is obvious: One hoped for fidelity; one's hope was (more or less flagrantly) disappointed. There often is, as well, the experience of abandonment, salt for the wound. Whether bitterness is justified in this case depends upon whether one's hope of sexual fidelity[6] was legitimate.

Is the hope of sexual fidelity a legitimate hope?

The answer is not obvious. One might say yes, because sexual fidelity is one of the commonly held assumptions of marriage, as usually practiced, and even if one is not married, an explicit promise may have been made. On the other hand, the answer might seem to be no, because of the well-known statistics: Lifelong sexual fidelity is not in fact the norm, whatever heartfelt promises we may make.

What constitutes a legitimate hope?

There are two senses of "norm" at issue here, one merely statistical, the other what might be called ideal, that is, part of some personal and/or moral ideal. Fidelity may not be the norm in the statistical sense, but it is part of an ideal many of us hold.

Which sense of "norm" does legitimacy of hope turn on—statistical norms or personal and/or moral ideals?

Clearly there must be some relation between the two. If an act is impossible (flying, for example, or being true to two lovers at the same time), then this should limit the legitimacy of a hope based on someone's statement of intention to do these things. And even if something is possible, its extreme unlikelihood should cast doubt on the legitimacy of a hope based on it. If I promise, for example, to give you the Golden Gate Bridge, my fulfilling such a promise would be extremely unlikely. "Extreme unlikelihood" of fulfillment should be made relative to the individual: An escape that is extremely unlikely for me would have been easy for Houdini. But even Houdini could not, as he allegedly promised to do, return from death. So there will be some things that are extremely unlikely for all of us, including those that are logically or physically impossible.

We can say that a hope is legitimate, then, if it is a hope that meets two conditions: (1) it is not extremely unlikely to be realized (either statistically or in the particular case), and (2) it has been raised by one person in another through an explicit statement of intention. Perhaps both conditions are not necessary (an implied intention, for example, might do), but that they are sufficient is all I need to support my thesis: Where one's legitimate hopes are disappointed, partial, passive bitterness is justified.

One might object that there are cases where one's hopes are legitimate on my account, but bitterness is clearly not justified. Suppose, for example, that I have promised to meet you in San Francisco on May 21, 1990. I have bought my ticket, confirmed my plans, and have every intention of going. But I am run over by a Mack truck on the way to the airport. Clearly, although your hope was legitimate, bitterness (toward me) would not be justified.[7] So my thesis should be qualified: Where one's important, legitimate hopes are disappointed, in the absense of excusing conditions, partial, passive bitterness is justified.

Thus, to return to the betrayed lover, we can say that, on the assumption that sexual fidelity is possible (and not better described as laziness), and assuming one's lover is not exceptionally gifted in respect of waywardness, and one's vows or other communications contained an explicit statement of intention to be "true," the lover who was betrayed had her legitimate, important hope of fidelity disappointed, and so partial, passive bitterness is justified.

What, then, is wrong with it?

One answer assimilates betrayal to death. Death is inevitable; betrayal, once accomplished, is irrevocable. So neither is amenable to change. To be bitter, one might argue, is to dwell on irrevocable wrongs, on something one cannot change, and is therefore wrong.

If we were to grant this objection, no backward-looking emotion, however powerful the grounds (for example, grief due to the death of one's child) would be justified, since *everything* past is irrevocable. But we do think some backward-looking emotions are justified. Grief, for one. So the above assimilation of betrayal to death should be rejected.

Further, even if one could justly criticize a person for dwelling on the past, the criticism might be answered by appealing to present consequences. The mere fact that the initial wrong was in the past does not show that present bitterness is unjustified. Consider, for example, the results of a botched job of surgery: the case of *Hawkins v. McGee*,[8] where the plaintiff, Hawkins, went to the defendant, Dr. McGee, with a burned hand and was promised complete restoration. He went home with a *burned and hairy hand*, due to the doctor's incompetence. McGee had used skin from the plaintiff's chest for the graft. One would not be surprised to hear that Hawkins was bitter, if he was, or that he did not respond well to the enraging advice to forget it, since the past is past and cannot be changed.

In this case, one might object, the harm is not irrevocable: Skin grafts can be redone. Still, my point stands if we rewrite the story slightly and say that due to the doctor's gross incompetence, Hawkins went home with no hand. Clearly the advice to forget it would be enraging and more enraging *because* the damage could not be undone.

It might be argued that bitterness is harmful to its host, and this is what makes it wrong. Is this plausible?

No. As Derek Parfit argues, that an attitude is bad for us does not show this attitude to be irrational. At most it shows that we should try to change it. "If the person whom I love most is killed, I should perhaps try, after a time, to reduce my grief. But this does not show that I have no reason to grieve. Grief is not irrational simply because it brings unhappiness. To the claim 'Your sorrow is fruitless,' Hume replied, 'Very true, and for that very reason I am sorry.' "[9]

If there is reasonable grief, then, I suggest, there is justified bitterness. For as grief is proof of love,[10] bitterness is proof of hope, since both love and hope can be well- or ill-grounded; so too can the emotions of grief and bitterness, which are responses to these losses.

But though this reply to the objection seems sound, we might question instead the assumption that underlies the objection—that bitterness is always bad for us. And here we may want to consider the harder case: active bitterness, bitterness that is more vocal and/or vindictive.

Is active bitterness always bad for us?

In *Wild Justice: The Evolution of Revenge*, Susan Jacoby questions the common view that forgiveness is always good for mental health and vindictiveness always bad. She cites Doris Donnelly, who, acknowledging that it may sound ludicrous to advise a battered wife to turn the other cheek, emphasizes her belief that, "ultimately, when that battered wife is out of danger, at some point she's going to have to address the question of forgiveness—or hang on to her outrage for the rest of her life."[11]

Jacoby cites Karen Horney, who makes similar claims: "In simplest terms the vindictive person does not only inflict suffering on others but even more so on himself. His vindictiveness makes him isolated, egocentric, absorbs his energies, makes him psychically sterile, and above all, closes the gate to his further growth. . . . Every vindictiveness damages the core of the whole being."[12] Horney seems to be talking not about partial, active bitterness, but about bitterness that characterizes the person, bitterness that is complete. Although complete bitterness may damage the core of the whole being, it's not clear why partial bitterness must.

Jacoby seems to agree. She says that the common view confuses particular acts of deserved forgiveness with a policy of unconditional forgiveness, and it confuses particular acts of retaliation with vengefulness as a way of life.

It is not the question of forgiveness a battered wife must address . . . but the question of how to free herself from the power of vengeful rage. One step toward such freedom, I believe, is the admission that forgiveness may, on occasion, be as inappropriate and self-destructive a response to injury as overweening vindictiveness. There are people who, in denying responsibility for their actions, abandon their claim upon human compassion.[13]

One cannot "come to terms" with brutality where there is no remorse; such terms are not acceptable. Hence, acceptance of one's fate is, in these circumstances, more than we can reasonably ask, and forgiveness is inappropriate and self-destructive. As responses to the infliction of undeserved suffering, forgiveness and active bitterness are on opposite ends of the continuum. Thus, it might be argued, where forgiveness is inappropriate and self-destructive, active bitterness may be appropriate and not self-destructive. So even active bitterness is not always bad for its host.

But clearly it can be harmful and generally is. To be bitter is to hold a grudge, vividly and continuously. Those who are bitter have, we might say, trouble in letting go of their pain. Like vindictiveness, it resists containment, tending toward excess, overgeneralization. As a response to a particular loss, bitterness may be justified, but it is liable to poison one's other perceptions, to corrupt one's judgments of people, life. One begins to *look* for the half-eaten worm in the rotten apple. Instead of hating one's deserving wife or brutal husband, one hates all women, all men. We have all known someone who has taken real loss and twisted it; no longer bitter about some harm or loss, he has become a bitter person. Bitterness is now part of his character. The emotion may survive even after its original object is forgotten, and perhaps it's this we fear in resisting the justification of bitterness.

But this is no objection to my account. I have argued that bitterness is justified where it is a response to the disappointment of an important, legitimate hope. One may be justifiably bitter *about* some action or omission on the part of another person, if there are no excusing conditions. This, however, rules out becoming a justifiably bitter *person*, unless all or most of one's important hopes are both legitimate and have been disappointed. Thus, in a society in which many are homeless or live in extreme poverty, or are members of despised minorities (or majorities), there will be a lot of justifiably bitter people.

And this consequence seems to me right. Only the saintly survive the disappointment of every important, legitimate human hope without becoming bitter, and even here we might question whether saintliness is something we should aim for, or whether it is preferable to fulfill our emotional responsibility to *feel things as they really are.*[14]

Honest rage has its place. In India, women who are raped may be put in prison. On the news recently was the story of a nine-year-old girl in northern California who was interviewed by a reporter interested in what it was like to be homeless. Later that week, she was rinsing her hair with kerosene, trying to kill the lice, when her hair caught on fire; she was burned on her face and two-thirds of her body.[15] Sometimes bitterness is a moral achievement.

One major objection to my defense of bitterness is that what I am talking about is not bitterness at all but unforgiving anger or deep sadness.[16] These may be justifiable but bitterness is not.

The thought here, I believe, is that bitterness is to grief as a grudge is to rage: meanness on a small scale. It is a pitiable reaction to loss with a touch of self-righteousness in it, even spite. Unforgiving anger or deep sadness can lack vindinctiveness, be "clean," and so can grief; bitterness cannot.

According to the *Oxford English Dictionary*, "bitterness" covers both active and passive forms. But the objection can be reformulated to take this into account: Passive bitterness can be justified, but active bitterness cannot.

Granted, active bitterness is less attractive, more mean-spirited, liable to do more damage; passive bitterness is cleaner, more admired, easier to live with. But is active bitterness always out of place?

The clearest cases of justified bitterness are of the blame-the-victim variety (the bitterness of rape victims, for example). This suggests that an abhorrence of active bitterness may have a suspect motive: It helps keep the victim in a position of weakness.

Ronald de Sousa gives an analysis of the emotion of anger that supports this view.

An angry man is a "manly man," but an angry woman is a "fury" or a "bitch." Or, worse, she is "hysterical," which denies her "real" anger altogether. This is necessarily reflected in the quality of the emotion itself. A man will experience an episode of anger characteristically as indignation. A woman will feel it as something less moralistic—guilt-laden frustration, perhaps, or sadness. Insofar as the conception of gender stereotypes that underlies these differences is purely conventional mystification, the emotions that embody them are paradigms of self-deceptive ones induced by social "deference."[17]

Thus, one might claim, active bitterness is a move away from self-deception and moral slavery in the direction of truth, a refusal to defer, and is therefore moral progress.

Some may find active bitterness lamentable, *even if justified*, in a category with suicide, for example, or justice that shows no mercy, or loyalty that demands one's death. But this is a different question—of whether justified bitterness should be encouraged or discouraged.

Many of us admire those who "forgive and forget" or who otherwise resist or overcome bitterness. (Our praise is generally aimed at some form of romantic stoicism: "What does not destroy me makes me stronger."[18] It equally well might make one meaner, more bitter.) The question is, Should we admire them? Or are we wrong to?

Bitterness hurts not only its host; it hurts others as well. The concentration on one's own pain must have its effect on those closest to the sufferer, whether directly or indirectly. At best it limits, through self-absorption, one's attention to others; at worst, it can foster what it is aimed against. Battered children, for example, often become battering parents. "There may be losses too great to understand / that rove after you and, faint and terrible, rip unknown through your hand."[19] Old wounds create new victims. This suggests that even if justified, bitterness should at some point be resisted, if not for one's own sake, then for the sake of others.

There is an objection to this view, however. Bitterness may help others, so its capacity for harm does not settle the issue of its wrongness, for it may be on balance beneficial. In the prose foreword to her poem, *Requiem,* Anna Akhmatova provides an argument for this claim:

> During the terrible years of the Yezhovshchina I spent seventeen months in the prison queues in Leningrad. One day someone recognized me. Then a woman with lips blue with cold who was standing behind me, and of course had never heard of my name, came out of the numbness whch affected us all and whispered in my ear—(we all spoke in whispers there):
> "Can you describe this?"
> I said, "I can!"
> Then something resembling a smile slipped over what had once been her face.[20]

The last lines of the poem reiterate the potential value of bitterness: bearing witness for those who cannot speak for themselves, the power in truth-telling, the powerful consolation in the articulation of pain.

A similar view is expressed in Milan Kundera's *The Book of Laughter and Forgetting.* The novel begins with Communist leader Klement Gottwald stepping out onto the balcony of a palace in Prague to address his fellow Czech citizens. Gottwald was bareheaded, it was cold, and his comrade Clementis took off his own fur cap and put it on Gottwald's head. Four years later Clementis was charged with treason and hanged. He was immediately airbrushed out of the photograph and out of history. Mirek says that "the struggle of man against power is the struggle of memory against forgetting."[21] This is his justification for keeping a diary and for preserving all correspondence, analyses of the political situation, minutes of meetings. Mirek is later arrested and this material is confiscated, but he doesn't repent. "They wanted to erase hundreds of thousands of lives from human memory and leave nothing but a single unblemished age of unblemished idyll. But Mirek is going to stretch out full length over their idyll, like a blemish. And stay there, like Clementis's cap on Gottwald's head."[22]

Truth-telling and bearing witness (saying, "I know who you are and I saw what you did") are forms of active bitterness; thus if truth-telling and bearing witness are justified, so is active bitterness.

Susan Jacoby claims that

to assume the burden of being a relentless keeper of the truth is to place a higher value on righteous anger and remembrance than on forgiveness. Such people arouse antagonism not only because the world is unprepared to hear what they have to say but also because the personality traits that lend themselves to a sharp recollection of past injustice are not considered the most appealing qualities in ordinary social intercourse. "Thorny," "abrasive," and "vindictive" are the adjectives most frequently applied to those who devote a substantial portion of their lives to detailing the facts of pain and injustice. Who would not prefer Jesus to Jeremiah as a dinner guest?[23]

"Bitter" could easily be added to the list. And, it might be noted, the qualities we desire in a dinner guest are not the same qualities we seek when attending a revolution.

So there is not just a low-class (self-serving) reason but a high-class (moral) reason to resist the gag, the temptations of silence. Whether the argument is a fist or the relatively minor complaint, "You're so bitter," we should consider the motivation: They may be attempts to shut us up, to get us to sell out our pain and the pain of others before we've had a chance to give it a name. Although the vocally bitter may cause others discomfort, may threaten their illusions (may do the former *because* they do the latter), the question that should be addressed, as in other cases of justified bitterness, is one of fidelity—to the truth. And where the truth is harsh, and of human origin, and avoidable, bitterness is a form of moral accounting, of naming the losses, that we can condone both in ourselves and others.

Is bitterness ever required? Assuming a choice is possible, should we encourage or resist its going? As grief is proof of love, so, one might say, bitterness is a *necessary* reminder that something hoped for and greatly valued has been lost.

Although bitterness may be a way of bearing witness to the truth and resisting evil, may have both personal and political justification based on that fact, it is never required. For there are other more admirable and more powerful forms of resistance. As the narrator says in John Hawkes's *Second Skin*: "Perhaps my father thought that by shooting off the top of his head he would force me to undergo some sort of transfiguration. But poor man, he forgot my capacity for love."[24] Love as a response to such loss may be rare, but where it is possible most would agree that it is preferable to bitterness.

And Nietzsche, for example, claims that instead of seeking revenge for a wrong, it is better to show our enemy that he's done us some good. Instead of resenting a harm, better to use it to turn what seemed a harm into an advantage. *Amor fati.* One should love one's fate, even when it's harsh, especially when it's harsh. What he seems to be advocating is not the simple and dangerous idea that because it took all the bad things that happened for a person to be what she is, those things are thereby transformed and made good. That would be an egocentric and morally unacceptable attempt to justify evil (the history of the world's suffering was so I could write this essay justifying bitterness). I believe what he's advocating is an attitude toward life that might be called "bitter love"[25]—love that comes out of strength rather than weakness, that does not expect something for nothing, that has no illusions, that is not built on trust. "It is the love for a woman who raises doubts in us."[26]

There are some instances of evil, however, to which even bitter love would be a ludicrous response: human slavery, for example, or the Holocaust. Here bitterness is an emotional understatement, and the novelist Kelly Cherry's lament seems more appropriate: "Surely, grief and rage, are our highest moral imperatives."[27]

But even in cases where the encouragement to forgive and forget or to love one's enemy is obscene, there are forms of vindication other than vindictiveness.[28] Samuel Pisar, one of the youngest survivors of Auschwitz, wrote about the forms of vengeance appropriate to a civilized life:

> I still was given to flashes of violence. One day, in chemistry class, when I dug into my jacket pocket for a piece of chalk, I pulled out instead a banana peel. At the desk behind, a boy named Bill Downey grinned, chomping on a banana. With the blood rushing in my head, I swung a Landsberg jailhouse punch at him; he was knocked from his chair to the floor. . . .
>
> I was mortified. Fool, I said to myself, what have you done? You have reacted as if he wanted to kill you. Have those Nazis succeeded after all? It's no life to remain a savage. If you really want to make a life for yourself, you've got to become civilized. You've got to learn some self-control. . . .
>
> We decided that continuing the moral and intellectual rehabilitation we had begun, the undoing of Hitler's destructive work, even on the infinitesimal scale of two individuals, was

perhaps the only meaningful form of vengeance. It seemed the best way to begin discharging our duty toward the Jewish people and to humanity as a whole.[29]

Many writers have spoken of their work as alternatives to or more benign forms of revenge. John Hawkes, for example, claims that "fiction should achieve revenge for all the indignities of our childhood."[30] Francine du Plessix Gray makes a similar claim: "I write out of a desire for revenge against reality, to destroy forever the stuttering powerless child I once was," although the indignities she is attempting to avenge include the humiliations of adulthood at the hands of men.[31] In the preface to a book about his wife's suicide,[32] Robert Dykstra speaks of his writing as a way of "avenging" his wife's death, which suggests that the coming to terms with reality that writing sometimes represents may be as much a method of forgiveness as of vengeance.

What are the limits of bitterness?

No general answer seems available. It will depend on the particular case: the object of outrage, its magnitude and scope, the time that has passed, aftereffects, and the positive or negative value of its continued expression. One day may be too long to suffer a slight insult and complain of it; a lifetime may not be long enough to tell of unacceptable losses.

When and if the bitterness goes, it may be experienced itself both as a loss (what we hate helps to define us) and a relief, as one may slowly begin to neglect one's grief, and be both sad and grateful to find it gone.[33] For most of us, even where bitterness is justified and serves a high moral purpose, the thought will eventually come, as it did for Coriolanus: "There is a world elsewhere."

NOTES

I would like to thank the members of my former ethics discussion group at the University of Texas at Austin as well as students and colleagues at Syracuse University for valuable criticisms of an earlier draft of this essay. I am especially indebted to Jonathan Bennett, Dan Bonevac, Claudia Card, Rebecca Holsen, Bob Kane, John Kekes, Joel Kidder, Emily Robertson, John Robertson, Tom Seung, and Michael Stocker. I have profited most, in reading, from the works of Susan Jacoby and Ronald de Sousa.

1. From an early draft of *Herzog* by Saul Bellow. Quoted by Anne Sexton as an epigraph to *Live or Die*, in *Sexton, The Complete Poems* (Boston: Houghton, Mifflin, 1981), 94.

2. See John Kekes, "True and False Hope," unpublished manuscript, 17.

3. Immanuel Kant, *Critique of Pure Reason*, trans. N. K. Smith (London: Macmillan, 1953), A805. The other two are "What can I know?" and "What ought I to do?"

4. See the *Compact Edition of the Oxford English Dictionary*, 885.

5. Dylan Thomas, *Collected Poems* (New York: New Directions, 1939), 128. For a good discussion of this question, see Thomas Nagel, "Death" and "The Absurd," in his *Mortal Questions* (London: Cambridge University Press, 1979), 1–23.

6. The concept of sexual fidelity may be problematic from a homoerotic perspective, but sexual infidelity is, I would guess, the most common case of betrayal, despite the existence of borderline cases; it's where the statistical sense and the ideal sense of "norm" most clearly conflict.

7. One may, however, raise the question of whether bitterness toward bad luck or death is justified.

8. The case of *Hawkins v. McGee* is discussed by Robert Fogelin in *Understanding Arguments* (New York: Harcourt, Brace, Jovanovich, 1978), 220.

9. Derek Parfit, *Reasons and Persons* (Oxford: Oxford University Press, 1985), 169. Quoted by Ronald de Sousa, *The Rationality of Emotion* (Cambridge and London: MIT Press, 1987), 167.

10. Ibid., 321.

11. Susan Jacoby, *Wild Justice: The Evolution of Revenge* (New York: Harper and Row, 1983), 351.

12. Ibid., 352.

13. Ibid.

14. This is de Sousa's point, *Rationality of Emotion*, 315.

15. In this case, there may have been no hope for a better life, and so no bitterness on her part. But isn't such a lack of hope more cause for bitterness; shouldn't we be bitter on her behalf?

16. This objection was raised by Jonathan Bennett (unforgiving anger) and Michael Stocker (deep sadness).

17. De Sousa, *Rationality of Emotion*, 259.

18. Friedrich Nietzsche, *The Portable Nietzsche*, trans. and ed. Walter Kaufmann (New York: Viking Press, 1968), 680.

19. William Stafford, *Stories That Could Be True* (New York: Harper and Row, 1977), 155.

20. Anna Akhmatova is quoted by Jacoby, *Wild Justice*, 356, and Terence Des Pres, *The Survivor* (New York: Pocket Books, 1977), 28.

21. Milan Kundera, *The Book of Laughter and Forgetting* (New York: Penguin Books, 1981), 3.

22. Ibid., 24.

23. Jacoby, *Wild Justice*, 358.

24. John Hawkes, *Second Skin* (New York: New Directions, 1963), 2.

25. "Bitter love" is a term from a poem by Richard Wilbur, "Love Calls Us to the Things of This World," *New and Collected Poems* (New York: Harcourt, Brace, Jovanovich, 1989), 233.

26. Nietzsche, *Portable Nietzsche*, 681.

27. Kelly Cherry, *The Lost Traveler's Dream* (New York: Harcourt, Brace, Jovanovich, 1984), 50.

28. This is Jacoby's point. See *Wild Justice*, 358–359, on the concept of the triumphant life as a form of vindication.

29. Samuel Pisar, *Of Blood and Hope* (New York: Macmillan, 1980), 122. Quoted by Jacoby, *Wild Justice*, 360.

30. John Hawkes interview, *The New Fiction: Interviews with Innovative American Writers*, ed. Joe David Bellamy (Urbana, Chicago, and London: University of Illinois Press, 1974), 108.

31. Francine du Plessix Gray, "I Write for Revenge against Reality," in *First Person Singular: Writers on Their Craft*, comp. Joyce Carol Oates (Princeton, N.J.: Ontario Review Press, 1983), 250.

32. Robert Dykstra, *She Never Said Good-Bye* (Wheaton, Ill.: Harold Shaw Publishers, 1932), xi.

33. De Sousa, *Rationality of Emotion*, 167.

10 / The Social Self and the Partiality Debates

MARILYN FRIEDMAN

"Moral impartialism" is a prominent view in contemporary moral philosophy. According to moral impartialism, moral thinking should be impartial, that is, it should be free of bias or prejudice. This means that it should involve the equal consideration of all persons and show no special favoritism toward anyone. In recent decades, most feminist and some nonfeminist moral philosophers have challenged moral impartialism. As part of their challenge, some feminist critics and nearly all nonfeminist critics defend the moral importance of partiality—that is, favoritism—to certain particular persons, in at least some areas of life. In addition, nearly all feminist critics and some nonfeminist critics base their challenge to moral impartialism on a conception of persons as inherently social selves. Let us call this the "social conception of the self," or, for stylistic variation, the "conception of the social self" (a concept I will explain later).

This conceptual overlap between feminist and nonfeminist critiques of the tradition of moral impartialism might suggest that the underlying concerns of both groups coincide. That appearance, however, is largely an illusion. What seems on the surface to be a shared project (challenging moral impartialism) in fact masks quite different underlying presumptions and concerns. My aim, in this essay, is to reveal some of those differences and to develop further the feminist alternative. In particular, I hope to clarify the social conception of the self in light of certain important issues brought up by nonfeminist critics of moral impartialism. For the most part, I will not take sides specifically on the challenge to moral impartiality or the defense of partiality. The social conception of the self is the focal point for this discussion of what some moral philosophers have begun to call the "partiality/impartiality debates."

THE PARTIALITY/IMPARTIALITY
DEBATES AND THE SOCIAL CONCEPTION
OF THE SELF: A SUMMARY

It has become a commonplace of contemporary mainstream ethics that we are each entitled to show favoritism, preferential treatment, partiality toward loved ones. Some philosophers would say even more strongly that we have the *obligation* to show such treatment, that it is not simply an option or a prerogative. This notion of partiality toward loved ones is lately gaining wide philosophical acclaim. (Ordinary people, fortunately, have held this view for quite some time.)

Although the appropriateness of partiality toward loved ones is itself uncontested, there is a lively debate growing in ethics over its theoretical justification. One of the hottest questions is whether partiality toward loved ones can adequately be justified by any of the dominant impartialist theories of modern moral philosophy. In the past two decades, both feminist and nonfeminist philosophers have been disputing the adequacy of those traditions to account for the moral value of personal relationships. The feature of these theories that seems to deny the legitimacy of partiality is their requirement of moral *im*partiality—the requirement to show equal consideration, in some specified sense, toward all persons.

Moral philosophers have used a variety of fictional images to express what it would be for moral thinking to be genuinely impartial. One image is that of the "ideal observer." According to Roderick Firth's classic 1952 depiction of it, the ideal observer is someone who is "omniscient with respect to nonethical facts," omnipercipient, disinterested, dispassionate, and consistent, but in all other respects, "normal."[1] A more recent image of impartial moral reasoning is R. M. Hare's "archangel," who can scan a novel situation and discern at a glance all its properties, including the future consequences of all alternative possible actions. Based on this superhuman knowledge, "he" frames a universal principle for behavior in that situation, a principle that would be acceptable to him from the standpoint of any role he might have to occupy in that situation.[2] Thomas Nagel's image of impartial moral thinking (he calls it "objective" or "impersonal" thinking) is "the view from nowhere": To attain this view, one detaches oneself from one's own personal perspective, transcends "one's time and place," and "escapes the specific contingencies of one's creaturely point of view."[3]

From the *im*partial standpoint, one is to reason about moral matters detached from the influence of one's own specific contingencies—one's wants, needs, loyalties, and so on. The impartial attitude is supposed to overcome what is traditionally regarded as the pervasive human tendency toward *self-serving* partiality and *egoism*. From the impartialist point of view, one is permitted to take account of one's own particularities—but only as contextual details of the moral matter under consideration, a sort of "grist" for the mill of moral judgment. One is not to reason *from* those particularities, that is, from a perspective that at the outset prejudicially favors those interests.

Treating everyone impartially appears to mean treating each person, including oneself, with the same consideration—no more, no less—as anyone else. One gives equal consideration to "every person as a person," according to Paul Taylor, when one refrains from "counting the basic interests of one individual as having greater (or lesser) weight than the basic interests of another."[4]

But this is hardly the way to treat loved ones. And so critics of moral impartialism charge that impartial theories call for attitudes that are alienating in close personal relationships—attitudes such as detachment from personal concerns and loyalties, disinterest, dispassion, and a regard for the generalized moral equality of all persons that abstracts from their particularity and uniqueness. Close relationships call instead for personal concern, loyalty, interest, passion, and responsiveness to the uniqueness of loved ones, to their specific needs, interests, history, and so on. In a word, personal relationships call for partiality rather than impartiality.

Impartialist theorists also tend to emphasize moral matters (such as justice), which pertain to a public world in which people interact as equal but mutually disinterested persons.[5] Furthermore, the impartialist ethical tradition that follows the work of Immanuel Kant is notable for its emphasis on a sense of duty as the primary moral motivation.[6] In close personal relationships, however, the need for care seems to overshadow the need for justice, and our loved ones may well be insulted by caring that is motivated by a sense of duty rather than loving concern.

Partialists have attacked moral impartialism and defended partiality with a variety of additional arguments. John Cottingham insists that partiality toward loved ones is essential to human integrity and fulfillment. John Kekes describes how the nature of intimacy renders impartiality inappropriate. Lawrence Blum and Charles Fried see intrinsic value in benefiting one's own friends and loved ones. In the opinion of Bernard Williams, devoting oneself preferentially to one's own ground projects, including personal relationships, is necessary in order to have character, integrity, motive force to face one's future, and reason for living. Andrew Oldenquist warns that equal concern for the whole of humanity is simply too weak a sentiment, in any case, to be effective as moral motivation.[7]

Those are typical nonfeminist arguments. Feminists, such as Sara Ruddick,[8] have generally endorsed partiality not so much for its own sake but rather as part of a larger project. This is the project of promoting esteem for the caring and nurturing activities that women have traditionally undertaken in such areas of life as family and health care. Those caring activities have essentially involved moral attention and responsiveness to the specific wants and needs of particular persons.

As if that entire array of charges against impartiality were not formidable enough,[9] some critics of moral impartiality—nonfeminists such as Alasdair MacIntyre and Michael Sandel and feminists such as Iris Young—have denied the very possibility of impartial reasoning.[10] (Young urges, further, that the rhetoric of impartiality should be distrusted because it has been used in practice by dominant social groups to disguise their de facto political and cultural hegemony.[11]) All three of these theorists argue that no self can reason as if dissociated from the contingencies that make her the self she is. There is no escape from the specifics of one's embodiment, historical situation, and relational connections to others. Impartial reasoning is impossible; the self is inherently partial.

Indeed, for MacIntyre, Sandel, and Young, the self is inherently *social* to some degree or other. In its identity, character, interests, and preferences, it is constituted by, and in the course of, relationships to particular others, including the network of relationships that locate it as a member of certain communities or social groups. This is the social conception of the self. According to Sandel's version of it, we each have "loyalties and convictions whose moral force consists partly in the fact that living by them is inseparable from understanding ourselves as the particular persons we are—as members of this family or community or nation or people, as bearers of this history, as sons and daughters of that revolution, as citizens of this republic."[12] For MacIntyre as well "we all approach our own circumstances as bearers of a particular social identity. I am someone's son or daughter, someone else's cousin or uncle; I am a citizen of this or that city, a member of this or that guild or profession; I belong to this clan, that tribe, this nation."[13] Relationships to others are intrinsic to identity, preferences, and so on, and the self can only reason *as* the social being she is.

The social conception of the self fits comfortably into the feminist project of incorporating women's moral perspectives into ethical theorizing. Caroline Whitbeck and Virginia Held argue that the social conception of the self, with its emphasis on the primacy of relationships, coincides with women's traditional experiences as mothers and caregivers.[14] The concept of the social self also provides a theoretical underpinning for the feminist view that gender in particular is a socially constructed aspect of human identity, one that may, therefore, diverge from our present gender arrangements of pervasive male dominance.

In addition, a social conception of the self makes a concern for other persons fundamental to the self and does not reduce it to a mere variety of self-concern. Indeed, the social conception of the self tends somewhat to blur the distinction between self and other. If my relationship to someone or some group is internal to who I am, then she or they are somehow a part of me—admittedly, a metaphor that needs substantial clarification. In my partiality for those who are in this way near and dear to me, I show a moral attitude that is neither egoism nor self-denying altruism. The flourishing of loved ones promotes my own well-being, yet my motivation to care for them does not require me to compute how their well-being will further my own interests; I simply am interested in them. J. L. Mackie, following C. D. Broad, called this attitude "self-referential altruism."[15] On this view, simple egoism is not the all-pervasive moral failing it has been theorized to be and far too much ethical work has been expended in disputing it.

Without doubt, the social conception of the self needs further development. The two issues raised by the partiality debate, which I deal with later in this essay, contribute toward that development.

Before turning to that discussion, I will highlight some features of the partiality debates that have special poignancy from a feminist perspective.

THE FLAVOR OF THE PARTIALITY DEBATES

To begin with, the social conception of the self is not shared by all critics of impartialism. Among nonfeminist partialists, conceptions of the self range from the individualistic atoms of libertarianism to the socially embedded subjects of communitarianism.

An example of an individualistic conception of the self is found in the works of Charles Fried, solicitor general under the Reagan administration and a formally trained philosopher. In his writings, Fried has puzzled over the limits of moral impartiality at least since 1970. Not surprisingly, he presents a libertarian view: Beyond the realm of justice, rights, and other duties to avoid injuring others, we are morally free to do what we want. On this view, morality has its limits, and beyond those limits, we may show partiality toward whomever we wish and ignore whomever we wish. Wants and wishes are left unexamined and the role of relationships in constituting wants and the wanting self is simply disregarded by Fried.[16]

Bernard Williams, a pioneering defender of partiality, has a conception of the self that is more social than that of Fried. Williams's conception of morality is richer as well and includes not only impartial moral demands but also matters of character and personal relations, which for him are not to be understood in impartial terms. One important matter of character is personal integrity. In Williams's view, the pursuit of integrity involves devoting considerable attention and energy to personal projects and commitments without which life would not be worth living. However, these projects *compete* with impartial moral concerns. A self who is too heavily encumbered with impartialist moral responsibilities to treat everyone with equal consideration will be alienated from close others and from her own self because she won't have time for her most fundamental, integrity-conferring relationships and projects.[17]

Wiliams's views[18] advance beyond Fried's in explicitly recognizing the importance of relationships to personal integrity and moral experience. But Williams's specific defense of his views is disturbing in virtue of the gender configurations that skew his examples. In an important essay on this topic, Williams argues that in a hypothetical dilemma in which there is time to save only one person, one should save one's drowning "wife" rather than a drowning stranger.[19] One obvious problem with this sad example is its reliance on the unfortunate social stereotypes of active male and passive, helpless female.

A second, not-so-obvious gender configuration problem emerges when this example is compared with other examples in Williams's writings. In his famous essay on moral luck, Williams argues that a painter who *abandons* wife and children altogether and heads off for Tahiti to develop his art will be retroactively justified if he thereby acquires the good fortune to create great paintings.[20] (Any resemblance between Williams's story of this hypothetical figure and the life of the painter Gauguin is not a coincidence.) Thus Williams's larger body of writing gives the true measure of his nonimperialist value hierarchy: wife trumps stranger, but great paintings trump wife.

Williams's writings aside, there are at least two more features of the partiality debates that are noteworthy from a feminist perspective. First, in mainstream ethics, partiality means favoritism or preferential treatment. Mainstream discussions presuppose a context of competing interests. The emphasis is on what I do for my wife or child *at the expense of* someone else, including other wives, other children.

Hypothetical disasters abound as thought experiments in these discussions. The moral world of mainstream ethics is a nightmare of plane crashes, train wrecks, and sinking ships! Wives and children drown in this literature at an alarming rate. The nonfeminist impartiality critics never acknowledge how infrequent these emergencies are in daily moral life, nor, therefore, how rare is the need to sacrifice someone else's wife in order to save one's own. And for these infrequent occasions, the nonfeminist impartiality critics never discuss the possibility of investing our moral energies in efforts to *reduce beforehand* those breathtaking contests for survival and love—for example, by better FAA regulation of airline safety.

Second, although there is broad consensus about the legitimacy of partiality toward family members and friends, there is no consensus about other special relationships. Some theorists defend partiality toward the members of one's local and national communities, such as neighborhood, city, and nation. Communitarians, as we have seen, especially favor these examples.[21] (It is astonishing how few non-feminist participants in the partiality debates mention gender or race; those few who do are usually *defenders* of moral impartialism, who point out that some forms of partiality are unjustified and who cite racism and sexism as examples.[22])

My point is that beyond the realm of close relationships, there is no consensus on the legitimacy of partiality. Note, however, that those who do defend partiality toward local or national communities ironically pay no attention to the historical specifics of interrelationships among communities and social groups—the hierarchies of group domination, the institutionalized oppressions, the imperialistic policies. Group loyalty is a form of partiality that covers a wide spectrum—for example, ethnic pride and group solidarity in the face of oppression, but also white supremacism, male chauvinism, and heterosexism. The moral worth of group loyalty varies with the relative needs, interests, powers, privileges, and history of the social group in question. At any rate, this issue has yet to find adequate treatment in the partiality debates.

ON BEING SOCIAL BUT NOT CONVENTIONAL

In this part of my essay, I turn to the first of two problems faced by a social conception of the self as suggested by the partiality debates. Many nonfeminist impartiality critics refer to certain conventionally defined roles and relationships as if the relationships as such legitimated the partiality shown within them. If my child or friend is in danger, then I may—or, rather, I should—help her first before I help others who are in lesser or equivalent or even slightly greater danger. According to most nonfeminist impartiality critics, that someone is related to me in certain ways *of itself* warrants partiality toward that person. On this view, certain conventional social relationships are intrinsically legitimate reference points for partiality.

The extreme form of appeal to social convention is expressed by communitarian critics of impartiality.[23] In their view, social traditions, practices, and roles determine the particulars of individual moral lives. I am someone's daughter, someone's friend, someone's mother, and I therefore have certain filial, friendship, and parental responsibilities toward certain individuals, responsibilities that I do not have to people to whom I am not thus related. The basis for these responsibilities is at least partly a matter of tradition, a matter of the way in which caretaking work is socially allocated. Impartiality calls for the humanly impossible detachment from those particulars about oneself that make certain social conventions relevant. Thus on the communitarian view, partiality in special relationships simply fulfills socially assigned responsibilities in the context of traditional relationship practices that define the "starting points" of individual moral identity.

In the nonfeminist literature on this topic, the consensus is that one should show special favoritism to people in the following relationships to oneself: spouse, child, parent, and friend. These are by far the most commonly invoked nonfeminist examples. Even nonfeminist theorists who disagree on how to justify partiality in these relationships nevertheless agree that partiality *is* legitimate in these relationships.

This approach, however, gives rise to a serious problem. Nonfeminist impartiality critics treat these traditionally sanctioned relationships as paradigms of partiality, betraying an uncritical attitude toward our traditions of intimate relationships.

This social conservatism, which merely lurks beneath the surface of many defenses of partiality, finds explicit statement in writings by Christina Hoff Sommers. In Sommers's view, feminists—together with contractarians!—are prime philosophical offenders against the traditional family. Sommers's discussion interweaves as a seamless undifferentiated whole the traditional family, traditional marriage, getting a man, and being feminine, with family in a more generic sense, marriage in a more generic sense, and having children. She treats the critique of any of the former institutions or practices as if it were also a wholesale rejection of each of the latter. Sommers denounces feminists for waging war on what women really want, namely "a man [and] children," and what "most women" really enjoy, namely "male gallantry, candlelit dinners, sexy clothes, [and] makeup." The feminist onslaught against these values, in Sommers's opinion, has supplanted and eliminated any worthwhile feminist analysis of the "economic and social injustices to which women are subjected."

Unfortunately, Sommers's unswerving loyalty to the traditional family and its gender roles (as well as to traditional marriage and femininity) occurs in a vacuum. She ignores the massive literature—more social science than philosophy—that documents difficulties and tragedies in traditional family life. Consequently, Sommers never directly refutes any substantive criticisms of those traditional relationships.[24]

Our traditions for interrelating closely with people, the traditions that make partiality legitimate for each of us toward certain others—especially but not solely in the context of the traditional family—are problematic in at least two ways. First, those traditions are restrictive. Only certain types of people can be related to each of us in specific ways. By legal and religious tradition, for example, no women are qualified to be a spouse of mine. Because of those restrictive traditions, lesbian and gay relationships are subjected to scorn and other social obstructions.

Second, even the permitted forms of traditional relationships can be morally treacherous. Shielded from public scrutiny by a veil of "privacy," conventional intimate relationships have permitted abuses as well as favoritism.[25] Many of the socially sanctioned relationships for partiality and favoritism have been sites of privatized power imbalances. The same social traditions that confer prerogatives of favoring loved ones have permitted, to those with greater power, privileges of hurting those same loved ones. Historically, men have been able to assault, batter, and rape the women to whom they were married, and parents can assault, batter, and impound their children. Traditional forms of partiality, or "preferential treatment," have often come at a price. The "favoritism" shown by husbands toward wives has not always been so favorable. However, most nonfeminist impartiality critics provide no critical evaluation of the social roles that they take to warrant partiality. They disregard the costs of that partiality for those "favored" by it—not to mention the costs of that partiality to those disfavored by it or excluded from it.[26]

To recap: The nonfeminist defenses of partiality generally show a complacency about our social traditions for close personal relationships. But these traditions are morally suspect in at least two different ways: First, they are too limited and by default seem to render illegitimate any close personal relationship that falls outside the bounds of convention; and, second, they sometimes harbor their own moral problems, problems that are ignored by nonfeminist partialists in their haste to endorse the partiality featured in those relationships. Thus the nonfeminist partialists inadvertently remind us of the need for a socially critical perspective on relationship traditions.

This need for a critical attitude toward relationships bears on the social conception of the self in an important way. The social self identifies herself, at least in part, by her relationships to others, including the social groups of which she is a part. She is, for example, someone's daughter, someone's sister, someone's aunt, she is Black, she is heterosexual, she is middle class, she's a Hoosier. Doubtless, she understands those relationships in terms of whatever, if any, social norms and conventions govern them. But if she has a socially critical perspective, then she does not necessarily act in accordance with those relational norms or with the conventions for her group. Instead, she may resist and subvert them.

This conception seems on the face of it mysterious. How can someone both identify in terms of certain relationships and, at the same time, cast doubt on those relationships by questioning the underlying social norms on which they are based? How can someone resist constituents of her very self? How can such independent attitudes be possible? Wouldn't they also be socially constituted? If so, wouldn't that negate the possible social independence of attitudes?

We know, however, that attitudes and behavior sometimes *are* independent. We know that there are social deviants. From that assumption, it is plausible to modify the social conception of the self to account for the existence of social criticism and resistance. What follows now is a brief excursion into speculative social theorizing aimed at beginning such an account.

The potential for deviating from relationship norms must lie in the complexity of selves and the diversity of ways in which we are constituted by our social contexts. A complex self can depart from this or that particular social influence, even those that (partially) constitute her identity, because of the combined effect of her *various and varied* identity-constituents. Selves do not simply replicate a small cohesive set of social norms.

What are some of those varied identity-constituents? First, as social beings, we reflect a *variety of relationships*—few people show the influence of only one formative relationship. But where there is variety, there is likely to be inconsistency. From political activist friends many years ago, I learned to distrust the patriotism I was taught in school. From love relationships, I learned to resist the sexual norms of femininity that gripped my teen-age consciousness. We can move back and forth among a plurality of partial identities, now interrogating this or that relational norm from the standpoint of other commitments.[27]

Second, this movement between aspects of identity is assisted in our culture by capacities for distrusting, doubting, interrogating, criticizing, and resisting that are socially learned to varying degrees. When someone finds out that she can "just say 'no' " to drug dealers, she is also learning how to say "no" to other demands. These techniques generalize and can be deployed against the conventional as well as the unconventional both to scrutinize others and in self-scrutiny.

Third, there are aspects of the *social* that are not normative, conventional, or rule-governed. Only some of what we derive from social origins is the orderly implementation of rules applied consistently across all social contexts. Our society is heterogeneous, complex, confused, contradictory, and sometimes incoherent. Some of what we derive from our social relationships is unregulated, disorderly, chaotic.

This social irregularity in turn has at least two dimensions. First, relational norms themselves are usually general and do not dictate the specific ways in which they are to be realized in any particular case; this must inevitably depend on the specifics of the persons involved. For example, we are taught to care for our parents when they are old and infirm, but there are no specific guidelines about exactly how to do this. The best *affordable* medical care might be available only in a nursing home, but your mother might rather be dead than enter one. Filial and other social norms are often general, and we are left to work out the specific applications for ourselves.

A second dimension of the unregulated nature of the social is the chaos of socially unsanctioned abuses. The sexual molestation of children is not explicitly condoned by our dominant cultural ideology or by our conventional norms of relations to children, but it is encouraged by suggestive advertising and inadequately punished by law. As we are socially constituted, we are influenced by these lawless social elements along with what is rule-bound, norm-governed.

And let us not forget the chaos of being constituted a woman, female, the "other"—lacking a sense of justice, lacking the authority of reason, lacking a you-know-what, fleshy, mysterious, and insatiable, the human source of original sin. Isn't our female embodiment socially constituted? And is it not the source of so much "female trouble"?

So. Selves are complex. Even though they are socially constituted, they can adopt points of view that are independent of this or that norm-governed relationship constituting their very identities. This complexity of selves includes (1) the *variety* of relationships that contribute to any one person's identity and that afford her differing and sometimes contradictory points of view; (2) learned techniques of doubt, critical reflection, resistance, and insubordination; and (3) elements of social life that exceed the limits of social regulation, elements of disorder within the heart of society and culture, including female nature and embodiment. It is because of conditions such as these that socially constituted selves can evade thorough social regulation.

If this survey of social influences on self-identity is correct, then the social conception of the self is consistent with the possibility that a self might criticize or resist this or that relationship constituting her very identity.

ON BEING PARTIAL BUT NOT
PAROCHIAL: GLOBAL MORAL CONCERN

In this final section, I turn to a different issue. I mentioned earlier that moral impartiality is currently understood in terms of giving equal consideration to all persons. As interpreted by most nonfeminist critics of impartiality, this requirement calls for the moral agent to devote literally equal amounts of time, energy, and resources to all persons. I should not be buying my own child such luxuries as toys when there are children (and adults) across town, or across the oceans, who don't even have food to eat. An equality of global moral concern, then, is an important part of what impartiality represents or entails for nonfeminist impartiality critics and is a primary target for them.

In opposing that view, many nonfeminist critics defend partiality with the fervor of political activists fighting for a social cause. In this case, the cause is "taking care of one's own." These philosophers have been especially troubled by the demand that we always consider the interests of all strangers and unloved acquaintances equally with the interests of loved ones. On the nonfeminist partialist view, the special obligations we have to those who are close to us have overriding moral priority when compared with general obligations to show concern for distant peoples. Nonfeminist partialists argue that special obligations to those who are close to us, to those who are "our own," should virtually eclipse those distant obligations in our moral attention.[28]

It should be noted that only a few moral *im*partialists have explicitly stated the requirement of impartiality in these demanding terms. William Godwin and Peter Singer are convenient targets for the partialists because they each profess an uncompromisingly thoroughgoing impartiality.[29] Peter Singer, especially in his earlier writings, argues that proximity and close relationship carry no moral weight and that moral responsibilities—for example, to those who are starving—extend equally to all members of the global village.[30]

William Godwin (ironically, the husband of the late-eighteenth-century British feminist Mary Wollstonecraft) was the one who invited us to consider this philosophically (in)famous dilemma: Should I rescue my beloved but socially worthless parent, a mere valet or chambermaid (depending on which edition one consults)? Or should I rescue instead François de Salignac de La Mothe-Fénelon, the archbishop of Cambray, in a disaster that prevents me from rescuing both? Godwin urges us to opt for the eminent archbishop. "What magic is there in the pronoun 'my,'" he asks, "that should justify us in overturning the decision of impartial truth?"[31] It is noteworthy how few such extreme defenders of the impartiality requirement there really are. (This suggests that moral impartiality means something else to most of its defenders and that its critics attack a straw person. But that is a discussion for another occasion.)

The point to emphasize here is that feminists who dispute the requirement of moral impartiality are not usually challenging the idea of global moral concern.[32] Global concerns and international connections among feminists have nourished our wider movement. Most feminists would insist on the importance of a cross-cultural variety of women's issues and of forging cross-cultural connections and solidarity among women. The responsibility to be concerned about distant peoples, then, is one implication of moral impartiality that, I think, most feminists would wish to retain. It is not in this respect that the notion of moral impartiality has worried feminists.

It is important to beware of possible equivocations over the notion of global moral concern. The difference between nonfeminist and feminist impartiality critics on this point is subtle. Some non-feminists, such as John Cottingham, are quick to point out that they do not oppose, for example, giving money to Oxfam. What Cotting-ham opposes is the idea that morality requires giving nearly *all* one's money to Oxfam, down to the point at which one has no more money than any of the starving beneficiaries of Oxfam relief—a radical divestment that he thinks is the ultimate logical outcome of the impartialist's insistence on giving equal weight to everyone's inter-ests.[33]

However, even feminists with money to burn and whose charity-giving histories are second to none are not usually relinquishing their resources at such a rate. So what exactly is the point at issue? The dispute seems to concern a matter of degree and a matter of what is honored and who the heroes are. Nonfeminist partialists, some of them at any rate, concede that it is all right to be charitable toward distant peoples; but on the whole, they downplay the importance of global concern and instead idealize favoring "one's own." By con-trast, feminist partialists devote much more theoretical attention to developing concern for those who are not "one's own." This is the significance of all the work that feminists put into theorizing "differ-ence" and into trying to incorporate a diversity of racial and class consciousness into feminist theory. Cross-cultural connections, theoretical and practical, are highly revered feminist achievements. Thus for feminists, "global moral concern" does not mean the prac-tice of exactly equal consideration of the interests of all individuals; but it does mean substantially more concern for distant or different peoples than is common in our culture and our time.

However, global moral concern raises a unique problem for the social conception of the self. A self whose identity is defined in terms of relationships to certain others is capable of having immediate and direct moral concern for those others. Her moral concern for them does not need to be mediated by calculations of how their well-being might serve her own interests. The question raised by the issue of global moral concern is whether concern for distant and unknown peoples is an immediate moral motivation of the social self.

The likeliest source of such a motivation is group identity and consciousness.[34] We are familiar with the sort of group consciousness that attaches to racial, ethnic, and national communities. What about consciousness of membership in the human community? Unfortunately, it is not clear just what role it plays in self-identity. Philosophy has been of no help on this question. Philosophical works that have inquired into what it means for us to be "men" and not brutes aim to clarify how we are different from (nonhuman) animals but not to foster among all human beings a sense of globally shared mutual interest. Human group consciousness is an aspect of the social conception of the self that awaits further clarification.

Virginia Held suggests that we acquire concern for, say, starving children elsewhere by *learning* to empathize with them.[35] One learns what it is like for children close to home to starve, and one recognizes that distant children are like those close to home. One's empathic capacities, developed in relationships with persons known closely, are engaged by more distant peoples through recognition of their similarity to those whom we know. This approach, however, does not spring solely from motives that are rooted in self-identity but requires, in addition, reasoning and analogical insight.

Interpreted in this way, global moral concern is a rational achievement but not an immediate motivation, and it is an achievement only for some selves. It is a result of moral thinking that has no necessary motivational source in the self and so not everyone will find it convincing. (Think about those who *fail to see* the similarity between "them" and "us.") Since so many people appear to lack global moral concern, Held's view is certainly plausible—regrettably so.

This result does not threaten the social conception of the self. However, it brings us face-to-face with one important limit of that concept: its inability to ground the widest sort of concern for others in unmediated constituents of the self. Thus we confront the apparent fragility of the human motivation of global concern.

NOTES

1. Roderick Firth, "Ethical Absolutism and the Ideal Observer," *Philosophy and Phenomenological Research* 12, no. 3 (March 1952): 333. For an illuminating critique of the limitations of this and several other rhetorical fictions that are supposed to illustrate the moral point of view, see Margaret Walker, "Partial Consideration: Some Images of Impartiality Re-examined" (unpublished manuscript).

2. R. M. Hare, *Moral Thinking* (Oxford: Clarendon Press, 1981), 44.

3. Thomas Nagel, *The View from Nowhere* (New York: Oxford University Press, 1986), 139, 9, and *passim.*

4. Paul Taylor, "On Taking the Moral Point of View," *Midwest Studies in Philosophy* 3 (1978): 37.

5. See John Rawls, *A Theory of Justice* (Cambridge, Mass.: Harvard University Press, 1971), and the massive literature generated by Rawls's work.

6. For contemporary defenses of this Kantian notion, see Barbara Herman, "On the Value of Acting from Duty," *Philosophical Review* 66, no. 2 (July 1981): 233–250; and Marcia Baron, "The Alleged Repugnance of Acting from Duty," *Journal of Philosophy* 81, no. 4 (April 1984): 197–220.

7. Citations, in the order of appearance, are to John Cottingham, "Ethics and Impartiality," *Philosophical Studies* 43 (1983): 87, 94; John Kekes, "Morality and Impartiality," *American Philosophical Quarterly* 18, no. 4 (October 1981): 299–302; Lawrence Blum, *Friendship, Altruism, and Morality* (London: Routledge and Kegan Paul, 1980), chap. 3; Charles Fried, *Right and Wrong* (Cambridge, Mass.: Harvard University Press, 1978), 172; Bernard Williams, *Utilitarianism: For and Against* (Cambridge: Cambridge University Press, 1973), 108–118, and "Persons, Character, and Morality," in Williams, *Moral Luck: Philosophical Debates, 1973–1980* (Cambridge: Cambridge University Press, 1981), 1–19; and Andrew Oldenquist, "Loyalties," *Journal of Philosophy* 79, no. 4 (April 1982): 181.

8. See Sara Ruddick, *Maternal Thinking: Toward a Politics of Peace* (Boston: Beacon Press, 1989).

9. Impartialists have responded to these charges in several ways. One prevalent theme, which appears in both deontological and consequentialist writings, is the view that moral thinking is two-leveled. Impartiality is a requirement only of the higher level of moral thinking at which moral rules, practices, or institutions are to be justified. At this level, some practices of partiality are justifiable, such as taking special care of one's own children—albeit in impartialist terms. At the lower level of moral thinking, which involves the application of moral rules or the implementation of practices, one may, therefore, show partiality in the justified ways. There are other impartialist rejoinders as well, but it is beyond the scope of this essay to discuss them or their adequacy; however, see my entry on partiality in Lawrence Becker, ed., *Encyclopedia of Ethics* (New York: Garland Publishing, forthcoming 1992).

10. See Alasdair MacIntyre, *After Virtue* (Notre Dame, Ind.: University of Notre Dame Press, 1981); Michael J. Sandel, *Liberalism and the Limits of Justice* (Cambridge: Cambridge University Press, 1982); and Iris Marion Young, "Impartiality and the Civic Public: Some Implications of Feminist Critiques of Moral and Political Theory," *Praxis International* 5, no. 4 (January 1985): 381–401. See also Marilyn Friedman, "The Impracticality of Impartiality," *Journal of Philosophy* 86, no. 11 (November 1989): 645–656.

11. Young, "Impartiality and the Civic Public," 385–386. The notion of the "rhetoric" of impartiality comes from Margaret Walker, "Partial Consideration: Some Images of Impartiality Re-Examined," unpublished manuscript

presented at the Conference on the Partiality/Impartiality Debates sponsored by *Ethics* and held at Hollins College, Roanoke, Virginia, June 1990.

12. Sandel, *Liberalism and the Limits of Justice*, 179.

13. MacIntyre, *After Virtue*, 204–205.

14. Caroline Whitbeck, "A Different Reality: Feminist Ontology," in *Beyond Domination*, ed. Carol Gould (Totowa, N.J.: Rowman and Allanheld, 1984), 64–88; and Virginia Held, "Non-Contractual Society," in *Science, Morality and Feminist Theory*, ed. Marsha Hanen and Kai Nielsen (Calgary: University of Calgary Press, 1987), 111–138.

15. J. L. Mackie, *Ethics* (Harmondsworth, England: Penguin Books, 1977), 132.

16. Charles Fried, *Anatomy of Values* (Cambridge, Mass.: Harvard University Press, 1970), 227; and *Right and Wrong* (Cambridge, Mass.: Harvard University Press, 1978), 169–175.

17. See Williams, *Moral Luck*, especially 1–19.

18. For an excellent feminist exploration of some of Williams's views, see Claudia Card, "Gender and Moral Luck," in *Identity, Character, and Morality: Essays in Moral Psychology*, ed. Owen Flanagan and Amélie Oksenberg Rorty (Cambridge, Mass.: MIT Press, 1990), 199–218.

19. Williams, *Moral Luck*, 17–18.

20. Ibid., 20–39. Alison Jaggar is another feminist philosopher who expresses concern over Williams's use of this example ("Feminist Ethics: Some Issues for the Nineties," *Journal of Social Philosophy* 20, nos. 1, 2 [Spring/Fall 1989]: 97).

21. See MacIntyre, *After Virtue*; Sandel, *Liberalism and the Limits of Justice*; and Oldenquist, "Loyalties."

22. See Alan Gewirth, "Ethical Universalism and Particularism," *Journal of Philosophy* 85, no. 6 (June 1988): 298. John Cottingham is a singular example of a nonfeminist partialist who argues that not all partialities are justified and who worries about racism and sexism (see his "Partiality, Favouritism, and Morality," *Philosophical Quarterly* 36, no. 144 [1986]: 357–373).

23. MacIntyre, *After Virtue*; and Sandel, *Liberalism and the Limits of Justice*.

24. See Christina Hoff Sommers, "Philosophers against the Family," in *Person to Person*, ed. George Graham and Hugh La Follette (Philadelphia: Temple University Press, 1989), 82–105. Quotations are from p. 90.

25. As far as I've been able to determine, among nonfeminist theorists in the partiality debate, this point is brought out only by Robert E. Goodin, "What Is So Special about Our Fellow Countrymen?" *Ethics* 98, no. 4 (July 1988): 663–686. Goodin's work is also noteworthy for not invoking conventional relationships uncritically; instead, he justifies partiality by referring to the underlying values that are supposed to be served by special relationships (see *Protecting the Vulnerable: A Reanalysis of Our Social Responsibilities* [Chicago: University of Chicago Press, 1985]).

Among feminist theorists, there is massive literature on the problems in traditional close relationships. See Irene Diamond, ed., *Families, Politics, and Public Policy* (New York: Longman, 1983).

26. Cottingham is an exception. See his "Partiality, Favouritism, and Morality."

27. This part of my discussion reveals one of many remaining areas of obscurity in the social conception of the self. If we conceive of the self as being *wholly* constituted by its complex of socially derived identity-constituents, then it is not clear who or what it is that moves "back and forth" among the "plurality of partial identities." I do not address this metaphysical problem in this essay.

28. See Williams, *Moral Luck;* Oldenquist, "Loyalties"; and Christina Hoff Sommers, "Filial Morality," *Journal of Philosophy* 83, no. 8 (August 1986): 439–456.

29. William Godwin, *Enquiry Concerning Political Justice*, ed. K. Codell Carter (Oxford: Clarendon Press, 1971); and Peter Singer, *Practical Ethics* (Cambridge: Cambridge University Press, 1979), 10–11.

30. Singer, *Practical Ethics*, 10–11; and Singer, "Famine, Affluence, and Morality," *Philosophy and Public Affairs* 1, no. 3 (Spring 1972): 229–243.

31. Godwin, *Enquiry Concerning Political Justice*, 71; Carter notes that Godwin's first edition used the terms "mother," "sister," and "chambermaid," whereas the later edition substitutes "father," "brother," and "valet" (see Carter's editorial note 2, ibid.).

32. But see the skepticism expressed over the notion of universal moral concern in Nel Noddings, *Caring: A Feminine Approach to Ethics and Moral Education* (Berkeley: University of California Press, 1984), 91–94. It is noteworthy that Noddings uses the word "feminine," rather than "feminist" in her subtitle.

33. Cottingham, "Ethics and Impartiality," 91.

34. On the moral nature and importance of group identity, see Larry May, *The Morality of Groups* (Notre Dame, Ind.: University of Notre Dame Press, 1987).

35. Virginia Held, "Feminism and Moral Theory," in *Women and Moral Theory*, ed. Eva Feder Kittay and Diana T. Meyers (Totowa, N.J.: Rowman and Allanheld, 1987), 118.

11 / *Integrity and Radical Change*

VICTORIA M. DAVION

In this essay I explore the relationship of abstract principles and unconditional commitments to integrity. I examine two accounts of integrity presented in the recent work of Lynne McFall and Sarah Hoagland, respectively.[1] One of these defines integrity in terms of unconditional commitment to a consistent system of action-guiding principles. The other attempts to separate integrity from unconditional commitments and abstract principles and even goes so far as to argue that principled action can undermine integrity altogether. My project is to sketch an understanding of integrity which takes into account important objections some feminists have voiced regarding the notion of abstract principles and unconditional commitment but does not get rid of these notions altogether, as I think they are central to an understanding of integrity. Finally, I examine the question of whether multiplicitous beings can have integrity. I argue that if multiplicitous beings cannot have integrity, this challenges the idea that integrity is always a good thing.

Lynne McFall argues that integrity depends upon a person's having some unconditional commitments that are identity-conferring in that they are conditions for the continuation of the self. This core of commitments makes us who we are, establishes our moral identity. She says:

> Unless corrupted by philosophy, we all have things we think we would never do, under any imaginable circumstances, whatever we may give to survival or pleasure, power and the approval of strangers; some part of ourselves beyond which we will not retreat, some weakness, however prevalent in others, that we will not tolerate in ourselves. And if we do that thing, betray that

weakness, we are not the persons we thought: there is nothing left that we may even in spite refer to as *I*.[2]

This so-called core of principles that is a necessary part of moral identity must be coherent in certain ways in order for one to have integrity. First, the various core commitments must be consistent with each other so that they form a consistent value system. Second, one's actions must be consistent with whatever general principles can be derived from one's set of unconditional and identity-conferring commitments. In addition, these commitments must motivate actions rather than simply being consistent with them. This last condition bars the possibility that I can have integrity simply by acting in ways that are consistent with my commitments but not motivated by them at all. Mere consistency between action and principle isn't enough; motivation is important.

As a feminist, I am disturbed by Lynne McFall's interpretation because of what it says about moral identity as well as integrity. First, I don't believe that one's moral identity necessarily changes with a change in one's unconditional commitments. I believe that the self can continue even when principles that one felt to be unconditional change. This brings me to a related point. The idea that moral integrity depends upon a core of unchanging commitments is inconsistent with the kind of radical change that many feminists have been trying to encourage. For change to be *radical*, it must take place at the roots, at the deepest level. This means at the core, where Lynne McFall says that change is incompatible with integrity. As a feminist, I seek a concept of integrity that can account for radical change. According to Lynne McFall, it seems that radical change must amount to a loss of integrity.

Many of us have a set of "unconditional commitments." There are things we believe we would never do under any circumstances. However, these commitments aren't the most interesting aspects of moral identity. For example, I cannot see myself committing mass murder as a way of expressing anger. I cannot imagine myself doing such a thing under any circumstances. However, this isn't a very interesting fact about my moral identity. It doesn't distinguish me from most people (I hope). It doesn't really *identify* me. Most of the other commitments I am willing to regard as unconditional are probably equally uninteresting. In fact, the entire core of unconditional commitments that constitutes my so-called moral identity, according to Lynne McFall, fails to distinguish me from many other people.

My reasons for wanting to keep unconditional commitments to a minimum relate to concerns I view as feminist. Many feminists have stressed the importance of paying attention to context in decision-making. This means not being committed to a great many things regardless of particular conditions. One sense of "unconditional" is "without exception." Truly recognizing the importance of context means recognizing that each situation is somewhat unique and making decisions based upon the particular features of the situation at hand. Being committed to certain things in advance, regardless of the particular features of a specific situation, is the opposite of paying attention to context in decision-making. Hence, an unwillingness to grant that individual situations might present exceptions to principles is not to take context seriously. In order to take context seriously, one must judge each situation individually, and this means one cannot have many principles that one regards as having no exceptions. Paying attention to context means paying attention to conditions.

Another concern that I regard as feminist and that is related to issues concerning context is my belief that even commitments that feel unconditional are conditional on my understanding of reality. If this understanding changes, then my commitments will change. Another sense of "unconditional" is "not being dependent upon something that might change." However, if one recognizes that one's perception of reality is conditioned by one's political position, something feminists have argued, then one must be prepared for radical change in one's perceptions of it.[3] My own experience in becoming a feminist and the experiences of many other feminists I have spoken to about this reflect what happens when one's understanding of reality changes radically. One finds oneself changing one's values in ways one might not have imagined. For example, before becoming a feminist, one might have seen the institution of marriage as a good thing for women generally, but now one sees it as dangerous to women.

Seeing reality as political means being willing to acknowledge that one's understanding of reality might change radically, even being open to such change. Thus one should be open to the possibility that even values one believes will never change might in fact change, which in turn means one should view few, if any, of one's commitments as totally unconditional. This is another reason why the number of commitments I am willing to accept as unconditional is small. It certainly doesn't mean that many of my commitments don't feel as if they are unconditional; it means that I am open to the possibility that my understanding of reality could change drastically enough to change even these commitments.

According to Lynne McFall's definition of moral identity, a change in these so-called core and unconditional commitments involves a change in moral identity. As I stated, I seek a concept of moral identity that can account for an agent's being able to change radically. Such an account must not take whatever commitments feel unconditional at a given time as necessary for moral identity. I believe that relying on a core of unconditional commitments to establish moral identity is a mistake anyway. One can tell at least as much about a person's character by looking at how she arrived at her beliefs as by looking at which beliefs or values she views as unconditional at any particular moment. This also explains why one should not write off someone with whom one disagrees even deeply.

My concerns about Lynne McFall's definition of integrity are similar to the ones I have about moral identity. It assumes that there must be a core of unconditional commitments, thus denying that even commitments that feel unconditional are conditional upon our understanding of reality at the time. It implies that changes in commitments that feel unconditional mean a loss of integrity and thus that radical change of the sort many feminists are trying to promote involves a loss of integrity. If integrity is to be seen as a positive thing from a feminist perspective, it must allow for radical change.

Perhaps most important of all, Lynne McFall's definition doesn't capture one central meaning of integrity, namely, *being true to oneself*. In order to be true to oneself, one must be willing to explore commitments and change them when necessary. This is what it means to acknowledge ourselves as the changing beings that we are. To insist on a core of unchanging commitments is to pretend that commitments that feel unconditional necessarily are unconditional, which isn't the case. It is also to deny that reality is political and to deny the importance of context.

In *Lesbian Ethics*, Sarah Hoagland appears not to rely on unconditional commitments and abstract principles. She says the following about abstract principles: "We set up principles and codes, and we begin to cease considering the transformations we go through in our lives as a result of our choices. We ignore a great deal. Acting from principle interferes with rather than enhances our ability to make judgments."[4] She continues: "When an appeal to principles works it's because we are already acting with integrity."[5] Obviously, Sarah Hoagland does not define integrity in terms of following principles, as integrity must create the possibility of following principles.

In her discussions of integrity, Sarah Hoagland talks a lot about growing and becoming. Change is very important. She states:

> Focusing on integrity means acknowledging ourselves which in no way is equivalent to regarding ourselves as fixed or unchanging. It means proceeding from self-understanding through attending how we are reflected in the perspectives of other lesbians. It means becoming aware of what parts of ourselves we want to change, what parts go on hold for now, what parts center us, and what parts we want to develop at any given point. It means periodically assessing ourselves in terms of our values and in relation to others and their values.[6]

Sarah Hoagland seems to be talking about a process here, one that appears not to rely on any particular unconditional commitment. The process involves working on oneself, caring about oneself in a certain way. It is the opposite of floating along unreflectively.

I find the idea of applying the concept of integrity to the process through which one grows and changes appealing for several reasons. First, as I stated earlier, I think the way in which I make choices, my general style of decision-making, is at least as revealing about my character as whatever particular commitments feel unconditional to me at any particular time. Those who pay no attention to the kind of persons they are becoming necessarily lack integrity according to Hoagland's account. However, one can maintain integrity even through radical changes in how one understands reality provided that one is committed to one's development in a certain way, namely, committed to being careful and paying attention to one's growth process.

The idea of applying integrity to the growth process is also true of another sense of integrity: integrity as *a whole from which no part can be taken.* When a person takes care to monitor her own development, the process of becoming can be seen as a whole process rather than simply as a set of random events. When a person doesn't take on this responsibility, there is no process, merely a series of happenings. If there is integrity in the process, the changes will make sense from one change to the next only if no part is left out. The process from one moment to the next will be connected; it is literally a process from which no part could have been taken and still yield the same result, namely, one's becoming the person one is at any given moment. There will be a certain consistency and coherence in the process.

It may seem that finally we have a concept of integrity that doesn't focus on abstract principles and unconditional commitments. However, there are certain ways that principles can be useful even in this account. In the sense that I am now using the concept of integrity, no one can be born with integrity, and those who develop it must choose at some point to do so. This requires paying attention to who one is and who one is becoming. A first step is to discover what one's present commitments are at a deep level. This involves figuring out how one's beliefs at a more superficial level fit together, if they do.

One way of doing this is to figure out what general principles one's particular beliefs imply and examine whether these are principles one can believe in. For example, in my contemporary moral issues class, many of the students enter with firm beliefs about the issues we will discuss but without ever having examined how they came to have those beliefs and whether they wish to keep or change them. My goal as an instructor is to encourage students to examine the deeper commitments their beliefs reflect so that they can begin the process of monitoring their beliefs. This involves helping them see that their beliefs about issues reflect deeper commitments and deeper principles. Getting in touch with these will be a necessary starting point for developing integrity. However, this means that the process of developing integrity presupposes some deep value commitments that are unlikely to change and that can be used in the assessment of more superficial beliefs. However, if the process is not free of abstract principles, perhaps it is free of the requirement that these must be unchanging.

I contend that the process of examining beliefs about various issues in order to discover what deeper commitments these beliefs imply doesn't require a person to be particularly verbal. One can imagine acting in various ways without words at all. This concept of integrity doesn't require polished verbal skills or any level of formal education, but it does seem to require a large degree of self-knowledge. A knowledge of what one's beliefs are and what general principles these beliefs imply is necessary for a person to have integrity. However, there seems to be no requirement that even the most fundamental beliefs must be unchanging. Therefore, there is no requirement against the growth and change that many feminists wish to promote. No core of unchanging and identity-conferring commitments appears to be necessary.

Earlier I stated that although I found the idea that integrity depends upon a core of unchanging and unconditional commitments disturbing, I think Lynne McFall is right in claiming that some kind of unconditional commitment is involved. Even though it appears that Sarah Hoagland's interpretation does away with unconditional and abstract commitments, there is an abstract and unconditional commitment present nevertheless. However, the sort of commitment I have in mind is consistent with growth and change and with stressing the importance of context in decision-making. This account of integrity depends upon an unconditional commitment to monitor who we are becoming in the ways Sarah Hoagland suggests. Lynne McFall's account requires a good deal of concern with who we are becoming as well. Thus according to both accounts, we are committed to paying attention to ourselves. This unconditional commitment doesn't have to commit us to any particular action in any particular situation. It is consistent with paying a great deal of attention to context in making decisions, yet it is extremely abstract.

This brings me to an essential point about some recent feminist criticism of abstract thinking. Although the principle that one should monitor who one is becoming is highly abstract, it allows for a great deal of concern with context, with the particulars of situations. In fact, it is precisely because it is so abstract that it allows this. The more concrete a principle is, the less room individuals have in deciding how to apply it. This means that abstract principles are not necessarily in opposition to very concrete thinking. This is important to see for feminist purposes. One might argue that the commitment to monitor oneself is so abstract as to be meaningless. However, I think if one takes the commitment seriously, it involves a great deal of work. In addition, making the abstract principle involved explicit allows one to deal with an important objection to the idea that integrity is a good thing. I now turn to this objection.

In an article on Sarah Hoagland's *Lesbian Ethics*,[7] María Lugones explains that at this time integrity is undesirable for her. She relates some of her personal experiences as a U.S. Latina lesbian who is grounded by the community of place of Hispanos and Hispanos Nuevomejicanos. She states that her identity as a U.S. Latina lesbian depends upon her ability to be a multiplicitous being, having two distinct yet connected selves. She states: "I do not know whether these two possibilities can ever be integrated so that I can become at least, in these respects, a unitary being. I don't even know whether that would be desirable. But it seems clear to me that each possibility need not exclude the other *so long as* I am not a unitary but a multiplicitous being."[8] Here we have a case where, at least according to some definitions, having integrity means losing one's identity, having to kill a part of oneself. It is clear that in writing about integrity as necessarily a good thing, we as feminists must speak to this if we do not wish to marginalize the experiences of those for whom multiplicity rather than unity is necessary for survival as a multicultural being. We will either have to give up the idea that integrity is always a good thing or come up with an account of it that allows multiplicitous beings to have it.

In *Lesbian Ethics*, Sarah Hoagland suggests that separation is a way for lesbians to prevent de-moralization in a heterosexualist society. Heterosexualism is "a way of living that normalizes the dominance of one person and the subordination of another."[9] Demoralization occurs when someone's ability to make choices is undermined. In internalizing the values of dominance and subordination, we are demoralized because we cease to make our own choices and follow the dictates of those higher in the hierarchy. By withdrawing from heterosexualism as a way of life, we can avoid demoralization by rejecting dominance and subordination.

The aim of separation is to render the old value system meaningless. María Lugones points out that it is not only individuals who live in a system of domination and subordination; whole cultures are involved in various systems of dominance and subordination as well. One example of this is the Anglo domination of la cultura Hispana Nuevomejicana. This domination includes, among other things, the idea that the only way for Hispanos to survive is to assimilate to

Anglo culture, which would have the effect of destroying la cultura Hispana Nuevomejicana.

In la cultura Nuevomejicana, lesbians are seen as abominations and will not be fully accepted and able to participate in the culture if openly lesbian. One possibility is to allow this heterosexualist culture to die. However, the possibility of being a Nuevomejicana lesbian includes not only the possibility of being lesbian but the possibility of being Nuevomejicana as well. This means fighting for the survival of the culture and participating in transforming it. This is why the preservation of the culture cannot simply be left to others. To allow the culture to die is to allow a victory of heterosexualism and to erase the possibility of being a Nuevomejicana lesbian.

In a lesbian community, it is or might be possible to separate from heterosexualism as a lesbian. However, it is not a place where one can struggle for the preservation and continuation of la cultura Nuevomejicana unless it is specifically a Nuevomejicana lesbian community. The struggle for the preservation of this culture requires participating in the culture itself.

According to Sarah Hoagland, moral agency requires *autokoenony,* which she defines as a sense of self in community. "It involves each of us as having a self-conscious sense of ourselves as moral agents in a community of other self-conscious moral agents."[10] María Lugones sees two possibilities of herself as a unitary being and rejects them both. She says that as a cultural participant in la cultura Nuevomejicana, she would be

> working to keep culture alive, working to undermine the demoralization that keeps people from the embracing aliveness of the culture and from strengthening it through critical and creative participation. In Hoagland's use of "autokoenonous," this work can only be accomplished by an autokoenonous self, a self in community, and this self can only be well if the community becomes actively engaged in its own well-being.[11]

The other possibility is herself as a participant in lesbian community:

> Self in separation from heterosexualism: from both racist, imperialist, capitalist, and anglo relationships, conceptual and social frameworks, and from Hispano heterosexualism, steeped in

poverty and ravaged by anglo racism and colonialism. I come to lesbian community with "my culture on my back," but this is not where I can struggle for the survival of Hispana culture and life. Thus, my autokoenonous self is also lacking in lesbian community.[12]

In order to fight for her survival, María Lugones must nourish both autokoenonous beings, both selves in community. This requires two autokoenonous selves.

I have spent a good deal of time explaining the nature of the duplicity involved in this particular example because I see it as a problem for those who need to participate in more than one culture in order to fight against domination and subordination, for the possibility of their identities, and for anyone wishing to support those needing to do this. If integrity requires that each person have only one autokoenonous self, then to see it as a good thing is to see as good the death of all but one autokoenonous self per person.

I suggest that in loooking at integrity as relating to the process of growth, there is a sense of integrity that multiplicitous beings can have. It is the sense of integrity that can be promoted by feminists who do not want to marginalize the experiences of people who need to participate in more than one culture in order to preserve what they value in their identities.

A striking aspect of María Lugones's analysis is the extent to which she understands her situation. She has taken great trouble to examine the possibility of allowing one of these two selves to die. She has revealed a great deal of self-knowledge and an understanding of what her fight against domination and subordination must include. This is the opposite of merely floating through life unreflectively. It is very much like the process Sarah Hoagland speaks of in her discussions of integrity. She exhibits the kind of commitment that I have argued forms the basis for integrity, a commitment to monitor who she is and who she is becoming.

María Lugones states that although they are not integrated in the sense of being unitary, these two selves are connected. Each can understand and critique the other from its own perspective: "Because the selves can connect, each can critique the other and avoid the demoralization of self-betrayal (for example by becoming assimilated to heterosexualism or being ignorant of slowly becoming culturally obsolete).''[13] Maintaining this connection is not a given; it takes a lot of work. She says, "Each one of these two selves understands the other. This is not a given. This requires significant work in the "borderlands."[14] That the existence of these two selves helps to prevent self-betrayal is significant, and that the connection between the selves is something that is consciously worked on is significant as well. Both of these facts reveal a sense in which a multiplicitous being might have integrity.

I have already noted that an important sense of integrity is being true to oneself. If having two selves somehow helps to prevent self-betrayal, then it helps one in being true to oneself, and the killing of one of the selves would constitute one of the worst kinds of self-betrayal, a literal turning against oneself. Therefore, it would not promote integrity in this important sense. In addition, the work done to continue the connection between the autokoenonous selves is work that involves a gaining of self-knowledge, which is also necessary for integrity according to both Lynne McFall and Sarah Hoagland. The work done to keep a connection between the selves prevents the process of becoming, in which both are involved, from fracturing. The two selves are part of a larger self that constitutes the multiplicitous being. This being keeps the two working together for its survival. The two don't have totally different goals, and they have at least one fundamental goal in common—the preservation of the identity of the being as multiplicitous. The two autokoenonous selves must remain connected, as they literally form a whole from which no part can be taken. The multiplicitous being has integrity if she can somehow keep a connection between her two selves alive, as long as one can critique the other. This connection coordinates the growth process of each autokoenonous self so that they do not work against each other, so that each process can be seen as a larger part of the growth of the multiplicitous being.

A multiplicitous being could not have integrity if each autokoenonous self wanted the death of the other or even simply wanted to undermine the fundamental projects of the other. The growth process of the multiplicitous being would be fractured rather than unitary; there could be no consistency in the overall process. A multiplicitous being can have integrity if a connection is maintained involving the commitment to monitor oneself. This, I have argued, forms the basis for integrity.

In examining the nature of the connection between these selves, one can see that the two selves that constitute the multiplicitous being must have certain values in common. This common valuing insures that the selves don't work against each other in the ways I have described. Hence, it may seem that we are back to the idea of uniting the concept of integrity to unconditional principles. However, only the commitment to keep the selves valuing together at a fundamental level must be abstract and unconditional. It is the commitment to monitoring oneself that I have argued forms the basis for integrity. This leaves open the possibility that many other values, even fundamental ones, may change without a loss of integrity as long as fundamental values change in both selves so that the projects of each are compatible and the selves do not work against each other's projects. Growth and change do not necessarily stand in the way of integrity, but one cannot change in just any direction and maintain it. Hence, the possibility of change that I as a feminist wished to incorporate into the notion of integrity is present.

The restrictions on change I have discussed seem also to apply to beings who are not multiplicitous. A single self can work against its own projects if its most fundamental values are in conflict. It can undermine itself in the same way that each self that is part of a multiplicitous being can undermine the other. Thus a certain consistency among fundamental values is necessary. However, this does not mean that a change in fundamental values means a loss of integrity. It means that fundamental values must change together to prevent a person from turning against herself. This restriction on change doesn't preclude the possibility that a person might change radically while maintaining integrity.

NOTES

Special thanks to Claudia Card for comments on earlier drafts of this chapter.

1. Lynne McFall, "Integrity," *Ethics* 98 (October 1987): 5–20; Sarah Lucia Hoagland, *Lesbian Ethics: Toward a New Value* (Palo Alto, Calif.: Institute of Lesbian Studies, 1988).

2. Lynne McFall, "Integrity," 12.

3. See, for example, Marilyn Frye, "The Politics of Reality," in Frye, *The Politics of Reality: Essays in Feminist Theory* (Trumansburg, N.Y.: Crossing Press, 1983).

4. Sarah Hoagland, *Lesbian Ethics*, 11.

5. Ibid.

6. Ibid., 286.

7. María Lugones, "Hispaneando y Lesbiando: On Sarah Hoagland's *Lesbian Ethics*," *Hypatia* 5, no. 3 (Fall 1990): 138–146.

8. Ibid., 138–139.

9. Sarah Hoagland, *Lesbian Ethics*, 29.

10. Ibid., 145.

11. María Lugones, "Hispaneando y Lesbiando," 141–142.

12. Ibid., 142.

13. Ibid., 145.

14. Ibid.

Part Three
Questions Concerning
Women's Voices and Care

12 / Gender and the Complexity of Moral Voices

MICHELE M. MOODY-ADAMS

On one very powerful conception, philosophical reflection about morality—like all moral reflection—is a species of *self*-reflection. It is a species of *sincere* and *rational* self-scrutiny that, if carried out in detail, could issue either in a clear account of a principle (or principles) for guiding reflection and action or in a general conception of the character traits, cognitive capacities, and emotions that ought to determine the shape of reflection and action. This kind of self-reflection has been at the center of philosophical reflection on the moral life at least since Plato reported Athenian resistance to Socrates' contention that the unexamined life is not worth living. Kant's moral theory provides a very different view of the kind of knowledge that results from the examined life. Kant believed that his account of the Categorical Imperative revealed the ideally rational and objectively valid structure of the ordinary moral consciousness. Indeed, he insisted that like Socrates he was making human reason "attend to its own principle" (Kant [1785] 1964, 71–72). Thus very different philosophical traditions have acknowledged the centrality of self-reflection to philosophical ethics.

On some versions of this conception of philosophical reflection, the self-scrutiny of an individual person engaged in moral reflection is crucially connected to the collective self-scrutiny of that person's culture. Socrates' activities as a "gadfly" on the neck of Athens might thus be viewed as attempts to encourage the collective (as well as individual) self-scrutiny that is inseparable from moral reflection. The same conception of philosophical reflection allows us to understand why Martin Luther King, Jr., compared the nonviolent civil disobedience movement in the United States during the mid-twentieth century to the Socratic conception of philosophical reflection. King viewed that movement as a catalyst for the moral self-scrutiny of a culture as well as an instrument of social change (King 1964). Moreover, the importance of this connection between individual reflection and a culture's collective self-scrutiny is borne out by the fact that a person's self-conception is in part dependent upon that person's social experience. Of course there is much disagreement over what difference the self-conceptions of empirical persons ought to make to the shape and content of *philosophical* reflection about morality. Kant would have found the very question anathema; whatever we are to make of the Socratic vision, it seems clear that Plato himself would have done the same. My own view, though I will not argue for it here, is that the best philosophical reflection about morality will issue from a view that treats the self-conceptions of empirical persons (conceptions shaped by a variety of influences) as starting points for reflection, even though the ultimate aim of such reflection will typically be to encourage some revision of those self-conceptions.

On this model of philosophical reflection about ethics, if women do indeed speak about morality "in a different voice," recognition of this fact cannot leave such reflection unchanged. Of course we sometimes find it easier to avoid considerations that complicate moral reflection or require reflection on what we have always taken for granted. Like Plato's Euthyphro, we are sometimes resistant to the urgings of a newly audible moral voice. But figures such as Socrates and King are emblematic of the extent to which the voices a culture seldom hears, or refuses to listen to, or even actively tries to silence, are most likely to serve as catalysts for sincere and rational self-scrutiny.

For many thinkers, the notion of a distinctively feminine moral voice has been given substance by Carol Gilligan's empirical research in developmental psychology. Yet I want to take issue with the confidence of the many theorists who believe that Gilligan's claims have been unequivocally established as fact. My aim in this essay is to inquire what we can make of Gilligan's claims to have found such a voice. In the first section I consider whether there can be any "disinterested" assertions of gender-specific differences in moral development, by specific reference to Gilligan's claims about her inquiry. In the second section, I consider how we might know whether there is a moral voice that is specifically female, and I ask whether the very idea might not lead us to miss the complexity of the moral domain—especially as women conceive of it. Finally, in the third section I consider the assumptions that underlie the design of Gilligan's research. I question whether Gilligan's results license some of the sweeping assertions many—including Gilligan—now make about women's patterns of moral thinking. I argue, ultimately, that we cannot discern the lessons of women's ways of thinking about morality unless we are sure that we have heard their *voices* correctly.

CAN THERE BE A DISINTERESTED ASSERTION
OF SEX DIFFERENCES IN MORAL DEVELOPMENT?

In the introduction to *In a Different Voice,* Carol Gilligan initially seems decidedly reluctant to assert that there are sexual differences in the way people conceive of and talk about morality. She contends at first that the moral voice described in the book is "characterized not by gender, but theme," and that the association of this voice with women is "an empirical observation" and is "not absolute" (1982, 2). In these same passages she further asserts that the contrasts between male and female voices discussed throughout the book are intended to "highlight a distinction between two modes of thought . . . rather than to represent a generalization about either sex" (1982, 2). Just a few paragraphs later, however, the reluctance to make generalizations about the sexes gives way to claims that are emphatically about gender. She expressly states that the research detailed in the book is intended, among other things, to provide psychologists with the tools to come up with a "clearer representation of women's development" *and* to present the women readers in her audience with "a clearer representation of their thought" that will enable them to see that thought's integrity and validity (1982, 3). Indeed, many of the most important aims and ends of Gilligan's research clearly rest on empirical generalizations about the role of gender in moral discourse—specifically, patterns of emotion, thought, and action that most women allegedly articulate and defend in the process of reasoning about moral issues. Much of the response to Gilligan's research would be unintelligible were this not the case.

Gilligan's recent essays suggest that she has become increasingly confident of the legitimacy and importance of her claims about the patterns of women's moral thinking. Yet in at least one important essay, she acknowledges that some of her readers continue to find the project problematic. Although uneasiness about the implications of Gilligan's project has been expressed in many quarters, she pays particular attention to recent work in the psychology of moral development that seems to have "shied away" from noting sex differences in moral development. Gilligan attributes this resistance, quite rightly, to fears of "the dangers of stereotyping, the intimations of biological determinism, and the fact that in recent discussions of sex differences there is no distinterested position" (Gilligan and Wiggins 1987, 278). Yet her attempts to allay such fears provide little comfort to those who share such concerns. In a revealing passage, she contends that

> stereotypes of males as aggressive and females as nurturant, however distorting and however limited, have some empirical claim. The overwhelmingly male composition of the prison population and the extent to which women take care of young children cannot readily be dismissed as irrelevant to theories of morality or excluded from accounts of moral development. If there are no sex differences in empathy or moral reasoning, why are there sex differences in moral and immoral behavior? (Gilligan and Wiggins 1987, 279)

Not only does such a response fail to allay the relevant concerns, it generates a host of doubts about whether it is possible to claim that there are sex differences in moral reasoning without at the same time organizing those differences hierarchically.

Note that in Gilligan's description, what purports to be a strictly empirical generalization about behavior abruptly turns into a claim about moral capacities. This claim about moral capacities, moreover, embodies two dubious presuppositions. First, it seems to presuppose that those who have not been imprisoned for a crime necessarily possess more highly developed moral sensibilities—a questionable assumption at best. Second, Gilligan's defense assumes that because women do not commit crimes at the same rate as men, they are somehow more moral than men—whatever the source of the tendency to behave more morally. To be sure, later in the same essay, Gilligan insists that she is not arguing for the moral superiority or inferiority of either sex. In fact, she contends that her research attempts to frame "the sex difference question" in such a way as to *reject* any suggestion that one sex is morally superior to the other (Gilligan and Wiggins 1987, 282). Yet how could the question about "sex differences in moral and immoral behavior" be relevant to the composition of the prison population unless one presupposes that these facts somehow point to the moral superiority of those who do not wind up in prison?[1] Now, let us grant for the sake of argument that at least in some circumstances it can be shown that women are more moral than men. In this instance, however, such a conclusion seems unjustified: Sex differences in "empathy and moral reasoning" may explain very little about the makeup of the prison population. People sometimes refrain from committing crimes simply for fear of going to jail. Indeed, a whole tradition of reflection on the nature of law—the classical legal positivism of Austin and Bentham—is built upon the assumption that, most of the time, fear of punishment can be a sufficient motive to obey the law. Moreover, it is certainly plausible that traditional social roles and conventions have simply given women fewer occasions to commit crimes and that changes in these roles and conventions might be accompanied by a rise in the number of women who commit serious crimes.

Equally problematic is Gilligan's failure to recognize that *precisely* the sorts of generalizations she invokes in this passage have historically been called upon to support theories about the biological "inevitability" of criminal behavior. Those of Gilligan's readers who are concerned about the dangers of racial stereotyping may wonder what one is to make, using Gilligan's logic, of the fact that the male prison population is disproportionately black. Such readers cannot overlook the uses of analogous generalizations about the *ethnic* or *socioeconomic* composition of the "overwhelmingly male" prison population to justify discrimination against certain males on the basis of race. To be sure, Gilligan does not wish to license any such appeals, but the passage is disturbing in its failure to acknowledge its affinities to such appeals. It simply is not clear why the makeup of the prison population could be relevant to reflection on "moral and immoral behavior" unless the intent of the passage is to suggest that not winding up in prison is evidence of superior moral capacities. Of course, the composition of the prison population may support generalizations about what groups of people display more criminal manifestations of aggression. But an adequate explanation of such data will certainly be far more complex than Gilligan's assumptions allow. Moreover, one must pause to reflect on the nature of aggression itself: Surely not all manifestations of aggression are either criminal or evidence of deficiencies in moral development. With the possible exception of the extreme pacifist, nearly everyone would agree that a woman who aggressively defends herself against rape, or a man who aggressively protects his children from an attacker, clearly behaves in a morally acceptable way. Indeed, a willingness to display aggression—in due measure and in appropriate circumstances—may be essential to revealing the depth of one's capacity to care for others.

It might be possible, of course, to provide a more sympathetic reading of the passage in question. One might simply argue, for instance, that it is an unintentional overstatement of the case. But the passage does more than take issue with existing hierarchies of alleged sex differences in moral development. The passage makes a claim of an altogether different kind: It asserts the moral deficiency of one sex. The juxtaposition of this view with Gilligan's insistence that she does not want to make hierarchical rankings of moral perspectives suggests a vacillation in her professed view of the equal worth of moral perspectives. This suggestion is borne out by one of the most striking passages in *In a Different Voice*—one in which Gilligan elaborates upon Erikson's criticism of Gandhi's treatment of his family. She first cites what she calls Gandhi's "blind willingness to sacrifice people to truth" as evidence of "the danger of an ethics abstracted from life." She then argues that "this willingness links Gandhi to the biblical Abraham, who prepared to sacrifice the life of his son in order to demonstrate the integrity and supremacy of his faith. Both men, in the limitations of their fatherhood, stand in implicit contrast to the woman who comes before Solomon and verifies her motherhood by relinquishing truth in order to save the life of her child" (1982, 104–105). Considerations of faith, this passage implies, cannot ground a moral perspective with as much integrity and importance as the perspective of care.[2] This implication is problematic enough. Even more problematic is the extent to which this passage confirms, as other commentators have noted, that Gilligan's account of sex differences in moral reasoning is *not* always disinterested (Flanagan and Adler 1983, 587). Here, Gilligan is clearly vulnerable to Debra Nails's objection that differences become deficiencies when we look through the lens of gender (1983, 643).

Some readers will no doubt respond that a suggestion of the moral superiority of women would not be a regrettable implication of Gilligan's research. They may note that much of the research to which Gilligan's project responds, at least in part, appeals to deprecatory generalizations about women's moral thinking. But we cannot ignore the worry expressed by some commentators that claims about women's allegedly superior moral capacities have been associated historically with the claim that these capacities best suit women for domestic pursuits—an association most vividly embodied in the Victorian conception of the "angel in the house." Nor can we ignore the extent to which, even apart from the problematic implication of women's moral superiority, the vision of morality that Gilligan believes to be dominant in women's thinking is bound up with rather limiting stereotypes (Williams 1989). Some of Gilligan's less sympathetic critics find the potential danger of this stereotype reason in itself simply to reject the theory (Nails 1983). Such a rejection is clearly problematic, however, since it avoids the question of whether Gilligan's generalizations might be true. But even if Gilligan has correctly described a predominantly female perspective on moral reasoning, a more important problem remains: Do the social, cultural, and economic conditions that generated that perspective place intrinsic limits on the normative value of that perspective? We must ask whether our conception of "the feminine" remains too entangled in a complex array of insufficiently disinterested assumptions to be a useful category for reflection.[3]

DOES THE NOTION OF A SINGLE GENDER-SPECIFIC VOICE MASK THE COMPLEXITY OF WOMEN'S MORAL REASONING?

The question of whether there is a distinctively feminine moral voice cannot be separated from the questions of how we might discover such a voice and how we could be assured that we had correctly heard its distinctive urgings. If it is a fact that most women consistently give priority in their moral reasoning to considerations of care and responsibility in relationships, that they define themselves primarily in terms of their attachments to other persons, and that they tend to view moral problems "contextually" rather than "categorically," then we must be able to say how we know these claims about women's moral perspective to be true. Gilligan has of course offered her empirical research as evidence in support of these claims about women's moral voice. I am going to suggest, however, that there are some important difficulties with the design of Gilligan's research that may require us to reassess her claims.

In *In a Different Voice*, some of the relevant evidence comes from two studies of subjects' responses to hypothetical moral problems, as well as their responses to questions about how the subjects viewed themselves and what they considered to be moral problems. Gilligan refers to these two studies as the "college student study" (of students who had chosen to take a college course on moral and political choice) and the "rights and responsibilities" study (a comparative study of females and males of various ages and educational levels). But she seems to place the most importance upon the results of a third study, the abortion decision study, which generated data about the reasoning and actions of women deciding whether or not to undergo an abortion. One of the most striking features of Gilligan's research—in view of her claim to have revealed a distinctively feminine moral voice—is the absence of sustained discussion of many other concerns about which many women have become increasingly vocal. Of course the abortion decision study sought to elicit information about how women reason morally in one such circumstance. Yet other, very different circumstances confront women with equally difficult choices, though Gilligan does not consider them except in passing. Little or no attention is devoted to discussing how women think about, or act in response to, such problems as rape, physical or sexual abuse inflicted by a spouse, sexual harassment in the workplace, or sexual discrimination in employment. My claim is not that these problems have greater moral significance than those concerns discussed in 'Gilligan's research. Rather, I want to suggest that women's responses to these problems might well reveal considerations discordant with some of Gilligan's findings. Considerations of care and responsibility in relationships might be important in some discussions of this sort, but it is possible that women's discussion of these problems would have very little to do with such concerns.

Moreover, reflection on such problems might reveal the limitations of a moral perspective that purports to place at the center of moral reflection the kind of considerations that Gilligan associates with a distinctively female moral voice. Three of the problems cited above—the problems of rape, sexual abuse, and sexual harassment—seem to focus moral reflection on duties of noninterference rather than duties of care. Further, duties of noninterference seem to have a special status in that they are duties owed to persons whatever the extent of our capacity to care for them, whatever our particular desires about how they ought to care for us, and whatever our beliefs about how they ought to lead their lives. As Kant might have argued, they are duties that require us to treat persons as objective ends (as ends-in-themselves), not merely as subjective ends ("whose existence as an object of our actions has value *for us*") (Kant [1785] 1964, 96). In less strictly Kantian language, such duties require respect for the integrity and worth of persons simply *as persons*. But this notion of respect for the integrity of persons—perhaps more than any other—is particularly resistant to reduction to the language of care.

To be sure, some of Gilligan's comments suggest that she thinks that this concept of the integrity of persons could simply be reinterpreted in terms of the concepts of care and responsibility in relationships.[4] But central elements of the care perspective turn out to be inadequate to the task of explaining or justifying the respect due to the integrity of individuals. A conception of the self as defined not through separation from but through interconnection with others is oddly unhelpful in deciding what is morally wrong with rape, abuse, and sexual harassment. Surely one of the principal features of such actions—what makes them so damaging beyond any physical harm they may or may not cause—is that they embody the perpetrator's refusal to respect the integrity and *separateness* of the victim. The rapist who says of his victim that "when she said 'no' she meant 'yes,' " fails to respect the integrity of this woman's expressed wishes, as well as her separateness as a person. Moreover, sexual discrimination in employment typically consists of actions that somehow treat women differently from men on the basis of characteristics that are arbitrary from the point of view of the requirements of the job. Moral condemnation of such conduct will typically stress that it rests on a failure to recognize that for reasons of employment, in most instances worth should be measured independently of gender. Sexual discrimination in employment embodies a failure to respect the integrity of an employee's desire to be judged on her ability to do the job. Gilligan argues at some length for the tendency of the female subjects in her studies to view moral problems "contextually" and not "categorically" (1982, 98–105). But surely most women would simply pronounce all of these actions, from rape to sexual discrimination in employment, categorically unacceptable. I am even willing to concede for the sake of argument that considerations associated with the care perspective might play a greater role in the typical woman's response to these actions. What I cannot concede is that this same woman would be unwilling to proclaim the absolute unacceptability of these actions.

One must also wonder what kinds of responses would have been generated by reflection on a topic less likely to reveal consensus—for instance, the topic of pornography. The question of the moral acceptability of pornography might have proven a particularly rich source of reflection on women's ways of reasoning, especially because it is a matter about which women disagree. Indeed, even those women who agree in condemning it cite a wide variety of moral considerations. Some allege a direct connection between pornography and specific instances of violence against women. Others argue that even if no such direct connection exists, pornography is intrinsically exploitative of women. Still others argue that independent of the possibilities of exploitation and violence, pornography embodies disrespect for the equal worth of persons. The voices of women who condemn pornography, especially those whose criticisms presume no direct connection between pornography and crime, sound quite different from the voices of those women who responded to Gilligan's abortion decision study. Moreover, the voices of those women who do not condemn pornography might surprise us in their willingness to cite the overriding importance of ideals such as liberty of conscience, thought, and speech. In short, these unexplored possibilities raise a crucial, persistent question: Might the dominance in her female subjects of what Gilligan describes as care reasoning be a function of the kinds of problems they were asked (or not asked) about rather than a function of the way they actually think?[5]

Just as the choice of questions might have affected the outcome of Gilligan's research, so, too, might her decisions about what kinds of women to interview. For instance, there are surely women whose vision of the moral landscape is shaped not by their understanding of the relation between the self and others but by their religious faith.

Such women might even ground considerations of care (for self and others) in a religious conception on which a *command* to care issues from their faith. Still other women choose lives devoted to the perfection of their faith—even when that life requires that they place limitations on their capacity to care for others. A woman who chooses life in a religious community demanding celibacy is one such example. But we find an equally important example in the instance of a mother who believes that seeking medical treatment—even for her children—would violate the demands of faith. No doubt some such woman might choose to violate the demand on specific occasions. But surely even such a woman might take the choices of Gandhi or Abraham to illustrate much more than simply "the limitations of fatherhood" or "the dangers of an ethics abstracted from life." Surely women of strong religious convictions, even those who might bridle at conventional representations of femininity bound up with such convictions, can see those choices as the result of sincere and coherent moral reflection.

But religious faith is only one kind of ideal not discussed by Gilligan that might complicate our picture of women's moral reasoning. Other ideals—of personal integrity and courage, or aesthetic perfection, or scientific truth, for instance—might produce a vision of a moral landscape that would be dramatically different from that associated with considerations of faith. Interviews of women whose lives have been structured by such concerns might well have yielded a much more diverse picture of women's ways of reasoning about morality. A great writer, a diligent scientific researcher—even one whose choices included motherhood and family—might convince us that the moral domain consists of a diversity of goods. Even those women whose lives are not structured by the pursuit of such ideals might well be able to acknowledge the moral worth of lives devoted to them. Still further, few if any of the women interviewed in Gilligan's study seem to have undergone either the economic hardships or the racial and ethnic exclusion—or in some cases both—that are constants of some women's experience. Their experience might well make them more insistent than other women on the importance of respect for the equal worth of persons. At any rate, their experience would surely complicate one's account of the moral landscape—as women see it—even further.

WHY DOES GILLIGAN FIND UNITY WHERE WE MIGHT EXPECT TO FIND DIVERSITY?

One of the principal reasons Gilligan fails to discern the complexity of women's ways of reasoning morally is her decision to give the abortion decision study such a central place in her project. For though she cites the results of other studies, both in *In a Different Voice* and in later essays, the argument in the book suggests that the kind of response that emerges in the abortion decision study was indeed central. She frames the central problem of that project's design in clear terms: In order to discover "whether women's construction of the moral domain relies on a language different from that of men," it is necessary to find "places where women have the power to choose and thus are willing to speak in their own voice" (Gilligan 1982, 70). She then argues that the abortion decision study should play a central role because it yields important data about one of the "places where women have the power to choose." The legality of abortion (like the availability of birth control), she contends, affects women's power to make choices about "the relationships that have traditionally defined women's identities and framed their moral judgment." Moreover, she believes, the power to make these choices creates special kinds of conflicts for women: Although it can release them "from a sexuality that binds them in dependence," it also "brings them into conflict with the conventions of femininity" (Gilligan 1982, 70). In Gilligan's view, then, reproductive choice creates a framework within which women will be "willing to speak in their own voice."

But do women speak in their own moral voice *only* when they contemplate choices that might bring them into conflict with the cultural conventions of femininity? Even within these conventions, women have always been able to make choices about a variety of matters other than their capacity to reproduce. Suppose a woman at a supermarket, accompanied by her observant child, receives too much money back in change: Even this outwardly simple situation might require the most serious exercise of moral judgment about the importance of honesty. Whether she decides to return the money or to keep it, justifications offered in support of the decision will surely have effects that transcend the situation itself. The child's understanding of this decision's coherence with other similar decisions; the child's understanding of the moral significance of the relation between what a parent says and what a parent does; even the child's eventual capacity to respect the moral authority of the parent—all these effects are surely implicated even in this apparently simple situation. The content of a woman's exercise of moral judgment in such a circumstance—not unlike the kinds of circumstances that frequently confront many women—is surely relevant to discerning women's patterns of moral reasoning.

More important, it is not only in deciding about birth control or abortion—or about reproduction in general—that women contemplate making choices that might bring them into conflict with cultural conventions of femininity. Gilligan is particularly concerned with the abortion decision study for the way it focuses women's thinking about cultural conventions according to which a woman's goodness is revealed in self-sacrifice (Gilligan 1982, 70). But other cultural conventions embody a very different view of the moral status of women. Cultural conceptions of female sexuality as an ever-present temptation to male immorality or of women as intrinsically forces of irrationality and disorder—solely in virtue of their biology—underlie many people's belief that women are to blame for the sexual or physical violence to which they are sometimes subject. Moreover, a woman who decides to press charges in a rape case will almost certainly come into conflict with these conventions; she may even need to fight her own unreflective acceptance of them. This phenomenon is made manifest when women who are victims of rape find it difficult to convince others—sometimes even themselves— that they are not responsible for the wrongdoing of the attacker. Surely the voice of a woman who finds the courage to confront this dangerous conception is as distinctively a woman's voice as are the voices of the women in Gilligan's abortion decision study.

In a different but equally important way, some cultural conventions seek to define women's identity *solely* in terms of their capacity for reproduction and, as a consequence, in terms of their historically typical roles as primary caretakers of children. At least some women will come into conflict with this convention merely in *deciding* to pursue work that takes them outside of the domestic realm. Ironically, those women who historically have worked outside the home for reasons of economic necessity are usually "exempted" from this convention—at least so long as they occupy certain kinds of jobs. But nearly all women who decide to seek advancement in careers typically dominated by males will most certainly come into conflict with this stereotype. Some employers even now will argue that women should not be promoted to certain jobs because when they "go off to have babies," they will lose interest in the demands of a competitive career. Indeed, some employers even claim to find empirical confirmation for their conviction in the work of theorists such as Gilligan who assert an empirical association between women and the ethics of care (Williams 1989, 813–821).[6] Surely the voice of a woman who decides to protest her employer's decision not to promote her on such a basis is as distinctively a woman's voice as any of the voices in Gilligan's abortion decision study.

One of the most puzzling facts about Gilligan's use of the abortion decision study is that although she interviewed a variety of women, and although some chose to have abortions and others chose not to, she insists that the study could not really be used to reveal "the way women in general think about the abortion choice" (Gilligan 1982, 72). No effort was made, she explains, to ensure in advance that the women interviewed for the study amounted to a representative sample of women considering abortion. In fact, Gilligan even suggests that the women interviewed may have been referred to the study because counselors suspected them to be "in greater than usual conflict" over the decision (Gilligan 1982, 72). But it is extraordinary that although her subjects' decisions could not be relied upon to reveal general truths about the way women decide about abortion, they could nonetheless be relied upon to provide data about the way most women *as a whole* think about *morality in general.*

A woman considering abortion is surely confronted with a serious moral decision. But so, too, is a woman who must find the moral courage to confront her attacker—and the cultural conventions that threaten to excuse him. So, too, is a mother who must consider what to say to her child about why she decides one way or another when she receives too much money in change at the grocery. One can defend Gilligan's assumptions about the importance of the abortion decision study only if one accepts that women's decisions about their reproductive capacities—about motherhood—are the central morally significant fact of their experience. But in accepting such a view one endorses—knowingly or not—a set of assumptions about women that would make the biology of sex definitive of their identity. It is a short step from this to the view that a woman's biology is her destiny. Does not Gilligan herself continue to bind women in dependence to cultural conventions of femininity by assuming that women's distinctive moral voices will be heard most clearly in their judgments about reproduction?

CONCLUSION

There is a special irony in the fact that a project intended to make women's ways of reasoning about morality audible and intelligible should neglect the plurality of women's voices. For one of Gilligan's primary aims, of course, was to point out the respects in which previous developmental psychologists had failed to notice the complexity of moral discourse. Lawrence Kohlberg argues that detailed cross-cultural studies on the development of moral thinking support the thesis that there is a single invariant sequence of moral development for human beings. He also argues that ideally the right kind of moral education could, "without indoctrination," move the student's judgment toward higher stages in this sequence—toward reasoning that relied on ever more "adequate" principles (Kohlberg 1981, 27). Gilligan insists that Kohlberg's assumptions lead to an unacceptable picture of women's moral capacities as developmentally inadequate relative to the capacities of the typical male. Her research is thus in part a plea for a more complex understanding of the moral domain.

Gilligan is surely right to start from the presupposition that Kohlberg's view fails to do justice to the complexity of moral discourse. Indeed, Kohlberg is far from convincing in his claim to be able to account for moral discourse by reference to a single, universal sequence of stages of moral development. His conviction that there is some one set of structures of thought that underlies our moral reasoning abilities, as well as his caricature of Aristotle's view of morality as "the bag of virtues" view, both suggest a reluctance to acknowledge that moral reasoning might be an extraordinarily complex phenomenon. Kohlberg's resistance to Aristotle is of particular importance, since Aristotle defends a view on which what the ethical life requires of us cannot be codified or reduced to a single principle or set of principles. One need not accept Aristotle's theory of the virtues to understand the force of this view of the complexity of the moral domain. Moreover, Gilligan makes a strong case for the moral importance of considerations of care. As Lawrence Blum has suggested, in much of our daily lives, we find ourselves in circumstances where considerations of impartiality and justice seem simply irrelevant (Blum 1988, 479–480). Still further, in families and in friendships, for instance, concern for the integrity of persons *merely* as persons seems morally insufficient.

But Gilligan's tendency to assume that we could capture the complexity of moral discourse simply by arguing that there is an additional, primarily female voice—one that speaks the contextual language of care rather than the (alternative) abstract language of rights—does not avoid some of the misconceptions that cast doubt on the adequacy of Kohlberg's view. Even independent of the problems attending claims about gender-specific differences in moral reasoning, it is surprising that Gilligan would reproduce—in a different context—Kohlberg's unwillingness to allow for the diversity of moral discourse. To be fair, in some recent work Gilligan suggests (in passing) that there are "at least two" moral perspectives—apparently intending to posit more complexity in moral reasoning than her empirical research has led her to talk about (Gilligan 1987, 20 and 26). Yet at the same time, her own recent studies, as well as studies carried out by her collaborators, reveal an increased confidence that moral thinking is strictly "bimodal": that (1) moral reasoning is carried out in terms of justice or care or some mixture of the two, and that (2) the care perspective is the dominant perspective in women's moral reasoning.[7]

Yet there is a very good case for thinking that both women and men structure the moral domain in a variety of ways. There is also reason to believe that in the actual practice of moral reasoning, individual women and men—sometimes confronted with choices between seemingly incommensurable goods—would reject the notion that moral problems can all be reduced to some one or two measures of significance. A number of contemporary philosophical voices are attempting to convince us that the empirical practice of moral reasoning may here be considerably wiser than some in philosophy have thought (Taylor 1982; MacIntyre 1981). In varied contexts,

Kohlberg and Gilligan have called attention to Piaget's notion that the child "is a philosopher" (Kohlberg 1981, 16; Kohlberg and Gilligan 1971). Women—in the empirical practice of moral reasoning as well as in the quiet of the study—can surely be philosophers, too. But we can understand what they are saying only if we let them speak in their distinctive moral voices.

NOTES

1. This presupposition is not an isolated instance in Gilligan's writings. Other commentators have noted in some of her essays a tendency to assert the moral superiority of the moral perspective she associates primarily with women (Flanagan and Adler 1983, 587).

2. Nel Noddings has taken an even more forceful stand on the biblical story of Abraham—especially on Kierkegaard's interpretation of that story; "For the mother . . . this is horrendous. . . . We love not because we are required to love but because our natural relatedness gives natural birth to love. It is this love, this natural caring, that makes the ethical possible. For us then, Abraham's decision is not only ethically unjustified but it is in basest violation of the supra-ethical—of caring" (1984, 43).

3. Genevieve Lloyd (1983, 1984) has asked whether the very idea of a distinctively feminine moral character is perhaps a *product* of the very intellectual traditions to which it purports to be a critical response. Moreover, Joan Williams (1989) attempts to show that it may be impossible to purge the vision of women's moral perspective defended by Gilligan, and others, of the socially and culturally limiting (and typically discriminatory) notions historically associated with it. My aim, of course, is to show why Williams may well be correct.

4. Gilligan is not entirely consistent on this point. Sometimes she suggests that she does not believe that all moral considerations could be reduced to the language of care. Sometimes she suggests otherwise. Her use of the duck-rabbit image from the Gestalt psychology of perception (Gilligan 1987) does little to clear up this confusion. Even defenses of Gilligan on this point do little to clear up this confusion (see, for instance, Blum 1988, 474–476).

5. What Gilligan cites as an advantage of her study (1982, 2) may thus be something of a liability.

6. Joan Williams cites testimony in a Title VII class action lawsuit in which empirical research—like that done by Gilligan—is cited in support of a claim that men and women do not have "equal interests and aspirations regarding work" (Williams 1989, 813–820).

7. This is particularly true of the research in *Mapping the Moral Domain* (Gilligan, Ward, and Taylor 1988).

REFERENCES

Blum, Lawrence. "Gilligan and Kohlberg: Implications for Moral Theory." *Ethics* 98 (April 1988): 472–491.

Flanagan, Owen, and Jonathan Adler. "Impartiality and Particularity." *Social Research* 50 (Autumn 1983): 576–596.

Flanagan, Owen, and Kathryn Jackson. "Justice, Care, and Gender: The Kohlberg-Gilligan Debate Revisted." *Ethics* 97 (April 1987): 622–639.

Gilligan, Carol. *In a Different Voice: Psychological Theory and Women's Development*. Cambridge, Mass.: Harvard University Press, 1982.

———. "Moral Orientation and Moral Development." In *Women and Moral Theory,* edited by Eva Feder Kittay and Diana T. Meyers, 19–33. Totowa, N.J.: Rowman and Littlefield, 1987.

Gilligan, Carol, Janie Victoria Ward, and Jill McLean Taylor, with Betty Bardige. *Mapping the Moral Domain*. Cambridge, Mass.: Harvard University Graduate School of Education, 1988.

Gilligan, Carol, and Grant Wiggins. "The Origins of Morality in Early Childhood Relationships." In *The Emergence of Morality in Young Children,* edited by Jerome Kagan and Sharon Lamb, 277–305. Chicago: University of Chicago Press, 1987.

Kant, Immanuel. *Groundwork of the Metaphysics of Morals,* translated by H. J. Paton. New York: Harper and Row, 1964; first edition, 1785.

King, Martin Luther, Jr. "Letter from Birmingham Jail." In King, *Why We Can't Wait,* 76–95. New York: New American Library, 1964.

Kohlberg, Lawrence. "Indoctrination versus Relativity in Moral Education." In Kohlberg, *The Philosophy of Moral Development,* vol. 1, 6–28. San Francisco: Harper and Row, 1981.

Kohlberg, Lawrence, and Carol Gilligan. "The Adolescent as a Philosopher." *Daedalus* 100 (1971): 1051–1086.

Lloyd, Genevieve. *The Man of Reason*. London: Methuen, 1984.

———. "Reason, Gender, and Morality in the History of Philosophy." *Social Research* 50 (Autumn 1983): 490–513.

MacIntyre, Alasdair. *After Virtue*. Notre Dame, Ind.: University of Notre Dame Press, 1981.

Nails, Debra. "Social Scientific Sexism: Gilligan's Mismeasure of Man." *Social Research* 50 (Autumn 1983): 643–666.

Noddings, Nel. *Caring: A Feminine Approach to Ethics and Moral Education*. Berkeley: University of California Press, 1984.

Taylor, Charles. "The Diversity of Goods." In *Utilitarianism and Beyond,* edited by Amartya Sen and Bernard Williams, 129–144. Cambridge: Cambridge University Press, 1982.

Williams, Joan C. "Deconstructing Gender." *Michigan Law Review* 87 (February 1989): 797–844.

13 / *The Virtue of Feeling and the Feeling of Virtue*

ELIZABETH V. SPELMAN

> The mother who taught me what I know of tenderness and love and compassion taught me also the bleak rituals of keeping Negroes in their place. —*Lillian Smith*[1]

We cannot be said to have taken women seriously until we explore how women have treated each other. But that means, too, how we have mistreated each other. The history of women, including the history of feminism and feminists, is hardly free of some women doing violence to others, of some women miserably failing other women in need.

Most feminists would insist that the history of women cannot be well told unless its tellers are not embarrassed to investigate and describe women's emotional lives: our joys, our griefs, our hopes, our fears, our loves, our hates. But such insistence on the importance of feeling amounts simply to a ringing, one-sided celebration of women's virtues—in having emotions and recounting them—unless we are willing, as Lillian Smith was, to look at the expression of emotions among women that reveal the less glorious side of our lives together.

As is well documented, nineteenth-century white, middle-class suffragists were ready and willing to use racist arguments in the name of advancing what they called "women's interests."[2] Some white women routinely beat black women who were their slaves.[3] Nazi women gave their all in the effort to eliminate the Jewish population of Europe—which included, of course, Jewish women.[4] At an international conference on women's history not long ago in Amsterdam, the organizers were asked why what in the conference brochure was referred to as "women's history" still really amounted to "white women's history." One of the white women responded: "We have enough of a burden trying to get a feminist viewpoint across, why do we have to take on this extra burden?"[5] At a recent feminist gathering in Minnesota, an able-bodied woman expressed her deep disappointment at the complaints by women in wheelchairs that all the papers presumed that women are able-bodied: in effect she said, "Here we finally have some time and space to talk about just 'us,' and you insist that we talk about something else." Can we be confident that women who demand the strictest scrutiny of the conditions under which they work and of the fairness of their salaries show the same concern for the working conditions of the women who take care of their children or clean their condos?

I do not wish to suggest here that white, middle-class, able-bodied, heterosexual Christian women have a monopoly on the mistreatment of other women. And by using these examples rather than others, I run the risk of making the sins of some women more important than those of others and thereby simply reasserting the privileged position of certain women in Western feminism. But it is startling that something as basic as some women's inhumanity to other women has not been a central concern for the variety of inquiries included under the rubric "feminist ethics." We give lots of attention to men's oppression of women but far too few sustained examinations of women's oppression or exploitation of other women.[6] As Berenice Fisher put it, when commenting on the growing use of "guilt" at feminist conferences: "Although we frequently employed the language of "guilt," virtually no one paid attention to guilt as a moral issue, that is, to the realities of wrongdoing and the responsibilities and consequences entailed by it."[7] I want to offer a few reasons in brief for this virtual silence and then suggest a way we might explore the moral dimensions of women's treatment and mistreatment of one another as at least a necessary part of whatever we include under the rubric "feminist ethics."

Why has the question of women's treatment of each other not been a burning issue for much of feminism? First of all, one of the bad raps about themselves that many women have had to battle is the image that they are catty and callous toward each other, really interested only in men and their money or their prestige or their bodies or in some cases all of those. So perhaps it has seemed hard to make a publicly understandable feminist case about the oppression of women without simultaneously remaining mute on the topic of some women's oppression of or plain meanness toward other women. According to this way of thinking, it is, to begin with, too difficult psychologically to talk about oneself or other women as both victim and victimizer. For example, perhaps it is not easy to feel sympathy for the abused wives of white slave-owners and at the same time be critical of some of their actions toward their female (and male) slaves. Moreover, under such circumstances it is awfully inviting to lay the blame for our own or others' shortcomings at the feet of those who have victimized us or them. But however we might explain the reluctance or caution about discussing women's bad treatment of other women, taking those groups of women seriously requires that we do so.

There aren't only psychological motives for shying away from examining women's mistreatment of one another. Many of the tools of feminist thinking work against the possibility of our taking to be of much theoretical or practical concern the absence of care or the presence of hostility, hatred, and contempt among women.

First of all, many of us feminists have done little to shake a habit we share with many of our fellow citizens: talking loosely about "men and women" as if these men and women had no racial, class, or cultural identity; talking about "women and blacks" or "women and minorities" as if there were no black women or no women in the groups called "minorities"; comparing relations between "men and women" to those between "whites and blacks" or "rich and poor" or "colonizer and colonized," which precludes us from talking about differences among women—between white and black, or Anglo and Latina, or rich and poor, or colonizer and colonized. In addition, much feminist theory and history is filled with incessant comparisons between "women" on the one hand and "blacks," the "poor," "Jews," and so on, on the other. Think for example of talk about "women" being treated like "slaves." Whenever we talk that way we are not only making clear that the "women" we're referring to aren't themselves slaves; we're making it impossible to talk about how the women who weren't slaves treated those who were.

If we aren't encouraged to talk about differences among women, indeed prohibited from doing so by the very terms we use or the allegedly crucial comparisons we make, then it becomes very hard, or apparently only peripheral to our central concerns, to talk about how women treat each other. But *that*, it seems to me, is what feminist ethics ought to be about, whatever else it might be about: how women treat each other. For again we must ask whether we can be said to have taken women seriously if we have not explored how women have treated each other.

Moreover, the effort by some feminists to delineate an "ethics of care,"[8] as well as the struggle to get the role of emotions in human life taken seriously, paradoxically (but perhaps not so accidentally) has diverted our attention from the history of the lack of care of women for women and has almost precluded the possibility of our looking at anything but love and friendship in women's emotional responses to one another. Some passages from Jane Austen's *Emma* illustrate what I have in mind.

Emma, our lively young protagonist, is deep in a debate with Mr. George Knightley about the behavior of Frank Churchill. Young Churchill did not grow up with his father and stepmother, who are part of Emma and Knightley's social circle. A visit by Churchill to his father and stepmother has been long awaited. Emma and Knightley disagree in their assessment of Churchill's delay in making the trip:

KNIGHTLEY: "I cannot believe that he has not the power of coming, if he made a point of it. It is too unlikely for me to believe it without proof. . . . If Frank Churchill had wanted to see his father, he would have contrived it between September and January. A man at his age—what is he? three or four-and-twenty—cannot be without the means of doing as much as that. It is impossible."

EMMA: "You are the worst judge in the world, Mr. Knightley, of the difficulties of dependence. You do not know what it is to have tempers to manage. . . . It is very unfair to judge of anybody's conduct without an intimate knowledge of their situation. Nobody, who has not been in the interior of a family, can say what the difficulties of any individual of that family may be."

KNIGHTLEY: "There is one thing, Emma, which a man can always do, if he chooses, and that is, his duty. . . . It is Frank Churchill's duty to pay this attention to his father."

EMMA: "... you have not an idea of what is requisite in situations directly opposite to your own.... I can imagine that if you, as you are ... were to be transported and placed all at once in Mr. Frank Churchill's situation, you would be able to say and do just what you have been recommending for him; and it might have a very good effect ... but then you would have no habits of early obedience and long observance to break through. To him who has, it might not be so easy to burst forth at once into perfect independence. ... Oh, the difference of situation and habit! I wish you would try to understand what an amiable young man may be likely to feel in directly opposing [the other adults who had brought him up]."

KNIGHTLEY: "Your amiable young man is a very weak young man, if this be the first occasion of his carrying through a resolution to do right against the will of others. It ought to have been a habit with him, by this time, of following his duty, instead of consulting expediency."

EMMA: "We are both prejudiced! you against, I for him; and we have no chance of agreeing till he is really here."

KNIGHTLEY: "Prejudiced! I am not prejudiced."

EMMA: "But I am very much, and without being at all ashamed of it. My love for [his father and stepmother] gives me a decided prejudice in his favour."[9]

I think anyone interested in the work of Carol Gilligan and those influenced by her work would find the constrasts between Knightley's and Emma's judgments about Frank Churchill to be at least on the face of it illustrative of two conceptions of morality that seem to be quite distinct.[10]

Knightley's concern for principled behavior, impartial judgment, and everyone's getting their due seems to exemplify an "ethics of justice" (said to be more likely held by men than women). For Knightley, there are at least two principles that ought to be brought to bear: the duty Churchill has to his father and the importance of Knightley himself remaining unbiased in his judgment of Churchill. Whatever relationship Churchill has to his more immediate family, that can't be as important as his duty to his own father; whatever the particular facts of the circumstances Churchill finds himself in, such facts cannot be used by Churchill, or by anyone else, to mitigate the full weight of his duty.

Emma's insistence on the contextual details of the situation and her concern for the importance of the many relationships involved (Churchill and his immediate family, Churchill and his father and stepmother, Emma and Churchill, Emma and Knightley) seem characteristic of an "ethics of care" (said to be more likely held by women than men). For Emma, Churchill's formal "duty" here is irrelevant. And Emma's relationship to both Churchill and his father cannot be erased by some formal obligation she might be said to have to remain "unprejudiced." Knightley's principled judgment of Churchill is not well grounded: He doesn't know enough about what Churchill is capable of or about the crucial details of Churchill's relationship to his immediate family.

I do not here wish to enter into the ongoing and very rich conversation about such apparently contrasting ethical orientations.[11] Instead, I feel obliged to point out what readers may miss about Emma if they are interested in her only to the degree that her words and actions illustrate an "ethics of care" in contrast to an "ethics of justice."

In the chapter immediately following the one in which we overhear the animated discussion between Emma and Knightley, Emma and her friend Harriet are out for a walk. Jane Austen invites us to eavesdrop again, this time on Emma's private thoughts:

They were just approaching the house where lived Mrs. and Miss Bates. . . . There was always sufficient reason for [calling upon them]; Mrs. and Miss Bates loved to be called on; and [Emma] knew she was considered by the very few who presumed ever to see imperfection in her, as rather negligent in that respect, and as not contributing what she ought to the stock of their scanty comforts.

She had had many a hint from Mr. Knightley, and some from her own heart, as to her deficiency, but none were equal to counteract the persuasion of its being very disagreeable—a waste of time—tiresome women—and all the horror of being in danger of falling in with the second and third rate of Highbury, who were calling on them for ever, and therefore she seldom went near them.[12]

If we get thoroughly caught up in comparing Emma's unapologetically biased, very particularized caring for Frank Churchill with Knightley's rather stern, impersonal principled response, we may fail to ask a very important question: But for whom does Emma care? What kind of treatment does she give those she regards as her social and economic inferiors? The fact, if it is one, that some women in reflecting on their moral problems show care and a fine sense of complexity appreciative of context tells us nothing about *who* they think worthy of their care nor whose situation demands attention to details and whose does not.

Moreover, there are forms of care that are not only compatible with but in some contexts crucial to the maintenance of systematic inequalities among women. Judith Rollins describes in some detail the "maternalism" expressed by white female employers towards their black female domestic employees:

> The maternalism dynamic is based on the assumption of a superordinate-subordinate relationship. While maternalism may protect and nurture, it also degrades and insults. The "caring" that is expressed in maternalism might range from an adult-to-child to a human-to-pet kind of caring but, by definition (and by the evidence presented by my data), it is not human-to-equal-human caring. The female employer, with her motherliness and protectiveness and generosity, is expressing in a distinctly feminine way her lack of respect for the domestic as an autonomous, adult employee. While the female employer typically creates a more intimate relationship with a domestic than her male counterpart does, this should not be interpreted as meaning she values the human worth of the domestic any more highly than does the more impersonal male employer.[13]

I have said in effect that by my lights one of the most fruitful understandings of "feminist ethics" is the investigation of how women treat each other—how well or badly we do in relation to one another. I have also said that feminist interest in exploring an "ethics of care" and in emphasizing the importance of emotions in our lives paradoxically has encouraged us to *ignore* the absence of care by women for other women, to *disregard* the presence of "negative" emotional reactions by women to other women. I now want to make my remarks much more specific by focusing on the ways in which our emotions reveal the moral dimensions of our relationships—in particular, how our emotions reveal how seriously we take the concerns of others, what we take to be our responsibility for others' plight, and the extent to which we regard others as even having points of view we need to take seriously.

Our emotions, or at least some of them, can be highly revelatory of whom and what we care or don't care about. They provide powerful clues to the ways in which we take ourselves to be implicated in the lives of others and they in ours. As this example from Aristotle reveals, many of our emotions locate us in moral relation to one another: One who doesn't get angry when the occasion calls for it "is thought not to feel things nor to be pained by them, and since he does not get angry, he is thought unlikely to defend himself; and to endure being insulted, and put up with insult to one's friends, is slavish."[14] Aristotle is insisting that if under certain conditions we don't feel anger, we may have failed to show proper respect for ourselves or proper concern for our friends.

Here is another example of what I have in mind when speaking of our emotions as revelatory of ways in which we take ourselves to be implicated in the lives of others and they in ours. At my own educational institution and many others, there have been blatant displays of racism—for example, messages left by cowards in protective anonymity—telling black, Latina, and Chinese-American students in no uncertain terms that they don't belong at Smith College and that if they don't like the way they're treated, they should "go home." (These represent only the obvious tip of an iceberg that is melting with what the Supreme Court in a related context called "all deliberate speed.") I do not wish to go into details of how my institution or yours actually has responded to what, in a revealing phrase, typically are called "incidents" (a term that suggests, perhaps insists, that such events are infrequent and anomalous). But by way of beginning to show what our emotions tell us about our moral relations to each other and the contours and quality of our care for one another, I'd like to run through some possible responses.

1. Ivylawn College regrets the occurrence of racist incidents on its campus.
2. Ivylawn College is embarrassed by the occurrence of racist incidents on its campus.
3. Ivylawn College feels guilty about the occurrence of racist incidents on its campus.
4. Ivylawn College feels shame for the occurrence of racist incidents on its campus.[15]

Surely you already notice some significant difference—yet to be explored in detail—between regret, embarrassment, guilt, and shame. Think also of the difference between

5. Ivylawn College regrets the occurrence of racist incidents on its campus.
6. Ivylawn College regrets the harm done to those hurt by the recent events on its campus.

If the first set of contrasts reminds us that different emotions imply different notions of responsibility and depth of concern, the second reminds us that the same emotion can have different objects—what the emotions are about. In going into all these differences in more detail, I turn to Gabriele Taylor's *Pride, Shame, and Guilt: Emotions of Self-Assessment.*[16]

Gabriele Taylor is one of a number of contemporary philosophers who hold or operate on the basis of what has been dubbed the "cognitive theory" of the emotions. Though cognitivists differ among each other on certain details, they share the conviction that emotions cannot simply be feelings, like churnings in our stomachs, flutterings of our hearts, chokings in our throats. Though such feelings may accompany my regretting having hurt you or my sense of shame in having hurt you, the difference between my regret and my shame cannot be accounted for by reference to such feelings; nor can the difference between my regret in having hurt *you* and my regret in having hurt *my father*. There is a kind of logic to our emotions that has nothing to do with whatever dumb feelings may accompany them (in many cases there don't even seem to be such feelings anyway).

It is the central tenet of what is currently known as the "cognitive theory" of emotions that our emotions are not a clue to or sign of poppings and firings and other gyrations—mental or physical—within us but rather indicate how we see the world. For emotions typically have identificatory cognitive states. For example, what identifies my emotion as *anger* is among other things a belief that some unjust harm has been done; what makes my emotion a matter of *fear* is among other things my belief that danger is imminent. I shall not go into more detail about the cognitive theory here—you shall see more of it in reflective practice below—but it is perhaps worth making explicit that we could not regard our emotions as very interesting facts about us—in particular, as deeply connected to ourselves as moral agents—if emotions were simply events, things happening in us like headaches or bleeding gums.[17]

That said, let us return to our earlier examples of regret, embarrassment, guilt, and shame. As Gabriele Taylor reminds us, if I regret that something happened, then I must regard what happened as in some sense undesirable. But I need not regard what happened as anything morally troubling—for example, I may now regret not taking a few more days of vacation. Or I can feel regret for something for which I was in no way responsible—Gabriele Taylor's example is the passing of summer.[18] Moreover, even though regretting that something happened means I must take it to be in some sense undesirable, it is still possible for me to think that nevertheless all things considered it is not something I think should not have happened. And it is perfectly possible for me to regret it without being at all inclined to take any actions in consequence. This is why we can perfectly sincerely send our regrets—indeed, even our "deepest regrets"—that a party occurs on a night we're out of town. It might have been fun to go to the party, and I might be a bit apprehensive about hurting the feelings of or disappointing a good friend, but it is more important to do what takes me out of town and I don't want my friend to change the date of the party. In all these ways, Gabriele Taylor points out, regret is quite different from remorse. You can't feel remorse about something for which you do not believe yourself responsible, or about something that doesn't appear to you to be morally wrong, or about something you don't wish to undo or attend to in some way.

So if Ivylawn College or any other institution expresses *regret* that a "racist incident" happened on its campus, all it is doing so far is acknowledging that such an event took place and allowing that it was in some unspecified sense undesirable. But it is not in any way assuming responsibility for the "incident" or indicating that there is anything morally troubling about it (as opposed to its just being undesirable for its nuisance value in terms of college publicity); nor is it indicating that any action is in consequence required. Note, by the way, that precisely because regret has these features, there are certain built-in limitations on the description of *what* is regretted: Though it is perfectly possible to "regret" something described as a "racist *incident*," I'm sure no institution would publicly say that it "regretted" the murder of one student by another.

Having sketched out what the presence of regret means, we can keep on the back burner what the absence of it means—that is, not acknowledging that anything of note happened at all, let alone that it was in some way undesirable.

I shall then, without regret, move on to *embarrassment.* My guess is that most institutions are embarrassed by the occurrence of racism on their campuses, but they would not describe themselves in just that way. The reasons for this will become clear as we look at the logic of embarrassment (here again with Gabriele Taylor's help). Unlike regret, embarrassment necessarily involves a sense that one has been exposed and in consequence is subject to an adverse judgment of oneself in some respect. Suppose a man is embarrassed about beating his wife. His being embarrassed is fully compatible with his finding nothing wrong in the fact that he beats his wife. He judges himself adversely not because he thinks he has done something wrong but because he does not yet know how to respond to the audience to whom he is or imagines himself exposed. If all he feels is embarrassed, he doesn't need to do any basic repair work on himself, only figure out a way to deal with the audience—perhaps tell them it is none of their business, or insist that women need to be pushed around, or laugh it off. Perhaps he'll express regret that it is necessary to beat his wife in order to keep her in her place (so the expression of regret might cancel embarrassment). His concern is not about what he is doing to his wife but about the kind of impression he is making on others.

What then does it mean if Ivylawn College is *embarrassed* by the racist incidents on its campus—and why might it or any other institution be unlikely to publicly describe itself in this way? If an institution is embarrassed by the occurrence of racist remarks and other behavior, then what it finds troubling is not the behavior itself but the exposure of the behavior. If there is anything wrong with the institution, it is that it does not know how to prevent adverse publicity or deal well with it once public notice is taken. When an institution is embarrassed, and only embarrassed, it puts its public relations department to work; it works not on changing the institution but on changing the perception of the institution. Admitting to embarrassment is usually not a good way of dealing with embarrassment, for it simply brings attention to the situation that the embarrassed party does not want others to see.

You can feel *embarrassed* without thinking that you have done anything wrong or anything you shouldn't do, but in general[19] you can't feel *guilty* without believing that you have failed to live up to some kind of standard or that you have done something that is forbidden according to an accepted authority (including your conscience). (Of course you can be guilty without feeling guilty, but here we are talking only about feeling guilty). There is something I have done or failed to do. According to Gabriele Taylor, in feeling guilt I certainly am judging myself adversely, but my situation is not hopeless—I am not less of a person than I thought I was. I simply did something I think I shouldn't have done or failed to do something I think I ought to have done. There is a blot on my record—but then blots only are blots against the background of an otherwise still morally intact person. That is connected to the fact that there are things I can do to repair the damage I've done. Indeed, the action I take is geared to restoring the blot-free picture of myself—so, Gabriele Taylor insists, if I feel guilty about harming someone else, the thought is not so much that "I have harmed *her*" but rather "*I* have harmed her"[20] and hence disfigured myself to some extent. In response, I may want to do something about the harm I did to her but—to the extent that my concern is more about myself than about her—as a means of restoring my status in my own eyes.

Gabriele Taylor's analysis, then, implies that the man who beats his wife and feels guilty about it, unlike the man who merely feels embarrassed, does believe that he has done something he ought not to do, and feeling this way he is inclined to take action to alleviate the feeling of guilt. But his concern is not directly for his wife but for himself. If her pain is the occasion for his thinking he has violated something he stands for, his ceasing to beat her or his otherwise atoning for what he has done is the means to his self-rehabilitation.

Could Ivylawn College feel *guilty* about the racism on its campus? Of course this sounds odd—in a way that ascribing regret to the institution does not. This seems related to the fact that feeling guilty involves a sense of direct responsibility for the deed, so that to ascribe feelings of guilt to an institution really amounts to ascribing it to particular individuals within the institution. Institutions can have regret precisely because regrets don't entail responsibility and where there is responsibility we look for particular agents. The president of Ivylawn, for example, could talk about the college's having regrets without implying that she herself has them, but it would take a lot of work for her to say that the college feels guilty about something without giving the impression that she was talking about herself or other highly placed officials. It certainly is possible that there might be reports of various officials feeling "very bad" about what went on—not simply embarrassed, much more than regretful. Insofar as this means something like "feeling guilty," then if Gabriele Taylor is right such officials believe that while nothing is basically wrong with the institution or with them, they or the institution bear responsibility for the racist events. The emphasis in any action will be on redeeming the good name of the institution and attending to the hurt done the injured parties as the means to redeeming the good name of the institution.

Let us go on to *shame.* Suppose the man who beats his wife feels shame for doing so. How is that different from his feeling embarrassed or guilty? According to Gabriele Taylor,[21] the identificatory belief in shame is that I am not the person I thought I was or hoped I might be. It is not simply, as in embarrassment, that I wish I hadn't been seen doing something (even though I don't think I've done anything wrong) or, as in guilt, simply that I have failed to live up to a standard I adhere to. If I thought the latter, I could still entertain the possibility that I can set the record straight, for in such a case what troubles me about what I've done is quite local: I've *done* something I don't approve of, but I'm not *someone* I don't approve of. As Gabriele Taylor puts it: "When feeling guilty . . . the view I take of myself is entirely different from the view I take of myself when feeling shame: in the latter case I see myself as being all of a piece, what I have just done, I now see, fits only too well what I really am. But when feeling guilty I think of myself as having brought about a forbidden state of affairs and thereby in this respect disfigured a self which otherwise remains the same."[22] So if Mr. Husband feels shame about beating his wife, he must think that his action is revelatory of the person he in fact is even though he had thought or hoped that he was someone else, someone better than he turns out to be.

And thus if Ivylawn College should feel shame about the racism existing on its campus,[23] it would indicate that the college or the people identified as its representatives thought it wasn't the institution it hoped it was. The racism on the campus is revelatory of what the institution really is and not simply a sign that the college can't always live up to what it says it stands for.

Perhaps that is why an institution is unlikely to feel or admit to shame: It may be unable to countenance the possibility that at root it is not what it purports, even to itself, to be.

So, then, our emotions, or at least some of them, can be highly revelatory of who and what we care or don't care about. They provide powerful clues to the ways in which we take ourselves to be implicated in the lives of others and they in ours. And their *absence* provides such clues as much as their presence does. For example, the conference organizers referred to at the beginning of this chapter who were asked why no women of color were included in a gathering on "women's history" seemed to have no regrets about their decision, let alone embarrassment, guilt, or shame. From their vantage point, there was nothing undesirable about the focus of the conference, and though not in any way disclaiming responsibility for that focus, they made no room for the implication that they had done anything wrong or that the conference or they weren't what they understood it or themselves to be. Indeed, from the remarks quoted earlier, it appears that they began to argue that the complaints and demands of the women of color were groundless: The conference was about "women," not about race. And if anything, there is a strong note of annoyance in the remarks of the woman who insisted that talking about race was an "extra burden" for feminism and that the women of color were both missing the point and adding to the load already carried by the conveners.

Let us suppose that as a convener I come to feel regret as a result of listening to the comments of the women of color. What would that show about what I care about and how I take myself to be implicated in the lives of others and others in mine? Well, that depends of course on *what* I regret. Do I regret having hurt the women of color? Having been made uncomfortable myself? That my theory turns out not to be adequate? In this connection María Lugones recently noted that in her experience many feminists, when asked to explain how their accounts of "women's experiences" apply to women of color, express considerable concern about the inadequacy of their theories—but the focus of concern, María Lugones reluctantly concludes, is not how they have hurt women of color but rather that they need to tidy up their theories.[24]

It is not news that white feminist conferences and conversations have been peppered, sometimes even smothered, with expressions of guilt—sometimes in reaction to the very lack of regret (or perhaps some other emotion) for the exclusionary practices and policies I have described.[25] Indeed, a great deal has been made of white women's feelings of *guilt* in the face of charges by black women, Latinas, Japanese-American women, and others that our theories have been heavily tilted in the direction and to the exclusive benefit of white, middle-class women. Reflection on Gabriele Taylor's work leads me to make three comments about the discussions about this guilt. First, if Gabriele Taylor is right about the point of action taken to get rid of the feeling of guilt, then guilt is not an emotion that makes us attend well to the situation of those whose treatment at our hands we feel guilty about. We're too anxious trying to keep our moral slate clean. Second, I think it worth asking whether in any given case people are feeling guilt or simply embarrassment. If the latter, then there is no sense that one has failed in any way to act in accordance with what one stands for. There are no amends to make, only appearances to create.

Third, I think that there is a very neat fit between feeling guilty and a particular way of conceiving the relation between one's gender and one's racial identity. This friendly cohabitation throws some very interesting light on the concept of "white guilt." According to Gabriele Taylor, in feeling guilt rather than shame, it is possible for me to think of a part of myself as not living up to what the rest of me stands for. Insofar as I see myself as a "doer of a wicked deed," I see the hint of an alien self; in order to make sure such a self does not emerge, I need to do whatever it takes to "purge" myself of this alien self.[26] If I have a metaphysical position according to which my gender identity is thoroughly distinct from my racial identity (what I elsewhere call a form of "Tootsie Roll metaphysics")[27] I very handily can rely on a neat distinction between myself as woman and myself as white person. The woman part of me is perfectly okay; it's being white that is the source of my wrongdoing. I assert my privilege over women of color not insofar as I am a woman but insofar as I am white. Note then that unless I am prepared to think of my womanness and my whiteness as folded inextricably into the person I am, I can think of myself and my responsibility for my acts in the following way: What really counts about me is that I am a woman, and my deeds do not show that I am not any less of a woman than I thought I was; it's only insofar as I am white, which isn't nearly as important a part of me, that I have failed other women. It's not the woman in me that failed the woman in you; it's the white in me that failed (for example) the black in you. I, woman, feel nothing in particular; but I, white person, do feel guilt. If feminism focuses on the "woman" part of me and the "woman" part of you, conceived of as thoroughly distinct from my white part and your black part, feminism doesn't have to pay attention to our relations as white and black. We never have to confront each other woman to woman, then, only white to black or Anglo to Latina.

Feminist ethics, I have been insisting, must at least address the history of woman's inhumanity to woman. This part of the history of women is shameful. However, I am not proposing a daily regimen of shame-inducing exercises. Nor do I think that the deep self-doubt that is part of shame can serve as the immediate ground of a vibrant feminist politics, a politics that expresses and promotes real care and concern for all women's lives. But I do not see how women who enjoy privileged status over other women (whether it be based on race, class, religion, age, sexual orientation, or physical mobility) can come to think it desirable to lose that privilege (by force or consent) unless they see it not only as producing harm to other women but also as being deeply disfiguring to themselves. It is not simply, as it would be in the case of guilt, that the point of ceasing to harm others is to remove a disquieting blot from one's picture of oneself. The deeper privilege goes, the less self-conscious people are of the extent to which their being who they are, in their own eyes as well as in the eyes of others, is dependent upon the exploitation or degradation or disadvantage of others. Seeing myself as deeply disfigured by privilege and desiring to do something about it may be impossible without my feeling shame. The degree to which I am moved to undermine systems of privilege is closely tied to the degree to which I feel shame at the sort of person such privilege makes me or allows me to be.

In sum, then, I have been urging these considerations to keep those of us who are feminists from hastening to quickly to feel virtuous about attending to the virtues of feeling, the marvel of care. Whatever we mean by "feminist ethics," it ought not to make it difficult for us to examine and evaluate how women treat or mistreat each other. However, there are elements in feminism that make such examination difficult. For example, there is a tendency to focus on the contrast between an "ethics of care" and ethical systems that seem not to take care seriously. So far the contrast tells us nothing about who cares or does not care for whom. Moreover, since it has been claimed that an ethics of care is associated strongly though not exclusively with the way "women" think and act in the moral domain, it makes it very hard even to suggest that some women have failed to care for others, let alone that they have done violence to others. There is also a reliance on an understanding of care that obscures the fact that some forms of care are not only compatible with but crucial to the maintenance of systematic inequalities among women. In this connection, Judith Rollins's book about relations between white female employers and their black domestic employees is very insightful.[28] Among other things, Judith Rollins describes ways in which the employers insist on the privilege of "caring" for their employees in ways that reflect and sustain their power over them. Finally, there is a rampant terminology of contrasts between "women" on the one hand and "slaves" or "minorities" or "the poor" or "Jews" or whatever on the other. Such contrasts (and for that matter similarities) obscure differences between free women and slave women, gentile women and Jewish women, and so on, making it hard to talk about how one group of women treated others. This is reinforced by theories within feminism according to which women are the same *as women* and are oppressed the same *as women* and so if white women mistreat, say, black women, it is seen as how whites treat blacks, not how some women treat other women.

I have proposed one way of looking at some of the moral dimensions of women's treatment of one another. Some emotions are called "moral emotions" because having them involves or can involve moral assessment of oneself and others. In Gabriele Taylor's words, a moral emotion "requires a sense of value on the part of the agent, an awareness, more or less developed, of moral distinctions, of what is right or wrong, honorable or disgraceful."[29] Our having such emotions toward others can reveal whether, how, and to what extent we have treated them or think we have treated them well or poorly—so does our not having them. Moreover, our political and metaphysical theories give shape and structure to our emotional lives. For example, our assumptions about what *feminism* is about will influence our beliefs about what is appropriate and inappropriate to bring up at feminist conferences, which will in turn influence the possibility of our feeling anger, regret, remorse, embarrassment, guilt, or shame. (As Arnold Isenberg says: "When you lack what you do not want, there is no shame."[30]) And as I stated earlier, assumptions about the relation between our gender identity and other aspects of our identity such as our race, class, and religion can influence how we describe our responsibility for the way we treat other women.

NOTES

1. Lillian Smith, *Killers of the Dream* (New York: Norton, 1949, 1961), 27.

2. See, for example, Eleanor Flexner, *Century of Struggle* (New York: Atheneum, 1972), especially chap. 13; Ellen Carol DuBois, *Feminism and Suffrage* (Ithaca, N.Y.: Cornell University Press, 1978); Angela Davis, *Women, Race, and Class* (New York: Random, 1981); Paula Giddings, *When and Where I Enter: The Impact of Black Women on Race and Sex in America* (New York: Morrow, 1984).

3. See, for example, Linda Brent, *Incidents in the Life of a Slave Girl*, ed. L. Maria Child (New York: Harcourt Brace Jovanovich, 1973); Solomon Northrup, *Narrative of Solomon Northrup, Twelve Years a Slave* (Auburn, N.Y.: Derby and Miller, 1853), quoted in Gerda Lerner, ed., *Black Women in White America* (New York: Vintage, 1972), 51.

4. See, for example, Claudia Koonz, *Mothers in the Fatherland: Women, the Family, and Nazi Politics* (New York: St. Martin's Press, 1987).

5. *off our backs* (feminist newspaper), July 1986, 3.

6. See notes 1–5 above; also, for example, bell hooks, *Feminist Theory: From Margin to Center* (Boston: South End Press, 1984); Audre Lorde, *Sister/Outsider: Essays and Speeches* (Trumansburg, N.Y.: Crossing Press, 1984); Helen Longino and Valerie Miner, eds., *Competition: A Feminist*

Taboo? (New York: Feminist Press, 1987); Elly Bulkin, Minnie Bruce Pratt, and Barbara Smith, *Yours in Struggle: Three Feminist Perspectives on Anti-Semitism and Racism*, (Ithaca, N.Y.: Firebrand Books, 1984). Simone de Beauvoir, by the way, had quite a lot to say about women with race and class privilege undermining or failing to support other women in order to maintain their race and class privilege, but that part of her work is rarely highlighted—even by herself (see Spelman, *Inessential Woman: Problems of Exclusion in Feminist Thought* [Boston: Beacon Press, 1988], chap. 3).

7. Berenice Fisher, "Guilt and Shame in the Women's Movement: The Radical Ideal of Action and Its Meaning for Feminist Intellectuals," *Feminist Studies* 10, no. 2 (Summer 1984): 186.

8. See Carol Gilligan, *In a Different Voice: Psychological Theory and Women's Development* (Cambridge, Mass.: Harvard University Press, 1982); Eva Feder Kittay and Diana T. Meyers, eds., *Women and Moral Theory* (Totowa, N.J.: Rowman and Littlefield, 1987).

9. Jane Austen, *Emma* (New York: Bantam, 1981; first edition, 1816), 133–139.

10. These are not incompatible conceptions, according to Gilligan and others. See Eva Kittay and Diana Meyers, eds., *Women and Moral Theory.*

11. See, for example, ibid.; Lawrence A. Blum, "Gilligan and Kohlberg: Implications for Moral Theory," *Ethics* 98 (April 1988): 472–491.

12. Jane Austen, *Emma,* 139–140.

13. Judith Rollins, *Between Women: Domestics and Their Employers* (Philadelphia: Temple University Press, 1985), 186.

14. Aristotle, *The Nicomachean Ethics of Aristotle,* tr. Sir David Ross (London: Oxford University Press, 1925), 97.

15. Two problems emerge here, even in the presentation of 1–4: One is what it means for institutions, as opposed to individuals, to have such reactions; and the other is that as long as we focus on institutions, we don't have to think about what our own reactions are. But we'll get to these below.

16. Gabriele Taylor, *Pride, Shame, and Guilt: Emotions of Self-Assessment* (Oxford: Clarendon Press, 1985).

17. See Elizabeth V. Spelman, "Anger and Insubordination," in *Women, Knowledge, and Reality,* ed. Ann Garry and Marilyn Pearsall (Winchester, Mass.: Unwin Hyman, 1989), 263–273.

18. Although regretting that something happened differs in some important ways from regretting having done something—since the latter, not the former, entails responsibility for having done the thing in question—I can fully regret that something happened without in any way implicating myself in having brought it about.

19. In "Cognitive Emotions?" Chesire Calhoun discusses the repair work necessary for certain versions of the cognitive theory in light of the fact that sometimes "one's doxic life and one's emotional life part company" (in *What is an Emotion? Classic Readings in Philosophical Psychology,* ed. Chesire Calhoun and Robert C. Solomon [New York: Oxford University Press, 1984], 333).

20. Gabriele Taylor, *Pride, Shame, and Guilt,* 92.

21. Ibid., 68.

22. Ibid., 92.

23. Note how odd it would be to refer to that about which one feels shame as merely an "incident."

24. See chapter 2 of this volume.

25. It may seem as if this is at odds with my claim at the beginning of the chapter that the history of hostile or uncaring relationships among women has not gotten the sustained attention it deserves. But passing, even frequent, expressions of regret, embarrassment, guilt, or shame are hardly the same as a thorough examination of the meanings of those emotions in the history of the social and political relationships among women.

26. Gabriele Taylor, *Pride, Shame, and Guilt,* 134, 135.

27. See Elizabeth Spelman, *Inessential Woman,* passim.

28. Judith Rollins, *Between Women,* passim.

29. Gabriele Taylor, *Pride, Shame, and Guilt,* 107.

30. Arnold Isenberg, "Natural Shame and Natural Pride," in *Explaining Emotions,* ed. Amélie Oksenberg Rorty (Berkeley: University of California Press, 1981), 370.

14 / *Whom Can Women Trust?*

ANNETTE C. BAIER

"But though the males, when united, have in all countries bodily force sufficient to maintain this severe tyranny, yet such are the insinuation, address and charms of their fair companions that women are commonly able to break the confederacy, and share with the other sex in all the rights and privileges of society."[1] For years, decades even, I referred to this claim of Hume's as a claim about women's power to break male confederacies. It took a male reader of the passage, Chris Williams, to point out to me that Hume does not say that the confederacy to be broken is one of males only. Males are those accused of tyranny over women in many societies, but the confederacy that supports the tyranny that needs to be broken may not be an exclusively male one, indeed has not been an exclusively male one. Women must distrust not only the men who have the bodily force to maintain severe tyrannies but also the women whose insinuation, address, and charms are used to keep in favor with the tyrants, to help maintain rather than to break the confederacy that, in the extreme case, reduces women to slavery "incapable of all property, in opposition to their lordly masters."

Not only is this a pretty obvious truth once it is pointed out, but it is indeed one that Hume explicitly draws attention to in the essays that he addressed particularly to the women of his time and culture. In "Of Love and Marriage," for example, he gently chides them for taking satires on the institution of matrimony to be satires on themselves. "Do they mean that they are the parties principally concerned, and that if a backwardness to enter into that state should prevail in the world, they would be the greatest sufferers?"[2] Then there is his "pretty remarkable instance of a philosophic spirit," the young woman who, "observing the many unhappy marriages among her acquaintances, and hearing the complaints which her female friends made of the tyranny, inconstancy, jealousy, or indifference of their husbands, being a woman of strong spirit and an uncommon way of thinking," resolved to avoid matrimony without avoiding motherhood and resolutely did so.[3] "Our philosophical heroine" had to be fairly uncommon in her way of thinking, given the more usual female complicity in maintaining the institutions that perpetuated the inferior social position of women. The most thoroughgoing complicity consisted, and consists, not merely in vowing obedience but in bringing up daughters to do the same. But as Nancy Chodorow points out to us,[4] a woman's mere willingness to be the primary caregiver, however radically one might try to bring up daughters no differently than one brings up sons, may be enough to guarantee to one's daughters unequal ability to cope in "a man's world" and to one's sons unequal ability to cope in "a women's world." The confederacy of sexists is not easy to leave. In this chapter, I shall explore only some aspects of this confederacy. My title question, "Whom can women trust?" will be narrowed to "When can women trust women?" and that narrowed even further to trust between mothers and daughters.[5]

Should girls distrust their loving mothers simply because their love has been expressed in their loving care, their being willing to take the main responsibility for caring for them when they were infants and young children? Is the only trustworthy parent a co-parent who is very careful to keep the parental partnership, at least when it is a heterosexual one, from becoming unequal in time spent with the children? Maybe. But punctiliously coequal parents might still be abusive,[6] neglectful, unloving, bigoted, tyrannical, or themselves distrustful of their children, so that equal time with each parent is at best a necessary not a sufficient condition for the well-foundedness of children's trust in parents and of young daughters' trust in mothers.

Women, precisely because they have so often themselves been victims, should not be trusted too readily by other women or by men. The fact that they have been the victims of lies, exploitation, betrayal, cannot be expected to make them less ready themselves to lie, cheat, and betray. Tit for tat is supposed to be a rational strategy. As Hume wrote, "Tyrants, we know, produce rebels; and all history informs us that rebels, when they prevail, are apt to become tyrants in their turn."[7] Women can scarcely be said to have "prevailed" in our culture, but there can be small rebel victories and so small tempta-

tions to tyranny, not just to engage in tit for tat against the earlier
tyrants but to seize any opportunity for a bit of conspicuous exercise
of power, to lord it over someone, male or female. This is the sorry
lesson of history and of our known psychology. Toppling tyrants is
not enough to end tyranny—we have to have more than a mere rebellion, a mere switch of elites; we have to alter the structure of
government, stage a revolution.

Have we done that? The governance that would need to be altered
would be not merely that of parents over children but governance in
all other places where the pernicious patriarchal model has affected
structures of power. In this nation, we seem a very long way from
having a woman president (and even if we did, if that were accompanied by no structural changes, it would not amount to much except
a symbolic victory). Even the rebellion is badly incomplete as long as
there is not equal representation of women at the top as well as in the
lower levels of all power hierarchies, in universities, in the media, in
the arts, in business, in banking, in the Senate and House, among the
president's cabinet and advisers. But the rebellion, the replacement of
at least half the powerful men by powerful women, is not likely to
happen without some revolutionary structural changes of a sort that
we have only begun to institute. Paid pregnancy leave for women,
parental leave for both parents after the birth of their child, and proper
allowance in promotion decisions for such parental time off are as
necessary as equal educational opportunities, equitable divorce
rights, settlements, and alimony. Equal pay for equal work is only the
beginning—we need equal allowance and compensation for equal
homemaking services, and we need to demand that the services in the
home *be* equally shared.

As fathers take on more of their share of household drudgery, which
women have always been expected to do even when they worked
outside the home, and as both parents share the privilege of responsibility for child care, then of course the task and burden that used to be
reserved for men—military service—must also be shared by women.
This is only fair. However, it presents some problems. It might seem
to be social suicide for a nation to put its pregnant young women and
its nursing mothers into the front line along with the young fathers
and fathers-to-be. Even Hitler realized that a nation needs its young
women for more important tasks than killing and being killed.
Decimating the ranks of young males need make no noticeable differ-

ence to the birth rate, but decimating the ranks of young females can decimate their collective offspring. As far as sheer biological reproduction is concerned, we do not need more than a few "studs."[8] This basic sociobiological fact will become relevant to decisions about conscription to military duty in war time, when it will be only sensible to find some alternative form of war work for pregnant women and breast-feeding mothers, perhaps also for any young women who prefer it to military service, just as any humane society will also provide such alternative service to any conscientious objectors to violent warfare. But that women must carry a fair share of the general burden of defense, and that military careers must be as open to women as to men, seems clear. If we want equality, we must refuse that historically fatal offer "Serve and obey us, and we will fight to defend you." We must defend ourselves or, at any rate, do our share of the collective defense.

If this still seems a crazy proposal, to allow the not-yet-pregnant young women to be conscripted and killed in wartime, just to satisfy the demands of equality, of equal burdens as well as equal rights, then we could well consider why in modern conditions of warfare it is still deemed socially desirable that the *young,* male or female, be the ones who run the greatest risk of death and injury. Is it really still the case, if it ever was, that it takes the hot blood of youth to do the sort of things that members of the military forces must do in war time? Why not conscript those between forty-five and fifty-five? Why not let the young live out their youth and let the older people, some of whom take the decisions to go to war, themselves face the greatest threats? Is is that we feel we need our "elder statesmen" more vitally than we need our young men? Once we have elder stateswomen, the whole rationale of sending the young to fight their elders' wars might well be radically rethought.

Whom, then, can women trust? If the ones most naturally expected to have their welfare at heart—namely, their parents—are likely to be patriarchs and patriarchs' accomplices, then the outlook seems fairly bleak. Let me make it quite clear that when I say that daughters cannot necessarily trust either their fathers or their mothers, I am not necessarily imputing ill will to either. To trust is to take both the trusted's will and competence to be good enough for them to be relied upon to look after some aspect of one's well-being or something of importance to one that one entrusts to their care.[9] With the best will in the world, some parents may yet be untrustworthy because they lack some crucial *competence* that parents need. If to mold a child's aspirations and sense of herself and her future properly, it takes a mother who has herself an exemplary sense of her own worth and her own options, or indeed if Nancy Chodorow is right and it takes a mother who insists on *sharing* the child rearing, not claiming exclusive right to it, then many mothers will be incompetent, however great their goodwill and dedication to their children. "The reproduction of mothering is the reproduction of women's location and responsibilities in the domestic sphere . . . that women mother is a fundamental organizational feature of the sexual division of labor and generates a psychology and ideology of male dominance as well as an ideology about women's capacities and nature."[10]

Stereotypically maternal, attentive mothers and stereotypically paternal, distanced fathers reproduce their own psychology in their daughters and sons just as, according to folk wisdom on this matter, the victims of child abuse tend to become victimizers. Parenthood essentially is a matter of transmitting some of one's own traits, and of one's own inheritance of potentialities, to one's children. If it is true that the very fact that the mother has taken on the main responsibility of child care limits the daughter's ability to compete successfully for the opportunity to take on any responsibilities except those of child care, then this happens behaviorally as well as genetically and whether or not the parent intends it to happen. How is this self-replicating pattern of gender roles to be stopped from going on and on, generation after generation?

According to Nancy Chodorow's theory, we should expect that this will occur either through the against-the-grain efforts of some women to share their nurturing role equally with their children's fathers and to take on other roles outside the home or by the agency of the lucky few whose upbringing was fairly evenly shared by father and mother. "My expectation is that equal parenting would leave people of both genders with the positive capacities each has, but without the destructive extremes these currently tend towards."[11] These will be the points of leverage for change, particularly for change in the social structures that have reinforced the gender roles that perpetuate inequality.

I am no psychologist or psychotherapist, so I have no way, except casual observation, of knowing whether Nancy Chodorow's theses are empirically confirmed. I tread warily here, since even if by and large her theses are correct, it still seems evident that some daughters of mothers who took almost the full responsibility for their children's care do succeed in careers and are willing to share parental responsibility, to divide their time between career and home, expecting the father of their children to do the same. We all know of instances where the pattern has been broken—by good luck, by special help, or by special ambitions. My own mother, for example, was the very embodiment of the nurturing mother, devoting all her time and care to home and children, content to let my father take over child care only in the evenings and on weekends and then under fairly close supervision. But she imbued four daughters with career ambitions, and all four continued these careers after marriage, two of my sisters bringing up, with their husbands' help, five children each, the girls as career-bent as the boys. So my own observation closest to home does not make me gloomy about the prospects for women's equality and for men's chances to share the child-rearing. By Nancy Chodorow's theory, my own mother was *not* the sort who should have had ambitious daughters, but she did, and indeed it was to a large extent her sense of what she herself had not had—educational training for a career—that fired her with ambition for her daughters, that motivated the efforts she made to encourage our ambitions and to keep us at our schoolwork when other temptations beckoned. She was as trustworthy a mother as a daughter could have had, if will and competence to turn out ambitious daughters is the criterion of trustworthiness, and this despite the fact that she did not fit Nancy Chodorow's specifications.

The power of the negative should not be discounted. Women throughout history have occasionally broken the fetters that they inherited. Discontent is the first step. To communicate to one's daughters the discontent one feels with the way things were for oneself, and the hope one has of a different way for them, clearly can be enough to empower those daughters to take a different way from their mothers', and it can sometimes empower the discontented ones themselves to bring about change. The women activists whom we have to thank for women's suffrage and for other hard-won changes were not themselves the products of the better conditions they tried

to bring into being and sustain. Servitude is not necessarily repro-
duced along with the reproduction of mothering. As Nancy
Chodorow herself says, social advances "depend on the conscious
organization and activity of all women and men who recognize that
their interests lie in transforming the social organization of gender
and eliminating sexual inequality."[12] Sometimes it is the daughters
who recruit the mothers into the struggle rather than vice versa or,
more generally, the younger women who spur the older women on to
action.[13]

In Francine du Plessix Gray's "Reflections (Soviet Women),"[14] we
get rather scary informal confirmation of some of Chodorow's general
theses about the bad effect it has on girls to be brought up primarily by
their mothers with little sharing of the responsibility by the fathers.
Extensive interviews with contemporary Soviet women, most of
them fairly successful career women and all of them women working
outside as well as inside the home, revealed that their lives were spent
in work outside the home (usually under men as top bosses), very
time-consuming shopping for scarce food, and very hard work inside
the home, where they live with their mothers and their children,
occasionally with a temporary husband as a sort of tolerated guest in
the matriarchal realm. Marriage is normal, but equally normal is its
fairly fast dissolution. There is a Russian proverb, "Women can do
everything; men can do the rest," and the women that Francine Gray
spoke with were mostly scathing about men's contributions to their
lives. A husband, one successful woman gynecologist said, is "how
can I say . . . an elective obligation," and her felicitous wording was
greeted with approving laughter from her women fellow-workers.[15]
To tolerate a husband in the home is to "take on an extra child," so
little contribution to home life is expected (or perhaps allowed) from a
Soviet husband. "Here's the way our order of priorities goes: first a
career; second a child. As for a man, that's irrelevant. He can go his
way as soon as the child is conceived," said one successful program
editor of a television station, who lives with her mother and her
twenty-year-old daughter.[16] Francine Gray, interviewing these
superwomen who themselves speak of their own matriarchal ways as
"chronic," finds the popular Russian gaily painted wooden *mat-
ryoshka* dolls-within-dolls a fitting symbol for Soviet women as she
saw them. They were like these dolls with "generations of parth-
ogenetic females fitting snugly into each other."

This matriarchal subsociety appears to be having a disheartening effect on the young sons of these superwomen, who perform less well than their sisters at school and seem passive and diffident in comparison with their more aggressive, more confident sisters. Their prospects do not include any permanent niche within the mutually supportive women's world; they are expected to become as burdensome to any women they will love when they are adult as their fathers proved to be to their mothers. Useless in the home, self-indulgent, exploitative, charmless, incapable of contributing anything important (except a child) to a woman's happiness, these miserable male creatures are nevertheless the ones to whom the running of the nation is relegated. A Leningrad woman, Olga Lipovskaya, who edits a feminist newsletter, told Francine Gray that "politics always struck me and my women friends as something deeply unethical, as dirty work."[17]

This division of function, where men do politics and, when they can, sponge off women and women look after each other and also look after those cowed, silent little boys, produces personality types that are neither those that Nancy Chodorow analyzed nor quite those that her theory would lead us to predict. The girls, reared mainly by strong women, become strong women—aggressive, competitive, and independent but not ambitious to enter the dirty male political arena. The boys, reared virtually without fathers, become like their absent fathers—boorish, domestically incompetent, sad, and drowning their sorrows in politics as well as vodka.

This is no improvement over having aggressive, ambitious boys and diffident, modest girls. The Soviet superwomen are not contented with their lot; neither are the men. Nor can there be much hope of structural change if the strong women eschew politics and the politically strong men either avoid or are banished from the homes where their children are growing up. One Soviet woman suggested that "a good feminist movement would make our women more gentle,"[18] and one of the effects of perestroika was seen to have been to enable "our men to feel less superfluous" by encouraging some male individualism. Such sentiments may bring some changes, but whether they will be changes that break the cycle of the reproduction of matriarchs and rogue males is not at all clear. For the women's discontent is not really with the chronic matriarchy but with the overwork it brings. "Of course we are grossly overburdened. But we wouldn't give it up for the world. We take such pride in surviving it," said a Siberian woman factory worker to Francine Gray.[19] Such pride in being able to do without men is not the best basis for the sort of cooperation with them that on Nancy Chodorow's theory is an essential feature of competent parenting.[20] As long as the superwomen pride themselves on their own aggressive independence, or rather on the independence of the new family unit of grandmother, mother, and daughters, they are not likely to want to have the fathers of their children playing a more active parental role.

What of trust? Is there mutual trust among the superwomen? Between mothers and daughters, mutual trust seems the norm, but in a wider female circle the attitude seems more a mixture of mutual respect and mutual suspicion. Ironically enough, competition for the few relatively "bearable" (that is, civilized and house-trained) males contributes to the lack of general female solidarity. When one rare happily married woman whom Francine Gray interviewed explained how her older husband had helped make it possible for her to study and shared the cooking and diaper changing, her fellow students gasped with envy and incredulity.[21] Collective action by Soviet women on behalf of Soviet women and on behalf of their children, both male and female, was not seen by the women Gray interviewed as very likely.

The strong mother-daughter ties—what one woman termed "the normal and absolute return of love"[22]—contrasted with the weakness of other social ties. Should these daughters trust their mothers so absolutely? Should a Soviet daughter "give to my daughter what my mother gave to me"?[23] If what is given is this toughness, this very selective capacity for trust, gentleness, and sharing of responsibility, this self-verifying expectation that men, if allowed in their homes, will merely "look at television and occasionally remember to play with the children,"[24] does not seem an altogether benign inheritance to pass on, not such a great cause for filial gratitude. And certainly the sons seem to have very little reason to trust these mothers who make them feel so marginal and superfluous, fit only for dirty politics and for taking out the garbage. There may *be* mutual trust in the matriarchal Soviet family, but to an outside eye it appears to be misplaced trust.

It is instructive to consider the pathology of another society's gender relations, to compare it with our own pathological gender relations in the United States. For we, though surely different from these Soviet women, are certainly not superior. Our faults, especially those of white, middle-class women, may run more to contented dependency on men than to exclusionary independence of them, more to false buildup of male egos than to ruthless deflation of them. Many of us vacillate between making sisterhood powerful and turning on our sisters in displays of petty infighting, squabbles for ascendancy, and secret leagues with the supposed enemies. If the Soviet women look rather fearsome, we look just plain ridiculous. Most of us have no good reason to trust ourselves to be trustworthy custodians of the welfare of women and children.

Are we at least *more* trustworthy custodians of our own and our children's welfare than those who traditionally put women and children first, at least in their protective activities? Even if we, or many of us, are part of any conspiracy to keep us from full equality, are we at least relatively innocuous members of that evil confederacy? Not if some of us voluntarily take on the role of spokeswoman for the paternalistic status quo, as some of us obviously do. Do we have more "excuse" for such action than do the men, who are the more obvious "confederates"?

If there were some advantage to men in keeping women down, commensurate with the disadvantage it entails for women, then we could treat women as an oppressed "class" whose interests are opposed to men as a "class" in the Marxist sense. It is difficult to see what clear overall advantage it did bring men to keep women uneducated or educated only in genteel womanly matters, to attempt to restrict woman's place to the home, and then have to employ spies and jailers to try to enforce the restrictions. The only conceivable advantages it brought were monopoly of rule, monopoly of most of the interesting work, and what Grotius, Pufendorf, and others gave as the justification of that male monopoly within marriage—perceived assurance to men that their wives' children were really their own, "not spurious or suppositious."[25] Today, the last assurance is no longer one that men can reasonably expect to get by any coercive means, so it really falls out of account as a factor. A woman's assurance on this matter is not likely to be more trustworthy simply because she chooses the role of subservient wife rather than free woman. What of the monopoly of nondomestic work and of rule? Is the latter not always an advantage to the ruler? Is it not always a loss of advantage to compete with twice as many competitors for any job and to move from being ruler to becoming co-ruler?

As far as the last goes, it depends on the strength of one's hunger for power over others. Hume teases the women of his day with an over-valuing of the advantage of being boss. So restricted were his Scottish women contemporaries to a domestic realm in which to exercise any dominion that some of them were charged by Hume with the folly of taking "a fool for a mate, that she might govern with less control."[26] If the cost of being sole ruler is having fools as the ruled, the cost is too high. What is true for the women is as true for the men. If their monopoly of rule entailed their need to keep women as foolish as they could be—simpering sillies rather than full participants in "the feast of reason"—then the advantage was very dubious. As far as the monopoly of nondomestic work goes, males do lose some advantages once they compete with women. But to waste the reason and the passion of half the human population by narrowing their scope to domestic concerns is a pathological case of the division of labor. "By the conjunction of forces, our power is augmented: By the partition of employments, our ability encreases: And by mutual succour we are less expos'd to fortune and accidents."[27] What abilities were increased by the partitioning of employment so that women got all and only the domestic work? Not child-rearing ability, if Nancy Chodorow is right. As for the ability to rule, that requires not just wisdom but power, and "by the conjunction of forces, our power is augmented."

Whom can women trust? Not ourselves, until we manage to get a partitioning of employments that really does increase the abilities that, on reflection, we really do want increased. We surely do want to increase our ability to raise free-spirited children, both boys and girls. To reflect properly on what abilities are worth increasing, we surely do need the power of conjoined forces, so we should be against *any* monopoly of rule, any sharp partition into ruler and ruled. The cooperative scheme, the conjunction of forces, cannot afford to exclude any, not even the old oppressors.[28] Soul-satisfying fantasies of reversing "the trade in women" so that those few desirable gentle men who like to cook[29] become a commodity that the women trade in while the rest are dumped as superfluous must, however reluctantly, be put aside if we really aim to give daughters good enough reason to want to pass on to their daughters what they got from their mothers.

NOTES

I am grateful to Chris Williams for getting this essay started and to Claudia Card for the correction of some of its errors.

1. This quotation and the next are from David Hume, *An Enquiry Concerning the Principles of Morals*, ed. L. A. Selby-Bigge and P. H. Nidditch (Oxford: Clarendon Press, 1975), 191.

2. David Hume, *Essays: Moral, Political, and Literary*, ed. Eugene Miller (Indianapolis: Liberty Classics, 1985), 557.

3. Ibid., 542.

4. Nancy Chodorow, *The Reproduction of Mothering* (Berkeley: University of California Press, 1978). Nancy Chodorow's study is of parenting by heterosexual couples.

5. Since I am appealing to Nancy Chodorow's findings and these are limited to parenting by heterosexual pairs of parents, my remarks will be yet further restricted to mothers and such daughters whose other provider of parental care is a father. I use "mother" and "father" and "parent" to include those who are not the child's biological parents. Since Nancy Chodorow's theory rests on acceptance of some Freudian views about the development of male and female self identification, her findings cannot be generalized to cases where children are reared by homosexual parents.

6. For a sensational account of a trusting and trusted team of stepfather and mother in relation to a daughter, see Shelley Sessions and Peter Meyer, *Dark Obsession: A True Story of Incest and Justice* (New York: G. P. Putnam's Sons, 1990).

7. Hume, *Essays*, 560.

8. For a wonderfully informative account of "the mystery of males, why they're here and what they're for," see Fred Hapgood, *Why Males Exist* (New York: Morrow, 1979).

9. I develop this account of what trust is in "Trust and Antitrust," *Ethics* 96 (January 1986): 231–260.

10. Nancy Chodorow, *Reproduction of Mothering*, 208.

11. Ibid., 218. The heterosexual assumptions are very evident in this passage.

12. Ibid., 219.

13. My own consciousness of women's situation in this country is due largely to the influence of a succession of women students, among whom Carol Donovan, Lynne McFall, and Lynne Tirrell stand out as the ones who taught me most.

14. Francine du Plessix Gray, "Reflections (Soviet Women)," *New Yorker*, February 19, 1990, 48–81.

15. Ibid., 75.

16. Ibid., 74.

17. Ibid., 60.

18. Ibid., 74.

19. Ibid., 62.

20. If Nancy Chodorow is wrong in believing that the shared parenting must come from a male and a female parent, then of course such pride may not be so bad.

21. Francine Gray, "Reflections," 77.

22. Ibid., 81.

23. Ibid.

24. Ibid., 74.

25. Samuel Pufendorf, *The Duty of Man and Citizen*, tr. Frank Gardner Moore (Oxford: Oxford University Press, 1927), bk. 2, chap. 2. See also *The Law of Nature and Nations*, tr. C. H. Oldfather and W. A. Oldfather (Oxford: Oxford University Press, 1934), bk. 5, chap. 1.

26. Hume, *Essays*, 559.

27. David Hume, *A Treatise of Human Nature*, ed. L. A. Selby-Bigge (Oxford: Clarendon Press, 1975), 485.

28. Of course, if there is evidence that the old oppressors are still more prone to violence than their ex-victims, we will have to monitor the amount of parenting, of any sort, that they are permitted to do.

29. Hapgood, *Why Males Exist*, relates how the male eastern scorpion fly, *Bittacus apicalis*, must provide a "nuptial meal" before any self-respecting female will consent to mate with him and if the meal provided is inferior, she will still refuse.

15 / *Some Thoughts about "Caring"*

SARAH LUCIA HOAGLAND

I wrote *Lesbian Ethics* after years of observing and participating in lesbian community. The analysis I developed yielded a critique of traditional anglo-european ethics as, among other things, designed to coerce "cooperation" among antagonists. In focusing on the concept "lesbian," I found myself challenging heterosexualism. What I call "heterosexualism" is not simply males having procreative sex with females but rather an entire way of living:

> "Heterosexualism is men dominating and de-skilling women in any of a number of forms; from outright attack to paternalistic care, and women devaluing (of necessity) female bonding as well as finding inherent conflicts between commitment and autonomy, and consequently valuing an ethics of dependence. Heterosexualism is a way of living (which actual practitioners exhibit to a greater or lesser degree) that normalizes the dominance of one person in a relationship and the subordination of another. As a result it undermines female agency. (Hoagland 1988, 29)

I found that one central problem resulting from heterosexualism is the question of female agency. (By "agency" I simply mean the ability to make choices and act in situations.)

Under the heterosexual model of femininity, the feminine virtues are self-sacrifice, vulnerability, and altruism (Hoagland 1988, chapter 3). Female actions are to be directed toward others, thus the female ability to act is located in others. Consequently, the primary mode of female agency is manipulation. And this, of course, is the stereotype men use to dismiss and criticize women when they behave in ways men have prescribed. The resulting situation is one of the double binds discovered as feminists developed an analysis of sexism.

The independence of the male agent, the model for anglo-european ethics, is possible in real life only presuming the dependence of the female agent who provides the necessary services to allow the male agent to pretend autonomy. The anglo-european model of male ethical agency is that of one who is isolated, egoistic, competitive, and antagonistic. And as a result of this model, Alison Jaggar notes, the central question of anglo-european political theory is, How do we ever get people to cooperate? (Jaggar 1983, 40). Further, if we start with such a model of moral agency, it is no wonder that male philosophers will argue that if there is no altruism, there is no ethics. Nevertheless, as one might suspect, altruism accrues to those with lesser power (Hoagland 1988, chapter 2). It is a feminine virtue.

To counter this ethics of independence, some heterosexual women philosophers have developed an ethics of dependence, partially in an attempt, I believe, to capture and explore the idea of community beyond the collection of independent antagonists attempted in much masculinist ethics. Significantly, this ethics of dependence is often explored within the framework of mothering in which the idea of dependency can be explored and is often romanticized, but in which the women as mothers are not the ones who are dependent. I question the mother model as a model for female agency as much as I question the masculine egoistic model.

What I want to do in this chapter is examine some of the pitfalls of using mothering as the model of female moral agency. I chose Nel Noddings's work because it is perhaps most directly involved in developing the masculine model of the feminine.

INTRODUCTION

Nel Noddings's book, *Caring,* has many fine points that I consider central to ethical theory and that I find missing for the most part from traditional, masculinist ethics. Perhaps most central is her shift of the source of ethical sentiment from rules to natural sentiment— especially, caring. This shift includes two elements of particular importance. First, there is a refusal to rely on principles and rules. In discussing a situation in which she lies to an authority about her son's absence from school, or another one in which she refuses to spy on a neighbor, Nel Noddings explains how considering the particulars of a situation helps one make a decision about what to do in that situation (Noddings 1984, 57). In short, principles don't tell us when to apply them, and in the long run, they work only when we don't really need them.

She argues that to accept the universalizability of principles, "we would have to establish that human predicaments exhibit sufficient sameness, and this we cannot do without abstracting away from concrete situations those qualities that seem to reveal sameness. In doing this, we often lose the very qualities or factors that gave rise to the moral question in the situation" (Noddings 1984, 85). This does not mean, however, that we reject principles altogether. It is just that we regard them as guidelines, not ultimate arbiters of behavior. "The one-caring displays a characteristic variability in her actions—she acts in a nonrule-bound fashion in behalf of the cared-for" (Noddings 1984, 25).

The second aspect of Nel Noddings's shift from rule-oriented ethics to an ethics of caring is her focus on interaction between ethical parties. Her position is that relation is ontologically basic and the caring relation is ethically basic (Noddings 1984, 3). She argues: "Taking *relation* as ontologically basic simply means that we recognize human encounter and affective response as a basic fact of human existence" (Noddings 1984, 4). She contrasts the philosopher who begins with a supremely free consciousness, one who has an aloneness and emptiness at the heart of existence, with one who recognizes and longs for relatedness (Noddings 1984, 6). She suggests that our efforts must be "directed to the maintenance of conditions that will permit caring to flourish" (1984, 5). And she suggests her concern is not on the judgment or the acts, but how we meet each other morally (Noddings 1984, 5).

In particular, she introduces in caring the idea of receiving the other, of apprehending their reality (Noddings 1984, 14). "Caring involves stepping out of one's own personal frame of reference into the other's. When we care, we consider the other's point of view" (Noddings 1984, 24).

As a result of this focus on caring, Nel Noddings offers many valuable insights about relatedness—for example, that caring requires maintenance of self (Noddings 1984, 105) and that knowledge of what gives us pain and pleasure precedes caring for others (Noddings 1984, 14). She also discusses how caring for others can become an assumption of burdens whereby one is only focused on oneself—when caring becomes simply a matter of "cares and burdens" and I have become the object of my own caring (Noddings 1984, 37; see also 14). Of particular interest is her notion that our moral agency is affected by others (Noddings 1984, 49) and that in certain respects we depend on others to enhance our moral self. And there is something to be said for the idea of interacting with others by acknowledging only good motives (Noddings 1984, 178).

In many respects I agree with this focus. However, if such a focus is going to serve us morally, it must have a way of assessing the values we reinforce through our interactions and a vision of how values can change. My criticism stems from Nel Noddings's analysis of caring, an analysis that uses mothering as a model, and from implications that derive from this analysis. My concern is twofold. First, I object to the unidirectional description of caring. Second, I do not think mothering can be properly used as the model for an ethics of caring.

I take time with this because my concern is not to challenge caring as a pivotal point for ethical theory but rather to question a particular portrayal of caring. Nel Noddings's analysis of caring involves several elements: acting, engrossment, and motivational displacement on the part of the one who cares (the one-caring) and reciprocity on the part of the one who is cared for (the cared-for) (Noddings 1984, 150).

The action component is the most elusive as it cannot be defined in terms of behavioral indications. It is here that the move away from rule-bound behavior is most significant. One must determine one's course of action in terms of the person and the situation: "To care is to act not by fixed rule but by affection and regard" (Noddings 1984, 24).

Engrossment, receiving, and motivational displacement concern the way we involve ourselves with an other. Engrossment and receiving involve apprehending the other's reality, and Nel Noddings distinguishes this from empathy—I need to apprehend the other's reality not as I would feel it in their shoes but as they feel it (Noddings 1984, 30). This is close to what María Lugones calles "playful world travel," through which we can learn to love cross-culturally and cross-racially. It involves being able to go into the world of another quite different from our own without trying to conquer or destroy it (men's idea of play) (Lugones 1987, 3–19).

According to Nel Noddings, the element of motivational displacement enters because if I go into another's world, then "I am impelled to act as though in my own behalf, but in behalf of the other" (Noddings 1984, 16). Or again: "I allow my motive energy to be shared; I put it at the service of the other" (Noddings 1984, 33).

Finally, reciprocity on the part of the cared-for is crucial to caring because caring must be completed in the other. Reciprocity is not a matter of the cared-for responding as one-caring. Rather, "caring is completed in all relationships through the apprehension of caring by the cared-for" (Noddings 1984, 65). A baby wiggling in delight as she is bathed exhibits the reciprocal efforts of the cared-for (Noddings 1984, 52).

UNEQUAL RELATIONSHIPS

Certainly there are arguments for focusing on mothering in considering ethical (and political) questions. Alison Jaggar argues that if we stop viewing individuals as isolated, solitary, and essentially rational and consider the facts of biology—namely, that mothers need cooperative effort in raising infants—then liberals would be puzzled by the existence of egoism, competitiveness, and aggressiveness rather than the existence of community and cooperation (Jaggar 1983, 41). Yet Nel Noddings's focus is not on the cooperation necessary among adults for child-rearing but rather on the unequal relationship between mother and child. She also brings in teacher/student and, later, therapist/client relationships.

Nel Noddings's interest in these relationships seems to be a matter of the child/student/client having a need the mother/teacher/therapist can fill (Noddings 1984, 66). In some respects, she equates caring with teaching, and her focus on the mother/child relationship as primary seems to be a matter of the dependency of the child, which elicits a response from the mother. Thus the mother cares—a natural caring that can be turned into a moral caring (Noddings 1984, 5). This relationship is unequal, however, because the child or student is "incapable of perceiving or understanding what the parent or teacher wants for herself" (Noddings 1984, 70).

Now, in the first place, the very purpose of parenting, teaching, and providing therapy is to wean the cared-for of dependency. Consequently, an ethics of caring whose model is a dependency relationship, ideally transitory, provides at best for an incomplete analysis of caring. More significantly, to the extent that it is true that the cared-for cannot understand what the one-caring needs or wants, the conclusion I draw is that such a relationship is ipso facto a diminished caring relationship. Second, Nel Noddings argues elsewhere that the authorization of the parent/teacher/therapist, combined with the situation of the cared-for, justifies the inequality and, by extension, the lack of expectation of real reciprocity from the cared-for (Noddings 1984, 66). But this portrays only one party as needing help in the relationship; unless we are talking about a mere development of skills, this is false.

Third, there tends to be an assumption that we value unequal relationships because they afford a means of addressing differences in ability. That is, we tend to justify relationships unequal in power by assuming that their function is acknowledgment of differences in abilities. Along with this goes the further assumption that in equal relationships, we treat our peers as having abilities equal to our own. However, this is not the case (Leighton 1987). When interacting with those we consider our peers, we do not treat each other as if our abilities were the same, and we do not treat each other as lesser or unequal because of it. More likely, we just treat one another as normal and get on with helping or teaching each other. My friend who is an accountant helps me with my accounting, but the relationship is not an unequal one. So when we interact with someone in a way that is premised on a difference of power, it is not simply because we perceive them as not having abilities we have. Often it is because we perceive them as incompetent or less competent than we are in being able to make decisions in general. Consequently, we must ask ourselves what values we promote when we encourage unequal relationships as an ideal rather than as something to be worked out of or even overcome.

In my opinion, caring must find its grounding in a relationship that is not "authorized" (Noddings 1984, 66) and indeed serve as a check on the power exercised in these "authorized" relationships. For we live in a society premised on dominance and subordination, and oppression emerges in many forms—from parental all the way to colonial relationships—when decisions are made "for another's own good."[1]

Finally, an unequal authorized relationship promoted in the name of benevolence yields problems concerning the trust the cared-for is supposed to place in the authority. For example, a child is expected to be honest with the mother, but the mother is not expected to be accountable to the child—she can lie, for example, often under the guise of not burdening the child. The problem is compounded with teachers and therapists upon whom others rely for judgments about their academic abilities and mental states.[2] The situation encourages the cared-for to believe that it is appropriate to trust someone who has power over her with personal information about herself upon which this someone can make decisions about her "well-being." This is not appropriate, at least not in a capitalist or socialist society.

Given the nature of our society, an ethics that focuses on how we meet each other morally must, in my opinion, carry with it values that will challenge oppression and induce change. Although I do not seek an ethics that begins with rules to define right and wrong, I do seek an ethics that is capable of bringing about change in the values we affirm—in particular, a diminishment of dominance and subordination.

ADULT/CHILD RELATIONSHIPS

Part of the challenge that can induce change concerns the adult/child relationship directly. Nel Noddings states that she is "working toward criteria that will preserve our deepest and most tender human feelings. The caring of mother for child, of human adult for infant, elicits the tenderest feelings in most of us" (Noddings 1984, 87). Now, if in changing from mother/child to human adult/infant, Nel Noddings means to include men as human adults, then it is important to note that in almost a third of the households that permit male adults access to female children, a male adult rapes one or more female children (Bart 1988; Stanko 1985; Russell 1984; Rush 1980). Certainly it is not the tenderest of feelings that leads an adult to rape a child; the sentiment as well as the material conditions behind this phenomenon have to do with power in the form of dominance. And although Nel Noddings would draw on only those feelings we consider good, an analysis using the adult/child relationship must take these other feelings into account in order to induce change in the relationship.

Nel Noddings does acknowledge the existence of abusive males and discusses a wife killing her abusive and incestuous husband. However, she suggests that having to act to end the abuse by withdrawing one-caring results in ethical diminishment (Noddings 1984, 114). I disagree and will return to this later. More generally, an analysis of caring that derives from the mother/child relationship must go further than Nel Noddings's discussion has in acknowledging the values underlying perhaps the most serious proximate dilemma facing mothers—whether to tolerate an abusive male because of economic need or defend a female child.

Third, a model of mothering that draws on tender feelings must also acknowledge the real conflict that at least some mothers feel between resentment and tenderness (Rich 1976, 21). If we are going to build an ethics on natural feelings, then I think we must consider all aspects of the feelings. More important, this model of mothering does not acknowledge the fact that a number of mothers abuse their children. Although not as extensive as male incest and child abuse, it is a dynamic that cannot be ignored. It may be that, materially, no one should be in a position to have such singular authority over anyone else and that group mothering is the key.

In fact, a less romanticized, more realistic view of the adult/child relationship suggests that male dominance, the nuclear family, and even the glorification of unequal power relationships are central elements that an analysis of caring must be capable of challenging. An ethics appealing to the mother/child relationship must take into consideration both the power in the relationship and the social context of the relationship. Ignoring these will only reinforce oppression through ethics regardless of whether the ethics is based on caring or on principle.

AGAPISM

Nel Noddings argues that hers is not an ethics of agape. I want to argue, on the contrary, that it is and that this is a problem. Even though Nel Noddings argues that the one-caring can also be a cared-for (Noddings, 1984 and 1990), the phenomenological analysis of caring is unidirectional. And my central thesis is that the unidirectional nature of the analysis of one-caring reinforces oppressive institutions.

Let me begin with the reciprocity of the cared-for; it is not a mutual engrossment and motivational displacement, not even a receiving of the other's world to the extent of understanding it. Reciprocity amounts to acknowledgment of the other's caring (Noddings 1984, 52, 65). Nel Noddings notes that the relationship can be heightened if the cared-for's acknowledgment includes involving the one-caring in the cared-for's projects. However, there is no need for the child to turn and exhibit concern for the mother's projects. Again, to the extent that the cared-for (child) cannot understand what the one-caring (mother) needs or wants, such a relationship is ipso facto a diminished caring relationship.

What I question is the promotion of infant nonreciprocity-beyond-acknowledgment as a model for ethically relating to others. When I have no real expectation of an intimate, when I have certain standards of caring for myself that I do not apply to the other, for example, then I am not showing respect.

Further, nonreciprocity-beyond-acknowledgment undermines the possibility of instilling the value of one-caring in the cared-for. I am not convinced that a child, especially a male child, who experiences one-caring from his mother will ever learn to be one-caring himself. Rather, as is more consistent with my observations, such children learn to expect more one-caring—unidirectional—from all females; in fact, that is what they seek in a wife. There is nothing to indicate that this type of caring is capable of undermining what Marilyn Frye calls "the arrogant eye of masculine perception" (Frye 1983, 66–82). In addition, in my observation and experience, the treatment a female child receives that produces individuals predisposed to one-caring is not itself the care of one-caring. It is not a warm concern for a girl's projects (for example, sports) but rather a curbing of her projects as well as her abilities and an instilling of both guilt about others and deep concern for others' opinions about her—elements of the socialization of females into the feminine role in a patriarchal society.

Second, engrossment and motivational displacement involve acting on behalf of the other: "When we see the other's reality as a possibility for us, we must act to eliminate the intolerable, to reduce the pain, to fill the need, to actualize the dream" (Noddings 1984, 14). This suggests that it is appropriate for us to take over another's situation and try to control it, try to make it all right. I question this, and in my work I have argued that trying to take over and control a situation for another undermines the moral ability of both parties

(Hoagland 1988, chapter 3). (There may be times when we judge we must intervene in a given situation, but I contend that this also results in moral harm and that we must subsequently act to undo the harm.) At any rate, the idea that it is appropriate to take over for another and act to control her situation contributes to the unidirectional nature of the caring relationship and hence to the idea that it is a form of agape.

Third, I question the sense of self that emerges from the analysis of one-caring. Nel Noddings argues that one-caring is not self-sacrificing because we are defined in relation and because it is appropriate for the one-caring to care for herself (1984, 99).

Although Nel Noddings certainly insists that we take care of ourselves, the moral basis for this is to become better ones-caring (Noddings 1984, 105). Thus we have an other-directed justification for self-concern that can encourage false information about what counts as health as well as what counts as moral good (Frye 1983, 70). Further, if my ethical self can emerge only through caring for others (Noddings 1984, 14), if self is defined only in relation (Noddings 1984, 99), and if ethics is built on caring that is always other-directed (Noddings 1984, 99), then the only time I may focus on my own goals and have that be an ethical matter is as a cared-for—when it is important to someone else that I pursue my goals as a way of having their caring received. In addition, insofar as I become able to care for myself only as I care for others and am cared for, then I get my ethical identity from always being other-directed (Noddings 1984, 49). But this is not significantly different from the situation of exploitation as Marilyn Frye analyzes it (Frye 1983, 60).

Certainly relation is central to ethics. However, to begin with, there must be at least two beings to relate. Moving away from oneself is one aspect of the dynamic of caring, but it cannot be the only defining element. Otherwise *relationship* is not ontologically basic, but *the other* is, as is the case with Nel Noddings's particular phenomenological analysis, and the self ceases to exist in its own ethical right—there is, as yet, no real relation. Certainly we are not individuals who remain essentially isolated and relate untouched. We develop as we interact, and this, as Nel Noddings indicates, is what makes relationship morally basic and is what is basically lacking in masculinist ethics. Nevertheless, we are in no more useful a position when the one-caring's ethical status and identity is located completely in the other. Again, the feminine is not an antidote to the masculine. Rather, it is a supporter and nurturer of the masculine. I am sympathetic with Nel Noddings's impetus away from masculine ethics. It's just that in a patriarchal world we need something far more radical than an appeal to the feminine—itself a product of that masculine world.

One who cares must perceive herself not just as both separate and related but as ethically both separate and related; otherwise she cannot acknowledge difference—for example, that one is black and the other white in a racist society. And denying difference will lead to undermining the connection and perpetuating racism as well as sexism, ageism, heterosexism, and many other aspects of our social structure (Lorde 1982, 1984). I argue that my ethical self emerges from pursuing my own integrity and goals as well as relating to others; it comes from my perceiving myself as one among many (Hoagland 1988, chapter 5).[3]

Fourth, as Nel Noddings describes it, withdrawal from a relationship involves a diminishment of the ethical ideal (Noddings 1984, 114). I want to suggest that there must be the possibility of withdrawal from a cared-for without a diminishment of the ethical idea, for at times a withdrawal is necessary to preserve my ideal. As Nel Noddings notes, the mother who receives the incestuous father is de-moralized, her ideal diminished. However, Nel Noddings argues that it is also diminished by withdrawing from him.

The idea seems to be that the man who rapes his daughters, for example, is otherwise a quite decent fellow. Aunt Phoebe who is smug in her hatred of blacks is otherwise a warm and generous person. However, multiple personality theory notwithstanding, these choices are not distinct from other choices such a person makes. I must be able to assess any relationship for abuse/oppression and withdraw if I find it to be so. I feel no guilt, I have grown, I have learned something. I understand my part in the relationship. I separate. I will not be there again. Far from diminishing my ethical self, I am enhancing it.

Withdrawal may also be the only way one can help another. One danger of caring is what Alcoholics Anonymous calls enablement: People who are close to an alcoholic often enable an alcoholic's dependency. As Celinda Cantu explains, enablers become co-alcoholics—those who are as "dependent on the alcoholic as the alcoholic is on alcohol"—for they "get a fix by taking care of and being needed by the drunk" (Cantu 1983, 85).

Fifth, I question the nonjudgmentalism of the analysis of one-caring. Nel Noddings notes that we receive the other without evaluation or assessment as nearly as possible (Noddings 1984, 34). In the first place, this simply is not true—even not to judge is to judge. To pretend a stance of nonjudgmentalism merely discourages awareness of one's environment and the values of the status quo—in therapy, often the value of blaming the victim.

Nel Noddings denies that there is judgment in the initial impulse to care; what she means by "judgment" is "assessment of right and wrong." Yet there is some form of assessment, for example, in a heterosexual woman's initial impulse of repulsion when confronted with a lesbian. Although possibly nonreflective, it is not preconscious. If the feeling of caring is to be totally nonreflective, then it is no different from a sneeze. As Naomi Scheman writes, anything more complex than twinges and pangs exists in relation to our social context (for example, capitalist patriarchy) and makes sense in relation to it (Scheman 1983, 226ff).

Nel Noddings argues that hers is not an ethics of agape. I suggest, on the contrary, that it is. The reason she considers it not agape is that there is no command to love (Noddings 1984, 28–29); however, this is not my understanding of agape. The essence of agape lies in the direction of loving. In direct contrast to eros, which is self-centered, agape is other-centered. The caring of agape always moves away from itself and extends itself unconditionally. Certainly Nel Noddings's analysis is that caring moves away from itself (Noddings 1984, 16). However, I would add that since there are no expectations of the cared-for beyond being acknowledged by the one-caring, since my ethical self can emerge only through caring for others, since withdrawal constitutes a diminished ideal, and since there is allegedly no evaluation in receiving the other, one-caring extends itself virtually unconditionally.

Perhaps the paradigm of unconditional loving lies in the stereotype of the mammy. bell hooks writes:

Her greatest virtue was of course her love for white folk whom she willingly and passively served. The mammy image was portrayed with affection by whites because it epitomized the ultimate sexist-racist vision of ideal black womanhood—complete submission to the will of whites. In a sense whites created in the mammy figure a black woman who embodied solely those characteristics they as colonizers wished to exploit. They saw her as the embodiment of woman as passive nurturer, a mother figure who gave without expectation of return, who not only acknowledged her inferiority to whites but who loved them. The mammy as portrayed by whites poses no threat to the existing white patriarchal social order for she totally submits to the white racist regime. Contemporary television shows continue to present black mammy figures as prototypes of acceptable black womanhood. (hooks 1981, 84–85)

Motivational displacement is one consequence of enslavement, and by implication from Nel Noddings's analysis, the care of one-caring is successful if the son of a slave owner grows up under the one-caring of the mammy to become a master.

Further, the unidirectional ideal of mothering undermines reciprocal interaction beyond acknowledgment between mothers and daughters and so also encourages incompetency and ageism among us. Recipients of unconditional loving—children and husbands—combine in exploiting mothers, helping to create an ageist response to older women:

The children learned an assumption of privilege from their father, and he in turn became one of the children—legitimately passive, irresponsible. . . . [M]y older daughters never witnessed an *exchange* of nurturance. In their view of how the world worked, mothers gave, and men/daughters received. Ours was such an isolated nuclear family that they literally never had an opportunity to witness me being nourished, sustained, taken care of, or emotionally supported. . . . My own daughters, now in their thirties, are dutiful wives but still do not know how to extend nurturance to me, or to negotiate when we have a difference of interest. . . . As the children grow up, they continue to relate to older women with the clear expectations of service. By then they have laid claim to a place of privilege in the power hierarchy. (Copper 1985, 57)

María Lugones writes of her failure to love her mother and suggests that until she became basically one-caring herself toward her mother and thereby met her mother in care, meaning could not arise fully between them (Lugones 1987, 8).

To pursue the feminine (a part of whose essence is agape and unconditional loving), to pursue this sense of female agency, is to pursue oppression. The masculine and the feminine are not significantly different in what they engender.

INSULARISM

Nel Noddings's analysis of caring appeals to the feminine, to receptiveness. A truly radical ethics will challenge not only the masculine but also the feminine, for the feminine is born of a masculinist framework and so does not, at a deep level, represent any change. Both the masculine and the feminine are central to heterosexualism. In general, I do not find the society of mothers preferable to the society of fathers. In contrasting mothers and amazons, Monique Wittig and Sande Zeig suggest, mythically, that there came a time when some would no longer ride with the amazons and instead stayed in the city and watched their abdomens grow, refusing other interests and calling themselves "mothers":

"During the Golden Age, everyone in the terrestrial garden was called amazon. Mothers were not distinct from daughters. They lived in harmony and shared pleasures. They enumerated every beautiful and pleasant place in the terrestrial garden and invited one another to visit them. They hunted together. They gathered together and they wandered together. They described their deeds and exploits in epics. There were no limits to their adventures and age had no meaning in their lives or in their poems. Everyone thought of herself as an amazon.

"After the first settlements in the cities everything continued as before. The amazons lived far from, rather than inside, their cities. After hunting or gathering, the food was prepared out of doors and a festival was held. Very often the city was completely deserted and vacant for several days.

"Then came a time when some daughters and some mothers did not like wandering anymore in the terrestrial garden. They began to stay in the cities and most often they watched their abdomens grow. This activity brought them, it is said, great satisfaction. Things went so far in this direction that they refused to have any other interests. In vain, their friends asked them to join them in their travels. They always had a new abdomen to watch. Thus they called themselves mothers. And they found qualifications corresponding to this function of childbearing, for example, mother the plenary, mother the one who engenders. The first generation of static mothers who refused to leave their cities, began. From then on, they called the others 'eternal, immature daughters, amazons.'

"They did not welcome them cordially when they came back from their travels. They did not listen to their accounts of discoveries or explorations anymore. The joy of hunting, gathering, and wandering had disappeared. At that time the mothers stopped calling themselves amazons and the mothers and the amazons began to live separately" (Julienne Bourge, *Comments on the Past*, Gaul, Glorious Age). (Wittig and Zeig 1979, 108–109).

In a sense I am charging the one-caring as Nel Noddings describes her with a lack of experience in the world (Noddings 1984, 46)—indeed, with a withdrawal from the public domain (Noddings 1984, 84). I am suggesting that hers is the focus of one who has limited her attention and who will not leave the city. But my criticism is not a criticism from the masculine ethics Nel Noddings abandons, because I am not appealing to principles to solve these problems. Acting from principle can be acting from an equal or even greater lack of experience. It is a lesbian criticism: Caring cannot be insular and it cannot ignore the political reality, material conditions, and social structure of the world.

Although I applaud Nel Noddings's focus on care and situations and away from rules and principles, as well as the care she exhibits in detailing her examples, I question her particular analysis of caring because it does not adequately challenge the proximate intimate, because it fears the proximate stranger, and because it ignores the distant stranger (Noddings 1984, 47). An ethics that leaves starving people in a distant land outside the realm of moral consideration is inadequate, especially when, as Claudia Card (1990) notes, we have had a hand in creating these conditions. And a stance that fears the proximate stranger means the caring is not capable of crossing politically and socially imposed barriers, such as racism, to promote change. In discussing the failure of love between white anglo women and women of color, María Lugones writes: "I am particularly interested . . . in those cases in which White/Anglo women . . . ignore us, ostracize us, render us invisible, stereotype us, leave us completely alone, interpret us as crazy. All of this *while we are in their midst*" (Lugones 1987, 7; emphasis in original).

If an ethics of caring is going to be morally successful in replacing an ethics located in principles and duty, particularly within the context of oppression, then it must provide for the possibility of ethical behavior in relation to what is foreign, it must consider analyses of oppression, it must acknowledge a self that is both related and separate, and it must have a vision of, if not a program for, change. In my opinion, care stripped of these elements isn't a caring that benefits us. Further, as long as we exist within a context of oppression, an ethics relevant to us must function under oppression. If we are to have a female-focused caring central to an ethical theory, a theory of value, particularly one functioning in a patriarchal society, I suggest it be the caring of amazons, a caring of those concerned with challenging the inequities resulting from the values of the fathers.

NOTES

An earlier version of this critical discussion of Nel Noddings's work was presented to the joint session of the Radical Philosophy Association and the Society for Women in Philosophy at the Central Division APA meetings in Cincinnati, April 1988. A shortened version was printed in *Hypatia* 5, no. 1 (Spring 1990): 109–114.

1. A good example is the behavior of Sharon Kowalski's father in making decisions about what is good for his daughter. (Sharon Kowalski is a lesbian who in 1983 suffered a brain stem injury after being hit by a drunk driver. Her lover, Karen Thompson, worked tirelessly to help Sharon recover but soon found herself fighting a losing battle to retain access to Sharon against the prejudices of Sharon's father and subsequently the medical and judicial communities [Thompson and Andrzejewski 1988].) In contrast is the care

Karen shows Sharon in her eforts to involve Sharon in decisions that affect her and so undermine the unequal nature of the relationship between one who is able-bodied and one who is paraplegic (ibid., chap. 2–4).

2. Perhaps the most poignant portrayal of this question of trust in terms of therapy and questions of sanity emerges in Kate Millett's *The Loony Bin Trip* (1990).

3. In this respect, although Nel Noddings criticizes existential freedom, I would note that Simone de Beauvoir's existential freedom is not a freedom from commitment; it is profoundly engaging (de Beauvoir 1972).

REFERENCES

Allen, Jeffner. 1984. "Motherhood: The Annihilation of Women." In *Mothering: Essays in Feminist Theory*, ed. Joyce Trebilcot, 315–330. Totowa, N.J.: Rowman and Allanheld. And in *Lesbian Philosophy: Explorations*. Palo Alto, Calif.: Institute of Lesbian Studies, 1986.

Bart, Pauline. 1988. Interview.

Beauvoir, Simone de. 1972. *The Ethics of Ambiguity*. Secaucus, N.J.: Citadel Press.

Cantu, Celinda. 1983. "In Sobriety, You Get Life." In *Out from Under: Sober Dykes and Our Friends*, ed. Jean Swallow, 84–92. San Francisco: Spinsters Ink.

Card, Claudia. 1990. "Caring and Evil." *Hypatia* 5, no. 1 (Spring 1990): 100–108.

Copper, Baba. 1985. "The View from over the Hill: Notes on Ageism between Lesbians." *Trivia* (Summer 1985): 48–63.

———. 1988. *Over the Hill: Reflections on Ageism between Women*. Freedom, Calif.: Crossing Press.

Frye, Marilyn. 1983. "In and Out of Harm's Way." In Frye, *The Politics of Reality: Essays in Feminist Theory*, 52–83. Freedom, Calif.: Crossing Press.

Hoagland, Sarah Lucia. 1988. *Lesbian Ethics: Toward New Value*. Palo Alto, Calif.: Institute of Lesbian Studies.

hooks, bell. 1981. *Ain't I a Woman?: Black Women and Feminism*. Boston: South End Press.

Jaggar, Alison M. 1983. *Feminist Politics and Human Nature*. Totowa, N.J.: Rowman and Allanheld.

Leighton, Anne T. 1987. Interview.

Lorde, Audre. 1982. *Zami*. Freedom, Calif.: Crossing Press.

———. 1984. *Sister/Outsider: Essays and Speeches*. Freedom, Calif.: Crossing Press.

Lugones, María. 1987. "Playfulness, 'World'-Traveling, and Loving Perception." *Hypatia* 2, no. 2 (Summer 1987): 3–19.

Millett, Kate. 1990. *The Loony Bin Trip*. New York: Simon and Schuster.

Noddings, Nel. 1984. *Caring: A Feminine Approach to Ethics and Moral Education.* Berkeley: University of California Press.

———. 1990. "A Response." *Hypatia: A Journal of Feminist Philosophy* 5, no. 1 (Spring 1990): 120–126.

Rich, Adrienne. 1976. *Of Woman Born: Motherhood as Experience and Institution.* New York: W. W. Norton.

Rush, Florence. 1980. *The Best Kept Secret: The Sexual Abuse of Children.* Englewood Cliffs, N.J.: Prentice-Hall.

Russell, Diana E. H. 1984. *Sexual Exploitation: Rape, Child Sexual Abuse, and Workplace Harrassment.* Beverly Hills, Calif.: Sage Publications.

Scheman, Naomi. 1983. "Individualism and the Objects of Psychology." In *Discovering Reality: Feminist Perspectives on Epistemology, Metaphysics, Methodology, and Philosophy of Science,* ed. Sandra Harding and Merrill Hintikka, 225–245. Boston: D. Reidel.

Stanko, Elizabeth. 1985. *Intimate Intrusions: Women's Experience of Male Violence.* Boston: Routledge and Kegan Paul.

Thompson, Karen, and Julie Andrzejewski. 1988. *Why Can't Sharon Kowalski Come Home?* San Francisco: Spinsters/Aunt Lute.

Wittig, Monique, and Sande Zeig. 1979. *Lesbian Peoples: Material for a Dictionary.* New York: Avon.

Bibliography

HISTORY AND REFERENCE

Bar On, Bat-Ami. "Violence against Women: A Bibliography," *American Philosophical Association Newsletter on Feminism and Philosophy* 88, 1 (Nov. 1988): 11–13.

Becker, Lawrence, with Charlotte Becker, eds. *Encyclopedia of Ethics.* New York: Garland, forthcoming 1992.

Daly, Mary, with Jane Caputi. Webster's First New *Intergalactic Wickedary of the English Language.* Boston: Beacon, 1987.

Elwell, Sue Levi. *The Jewish Women's Studies Guide.* 2d ed. Lanham, Md.: University Press of America, 1987.

Giddings, Paula. *When and Where I Enter . . . The Impact of Black Women on Race and Sex in America.* New York: Morrow, 1974.

Grier, Barbara. *The Lesbian in Literature.* (Bibliography). 3d ed., rev. Naiad Press, 1981. (Printed by Iowa City Women's Press).

James, Edward T., Janet Wilson James, and Paul S. Boyer, eds. *Notable American Women: A Biographical Dictionary.* 3 Vols. Cambridge, Mass.: Harvard University Press, 1971.

Kersey, Ethel M., ed. *Women Philosophers: A Bio-Critical Source Book.* New York: Greenwood Press, 1989.

Kuzmack, Linda Gordon. *Woman's Cause: The Jewish Woman's Movement in England and the United States, 1881–1933.* Columbus: Ohio State University Press, 1990.

Laska, Vera. *Women in the Resistance and the Holocaust: The Voices of Eyewitnesses.* Westport, Conn.: Greenwood Press, 1983.

Lerner, Gerda, ed. *Black Women in White America: A Documentary History.* New York: Pantheon, 1972.

———., ed. *The Female Experience: An American Documentary.* Indianapolis: Bobbs-Merrill, 1977.

McKay, Nellie. *Introduction to Afro-American Literature of the Twentieth Century* (Study Guide and Anthology). Madison.: University of Wisconsin Extension, 1988.

Marsh, Margaret. *Anarchist Women, 1870–1920*. Philadelphia: Temple University Press, 1981.

Menage, Gilles. *The History of Women Philosophers*. Trans. Beatrice H. Zedler, Lanham, Md.: University Press of America, 1984.

Moraga, Cherríe. "Third World Women in the United States—By and about Us: A Selected Bibliography," *This Bridge Called My Back: Writings by Radical Women of Color*, ed. Cherríe Moraga and Gloria Anzaldúa (Watertown, Mass.: Persephone Press, 1981), pp. 251–261.

Moulton, Janice, ed. *Philosophy and Feminism: Bibliography of Recent Papers in Philosophy and Feminism*. Produced with the support of the Society for Women in Philosophy and the American Philosophical Association Committee on the Status of Women in the Profession. 1976.

Potter, Clare, ed. *The Lesbian Periodicals Index*. Naiad Press, 1986.

Roberts, JR, comp. *Black Lesbians: An Annotated Bibliography*. Naiad Press, 1981. (Printed by Iowa City Women's Press.)

Schwartz, Judith. *Radical Feminists of Heterodoxy: Greenwich Village 1912–1940*. Lebanon, N.H.: New Victoria, 1982. Rev. ed. Norwich, Vt.: New Victoria, 1986.

Sicherman, Barbara, and Carol Hurd Green, eds., with Ilene Kantrov and Harriette Walker. *Notable American Women/The Modern Period: A Biographical Dictionary*. Cambridge, Mass.: Harvard University Press, 1980.

Tierney, Helen, ed. *Women's Studies Encyclopedia*. Westport, Conn.: Greenwood Press, 1989.

Waithe, Mary Ellen, ed. *A History of Women Philosophers, Vol. I/600 BC–500 AD*. Dortrecht: Martinus Nijhoff, 1987.

Warren, Mary Anne, ed. *The Nature of Woman: An Encyclopedia and Guide to the Literature*. Inverness, Calif.: Edgepress, 1980.

Wittig, Monique, and Sande Zeig. *Lesbian Peoples: Material for a Dictionary*. New York: Avon, 1979.

Uglow, Jennifer S., ed. *The International Dictionary of Women's Biography*. New York: Continuum, 1982.

SELECTED CLASSICS: 1770–1970

Arendt, Hannah [1906–1975]. *The Human Condition*. Chicago: University of Chicago Press, 1958.

Beauvoir, Simone de [1908–1986]. *The Second Sex*. Trans. H. M. Parshley. New York: Knopf, 1952.

———. The Ethics of Ambiguity. Trans. Bernard Frechtman. New York: Philosophical Library, 1948.

Cooper, Anna Julia [1858–1964]. *A Voice from the South*. Xenia, Ohio: Aldine Printing House, 1892.

Douglass, Frederick [1817–1895]. *Frederick Douglass on Women's Rights*. Ed. Philip S. Foner. Westport, Conn.: Greenwood Press, 1976.

Engels, Friedrich [1820–1895]. *The Origin of the Family, Private Property and the State in the Light of the Researches of Lewis H. Morgan.* Trans. Alec West. New York: International Publishers, 1942.

Fuller [Ossoli], (Sarah) Margaret [1810–1850]. *Woman in the Nineteenth Century and Kindred Papers Relating to the Sphere, Condition and Duties, of Woman.* Ed. Arthur B. Fuller. Boston: Jewett, 1855. Reprinted with an Introduction by Bernard Rosenthal. New York: Norton, 1971.

Gage, Matilda Joslyn [1826–1898]. *Woman, Church, and State: The Original Expose of Male Collaboration Against the Female Sex.* (1893). Reprinted with a Foreword by Mary Daly and Introduction by Sally Roesch Wagner. Watertown, Mass.: Persephone Press, 1980.

Gilman [Stetson], Charlotte Perkins [1860–1935]. *Women and Economics: The Economic Factor between Men and Women as a Factor in Social Evolution.* 2d ed. of 1898, ed. Carl N. Degler. New York: Harper & Row, 1966.

———. *Charlotte Perkins Gilman Reader: "The Yellow Wallpaper" and Other Fiction.* Ed. Ann J. Lane. New York: Pantheon, 1980.

———. *Herland.* New York: Pantheon, 1979.

Goldman, Emma [1869–1940]. *Anarchism and Other Essays.* Reprint, with Introduction by Richard Drinnon, of 3d rev. ed. New York: Mother Earth Publishing Association, 1917. New York: Dover, 1969.

Grier, Barbara, and Coletta Reid, eds. *The Lavender Herring: Lesbian Essays from* The Ladder. Baltimore: Diana Press, 1976.

Hurston, Zora Neale [1901–1960]. *Their Eyes Were Watching God.* New York: Lippincott, 1937.

Loewenberg, Bert James, and Ruth Bogin, eds. *Black Women in Nineteenth-Century American Life: Their Words, Their Thoughts, Their Feelings.* University Park: Pennsylvania State University Press, 1976.

Mill, John Stuart [1806–1873], and Harriet Taylor Mill [1808–1858]. *Essays on Sex Equality,* ed. with introductory essay by Alice Rossi. Chicago: University of Chicago Press, 1970.

Rossi, Alice S., ed. *The Feminist Papers: From Adams to de Beauvoir.* New York: Columbia University Press, 1973.

Schneir, Miriam, ed. *Feminism: The Essential Historical Writings.* New York: Random House, 1972.

Schreiner, Olive [1855–1920]. *Woman and Labour.* London: T. Fisher Unwin, 1911.

Stein, Edith [1891–1942]. *Essays on Woman,* Vol. II of *Collected Works,* ed. Dr. L. Gelber and Romaeus Leuven, OCD. Trans. Freda Mary Oben Washington, D.C.: ISC Publications, 1987.

———. *On the Problem of Empathy.* Trans. Waltraut Stein. 2d ed. The Hague: Martinus Nijhoff, 1970.

Weil, Simone [1903–1943]. *Gravity and Grace.* (1st French ed. 1947). Trans. Emma Craufurd. London: Routledge, 1963. Reprint ed. London: Ark, 1987.

———. *The Need for Roots.* New York: G. P. Putnam's Sons, 1952.

———. *Simone Weil: An Anthology.* Ed. Sian Miles. New York: Weidenfeld & Nicolson, 1986.

Wollstonecraft [Godwin], Mary [1759–1797]. *A Vindication of the Rights of Woman: An Authoritative Text, Backgrounds, Criticism*. 2d ed. of 1792, ed. Carol H. Poston. New York: Norton, 1975.

Woolf [née Stephen], (Adeline) Virginia [1881–1941]. *Orlando: A Biography*. New York: Harcourt Brace Jovanovich, 1928. (A fantasy novel about Orlando, who lives through hundreds of years, beginning as a man and concluding as a woman.)

———. *A Room of One's Own*. New York: Harcourt, Brace, & World, 1929.

———. *Three Guineas*. New York: Harcourt Brace Jovanovich, 1938.

ANTHOLOGIES OF RECENT WORK

Allen, Jeffner, ed. *Lesbian Philosophies and Cultures*. Albany: State University of New York Press, 1990.

Allen, Jeffner, and Iris Marion Young, eds. *The Thinking Muse: Feminism and Modern French Philosophy*. Bloomington: Indiana University Press, 1989.

Anzaldúa, Gloria, ed. *Making Face, Making Soul*/Haciendo Caras: *Creative and Critical Perspectives by Women of Color*. San Francisco: Aunt Lute, 1990.

Asian Women United of California. *Making Waves: An Anthology of Writings by and about Asian American Women*. Boston: Beacon, 1989.

Bar On, Bat-Ami, ed. *Engendering Origins: Critical Feminist Readings in Plato and Aristotle* (tentative title). Albany: State University of New York Press, forthcoming 1991.

———, ed. *Modern Engendering: Critical Feminist Essays in Modern Western Philosophy* (tentative title). Albany: State University of New York Press, forthcoming 1991.

Beck, Evelyn Torton, ed. *Nice Jewish Girls: A Lesbian Anthology*. Rev. and updated. Boston: Beacon, 1989. (First published Watertown, Mass.: Persephone, 1982).

Birkby, Phyllis, Bertha Harria, Jill Johnston, Esther Newton, and Jane O'Wyatt, eds. *Amazon Expedition: A Lesbianfeminist Anthology*. New York: Times Change Press, 1973.

Bishop, Sharon, and Marjorie Weinzweig, eds. *Philosophy and Women*. Belmont, Calif.: Wadsworth, 1979.

Brant, Beth. ed. *A Gathering of Spirit: North American Indian Women's Issue*. Amherst, Mass.: Sinister Wisdom, 1983. (*Sinister Wisdom*, no. 22/23).

Browne, Susan E., Debra Connors, and Nanci Stern, eds. *With the Power of Each Breath: A Disabled Women's Anthology*. Pittsburgh: Cleis Press, 1985.

Bunch, Charlotte, and Nancy Myron, eds. *Class and Feminism: A Collection of Essays from* The Furies. Baltimore: Diana Press, 1974.

Curb, Rosemary, and Nancy Manahan, eds. *Lesbian Nuns: Breaking Silence.* Naiad Press, 1985.

Covina, Gina, and Laurel Galana, eds. *The Lesbian Reader: An Amazon Quarterly Anthology.* Oakland, Calif.: Amazon Press, 1975.

Fineman, Martha Albertson, and Nancy Sweet Thomadsen, eds. *At the Boundaries of Law: Feminism and Legal Theory.* New York: Routledge, 1991.

Garry, Ann, and Marilyn Pearsall, eds. *Women, Knowledge, and Reality: Explorations in Feminist Philosophy.* Boston: Unwin Hyman, 1989.

Geok-lin Lim, Shirley, Mayumi Tsutakawa, and Margarita Donnelly, eds. *The Forbidden Stitch: An Asian American Women's Anthology.* Corvallis, Ore.: Calyx Books, 1989.

Gilligan, Carol, Janie Victoria Ward, and Jill McLean Taylor with Betty Bardige. *Mapping the Moral Domain: A Contribution of Women's Thinking to Psychological Theory and Education.* Cambridge, Mass.: Center for the Study of Gender, Education and Human Development, Harvard University Graduate School of Education, 1988.

Gilligan, Carol, Nona P. Lyons, and Trudy J. Hanmer, eds. *Making Connections: The Relational Worlds of Adolescent Girls at Emma Willard School.* Troy, N.Y.: Emma Willard School, 1989.

Gornick, Vivian, and Barbara K. Moran, eds. *Woman in Sexist Society: Studies in Power and Powerlessness.* New York: Basic Books, 1971.

Gould, Carol C., and Marx W. Wartofsky, eds. *Women and Philosophy: Toward A Theory of Liberation.* New York: G. P. Putnam's Sons, 1976.

Hanen, Marsha, and Kai Nielsen, eds. *Science, Morality and Feminist Theory (Canadian Journal of Philosophy,* Supplementary vol. 13). Calgary, Alberta: University of Calgary Press, 1987.

Hibri, Azizah al-, and Margaret A. Simons, eds. *Hypatia Reborn: Essays in Feminist Philosophy.* Bloomington: Indiana University Press, 1990.

Hoagland, Sarah Lucia, and Julia Penelope, eds. *For Lesbians Only: A Separatist Anthology.* London: Onlywomen Press, 1988.

Hull, Gloria T., Patricia Bell Scott, and Barbara Smith, eds. *All the Women Are White, All the Blacks Are Men, But Some of Us Are Brave: Black Women's Studies.* Old Westbury, N.Y.: Feminist Press, 1982.

Jaggar, Alison M., and Paula S. Rothenberg, eds. *Feminist Frameworks: Alternative Theoretical Accounts of the Relations between Women and Men.* New York: McGraw-Hill, 1978, 1984.

Jaggar, Alison M. and Susan R. Bordo, eds. *Gender/Body/Knowledge: Feminist Reconstructions of Being and Knowing.* New Brunswick, N.J.: Rutgers University Press, 1989.

Kaye/Kantrowitz, Melanie and Irena Klepfisz, eds. *The Tribe of Dina: A Jewish Women's Anthology (Sinister Wisdom* no. 29/30). Montpelier, Vt: Sinister Wisdom, 1986.

Kittay, Eva Feder, and Diana T. Meyers, eds. *Women and Moral Theory.* Totowa, N.J.: Rowman & Littlefield, 1987.

Koedt, Ann, Ellen Levine, and Anite Rapone, eds. *Radical Feminism*. New York: Quadrangle, 1973.

Lederer, Laura, ed. *Take Back the Night: Women on Pornography*. New York: Morrow, 1980.

Leidholdt, Dorchen, and Janice G. Raymond, eds. *The Sexual Liberals and the Attack on Feminism*. New York: Pergamon, 1990.

Linden, Robin Ruth, Darlene R. Pagano, Diana E. H. Russell, and Susan Leigh Star, eds. *Against Sadomasochism: A Radical Feminist Analysis*. East Palto Alto, Calif.: Frog in the Well, 1982.

Lobel, Kerry, ed. *Naming the Violence: Speaking Out about Lesbian Battering*. Seattle: Seal Press, 1986.

McKay, Nellie, ed. *Critical Essays on Toni Morrison*. Boston: G. K. Hall, 1988.

Marks, Elaine and Isabelle de Courtivron, eds. *New French Feminisms: An Anthology*. Amherst: University of Massachusetts Press, 1980.

Miner, Valerie, and Helen E. Longino, eds. *Competition: A Feminist Taboo?* New York: Feminist Press, 1987.

Moraga, Cherríe, and Gloria Anzaldúa, eds. *This Bridge Called My Back: Writings by Radical Women of Color*. Watertown, Mass.: Persephone, 1981.

Morgan, Robin, ed. *Sisterhood Is Powerful: An Anthology of Writings from the Women's Liberation Movement*. New York: Vintage, 1970.

Myron, Nancy, and Charlotte Bunch, eds. *Lesbianism and the Women's Movement*. Baltimore: Diana Press, 1975.

Nebraska Sociological Feminist Collective. *A Feminist Ethic for Social Science Research*. Lewiston, N.Y.: Edwin Mellen Press, 1988.

Pearsall, Marilyn, ed. *Women and Values: Readings in Recent Feminist Philosophy*. Belmont, Calif.: Wadsworth, 1986.

Pierce, Christine, and Donald VanDeVeer, eds. *AIDS: Ethics and Public Policy*. Belmont, Calif.: Wadsworth, 1988.

Quest Collective. *Building Feminist Theory: Essays from* Quest. New York: Longman, 1981.

Rhode, Deborah L., ed. *Theoretical Perspectives on Sexual Difference*. New Haven, Conn.: Yale University Press, 1990.

Saxton, Marsha, and Florence Howe, eds. *With Wings: An Anthology of Literature by and about Women with Disabilities*. New York: Feminist Press, 1987.

Schoenfielder, Lisa, and Barb Wieser, eds. *Shadow on a Tightrope: Writings by Women on Fat Oppression*. Iowa City: Aunt Lute, 1983.

Stambolian, George, and Elaine Marks, eds. *Homosexualities and French Literature: Cultural Contexts/Critical Texts*. Ithaca, N.Y.: Cornell University Press, 1979.

Trebilcot, Joyce, ed. *Mothering: Essays in Feminist Theory*. Totowa, N.J.: Rowman & Allanheld, 1984.

Vetterling-Braggin, Mary, ed. *"Femininity," "Masculinity," and "Andro-*

gyny": *A Modern Philosophical Discussion.* Totowa, N.J.: Littlefield, Adams, 1982.

————, ed. Sexist Languge: A Modern Philosophical Analysis. Totowa, N.J.: Littlefield, Adams, 1981.

Vetterling-Braggin, Mary, Frederick A. Elliston, and Jane English, eds. *Feminism and Philosophy.* Totowa, N.J.: Littlefield, Adams, 1977.

ARTICLES: 1960–1990

Addelson, Kathryn Pyne (Parsons). "Moral Passages," in *Women and Moral Theory,* ed. Eva Feder Kittay and Diana T. Meyers (Totowa, N.J.: Rowman & Littlefield, 1987), pp. 87–110.

————. "Moral Revolution," in *The Prism of Sex: Essays in the Sociology of Knowledge,* ed. Julia Sherman and Evelyn Torton Beck (Madison: University of Wisconsin Press, 1977), pp. 189–227.

————. "Words and Lives," *Signs* 7, 1 (Autumn 1981): 187–199. (Contribution to a symposium on Adrienne Rich, "Compulsory Heterosexuality and Lesbian Existence," *Signs* 5, 4 (Summer 1980): 631–660.)

Allen, Jeffner. "An Introduction to Patriarchal Existentialism: A Proposal for a Way out of Existential Patriarchy," in *The Thinking Muse: Feminism and Modern French Philosophy,* ed. Jeffner Allen and Iris Marion Young (Albany: State University of New York Press, 1989), pp. 71–84.

————. "Lesbian Economics," *Trivia: A Journal of Ideas* 8 (Winter 1986): 37–53.

————. "Poetic Politics: How the Amazons Took the Acropolis," *Hypatia* 3, 2 (Summer 1988): 107–122.

————. "Women Who Beget Women Must Thwart Major Sophisms," in *Women, Knowledge, and Reality: Explorations in Feminist Philosophy,* ed. Ann Garry and Marilyn Pearsall (Boston: Unwin Hyman, 1989), pp. 37–46.

Baier, Annette C. "Hume, The Women's Moral Theorist?" in *Women and Moral Theory,* ed. Eva Feder Kittay and Diana T. Meyers (Totowa, N.J.: Rowman & Littlefield, 1987), pp. 37–55.

————. "The Need for More than Justice," in *Science, Morality and Feminist Theory,* ed. Marsha Hanen and Kai Nielsen (Calgary, Alberta: University of Calgary Press, 1987), pp. 41–56. (*Canadian Journal of Philosophy,* Supp. vol. 13.)

————. "Trust and Antitrust," *Ethics* 96, 2 (Jan. 1986): 231–260.

————. "What Do Women Want in a Moral Theory?" *Nous* 19, 1 (Mar. 1985): 53–63.

————. "Why Honesty Is a Hard Virtue," in *Identity, Character, and Morality: Essays in Moral Psychology,* ed. Owen Flanagan and Amélie Oksenberg Rorty (Cambridge, Mass.: MIT Press, 1990).

Bar On, Bat-Ami. "Balancing Feminism and the Philosophical Canon," *American Philosophical Association Newsletter on Feminism and Philosophy* (Apr. 1988): 20–25.

———. "Could There Be a Humean Sex-Neutral Idea of Man?" *Philosophy Research Archives* 18 (1987–88): 367–377.

———. "Feminism and Sadomasochism: Self Critical Notes," in *Against Sadomasochism,* ed. Robin Ruth Linden et al. (East Palo Alto, Calif.: Frog in the Well, 1982), pp. 72–82.

———. "Holocaust and Resistance," in *Inquiries into Values: The Inaugural Session of the Inernational Society for Value Inquiry,* ed. Sander H. Lee (Lewiston, N.Y.: Edwin Mellen Press, 1988), pp. 495–508.

———. "Notes on a Feminist Economics," *Quest: A Feminist Quarterly* 2, 4 (Spring 1976): 46–58.

———. "*Platoon* and the Failure of War," in *Sexual Politics and Popular Culture,* ed. Diane Raymond (Bowling Green, Ohio: Bowling Green University Press, 1990).

———. "Transforming the Philosophy Curriculum: Studying Sexual Violence," *APA Newsletter on Feminism and Philosophy* 88, 1 (Nov. 1988): 13–15.

———. "Violence against Women: Philosophical Literature Overview," *APA Newsletter on Feminism and Philosophy* 88, 1 (Nov. 1988): 8–11.

Bar On, Bat-Ami, with Caroline Sparks and Cherlyn B. Paul. "Designs for Income Sharing," *Quest* 2, 3 (Winter 1976): 58–67.

Bar On, Bat-Ami, and other members of Community Action Strategies to Stop Rape. "A Rape Prevention Program in an Urban Area," *Signs: Journal of Women in Culture and Society* 5, 3 (Spring 1980): s238–s241.

Bartky, Sandra Lee. "Feminine Masochism and the Politics of Personal Transformation," in *Hypatia Reborn: Essays in Feminist Philosophy,* ed. Azizah Y. al-Hibri and Margaret A. Simons (Bloomington: Indiana University Press, 1990), pp. 115–134.

———. "On Psychological Oppression," in *Philosophy and Women,* ed. Sharon Bishop and Marjorie Weinzweig (Belmont, Calif.: Wadsworth, 1979), pp. 33–41.

———. "A Research Agenda for Philosophy," *APA Newsletter on Feminism and Philosophy* 89, 1 (Fall 1989): 78–81.

———. "Shame and Gender: Contribution to a Phenomenology of Oppression." Working Paper no. 7. Milwaukee, Wis.: Center for 20th Century Studies, 1989.

———. "Toward a Phenomenology of Feminist Consciousness," in *Feminism and Philosophy,* ed. Mary Vetterling-Braggin et al. Totowa, N.J.: Littlefield, Adams, 1977.

Basehart, Mary Catherine. "Edith Stein's Philosophy of Woman and of Women's Education," *Hypatia* 4, 1 (Spring 1989): 120–131.

Bergmann, Merrie. "How Many Feminists Does It Take to Make a Joke? Sexist Humor and What's Wrong with It," *Hypatia* 1, 1 (Spring 1986): 63–82.

Bishop, Sharon. "Connections and Guilt," *Hypatia* 2, 1 (Winter 1987): 7–23.

Card, Claudia. "Caring and Evil," *Hypatia* 1, 1 (Spring 1990): 101–108. (Contribution to a symposium on Nel Noddings, *Caring: A Feminine Approach to Ethics and Moral Education* [Berkeley: University of California Press, 1989].)

———. "Defusing the Bomb: Lesbian Ethics and Horizontal Violence," *Lesbian Ethics* 3, 3 (Summer 1989): 91–100.

———. "Female Friendship: Separations and Continua," *Hypatia* 3, 2 (Summer 1988): 123–130.

———. "Fidelity," in *Encyclopedia of Ethics*, ed. Lawrence Becker with Charlotte Becker (New York: Garland, forthcoming 1992).

———. "Finding My Voice: Reminiscence of an Outlaw," in *Falling in Love with Wisdom* (tentative title), ed. Robert G. Shoemaker and David D. Karnos (New York: Oxford University Press, forthcoming 1991).

———. "Gender and Moral Luck," in *Identity, Character, and Morality: Essays in Moral Psychology*, ed. Owen Flanagan and Amélie Oksenberg Rorty (Cambridge, Mass.: MIT Press, 1990), pp. 197–216.

———. "Gratitude and Obligation," *American Philosophical Quarterly* 25, 2 (April 1988): 115–127.

———. "Intimacy and Responsibility: What Lesbians Do," in *At the Boundaries of Law: Feminism and Legal Theory*, ed. Martha Fineman and Nancy Thomadsen (New York: Routledge Press, 1991), pp. 77–94.

———. "Lesbian Attitudes and *The Second Sex*," in *Hypatia Reborn: Essays in Feminist Philosophy*, ed. Azizah Y. al-Hibri and Margaret A. Simons (Bloomington: Indiana University Press, 1990), pp. 290–299.

———. "Lesbian Battering," *American Philosophical Association Newsletter on Feminism and Philosophy* 88, 1 (Nov. 1988): 3–7.

———. "Lesbian Ethics," in *Encyclopedia of Ethics*, ed. Lawrence Becker with Charlotte Becker (New York: Garland, forthcoming 1992).

———. "Oppression and Resistance: Frye's Politics of Reality," *Hypatia* 1, 1 (April 1986): 149–166.

———. "Pluralist Lesbian Separatism," in *Lesbian Philosophies and Cultures*, ed. Jeffner Allen (Albany: State University of New York Press, 1990), pp. 125–141.

———. "Rape as a Terrorist Institution," in *Violence, Terrorism, and Justice*, ed. Christopher Morris and R. G. Frey (Cambridge, Eng.: Cambridge University Press, forthcoming 1992).

———. "Removing Veils of Ignorance" (abstract), *Nous* 25, 2 (forthcoming Apr. 1991).

———. "Sadomasochism and Sexual Preference," *Journal of Social Philosophy* 9, 2 (Summer 1984): 42–52.

———. "Why Homophobia?" *Hypatia* 5, 3 (Fall 1990): 110–117.

———. "Women's Voices and Ethical Ideals: Must We Mean What We Say?" *Ethics* 99, 1 (Oct. 1988): 125–135. (Review essay on *Women and Moral Theory*, ed. Eva Feder Kittay and Diana T. Meyers [Totowa, N.J.: Rowman & Littlefield, 1987].)

Davion, Victoria M. "Competition, Recognition and Approval-Seeking," *Hypatia* 3, 3 (Summer 1988): 165–66.

———. "Do Good Feminists Compete?" *Hypatia* 2, 2 (Summer 1987), 55–63.

———. "Pacifism and Care," *Hypatia* 5, 1 (Spring 1990): 90–100.

English, Jane. "Review Essay: Philosophy," *Signs* 3, 4 (Summer 1978): 823–831.

———. "Sex Equality in Sport," *Philosophy and Public Affairs* 7, 3 (Spring 1978): 269–277.

Flanagan, Owen, and Kathryn Jackson. "Justice, Care, and Gender: The Kohlberg-Gilligan Debate Revisted," *Ethics* 97, 3 (Apr. 1987): 622–637.

Foot, Philippa. "The Problem of Abortion and the Doctrine of the Double Effect," *Virtues and Vices and Other Essays in Moral Philosophy* (Berkeley: University of California Press, 1978), pp. 19–32.

Friedman, Marilyn. "Autonomy and the Split-Level Self," *Southern Journal of Philosophy* 24, 1 (Spring 1986): 19–35.

———. "Beyond Caring: The De-Moralization of Gender," in *Science, Morality and Feminist Theory*, ed. Marsha Hanen and Kai Nielsen (Calgary, Alberta: University of Calgary Press, 1987), pp. 87–110. (*Canadian Journal of Philosophy*, Supp. vol. 13)

———. "Care and Context in Moral Reasoning," in *Women and Moral Theory*, ed. Eva Feder Kittay and Diana T. Meyers (Totowa, N.J.: Rowman & Littlefield, 1987), pp. 190–204.

———. "Feminism and Modern Friendship: Dislocating the Community," *Ethics* 99 (Jan. 1989): 275–290.

———. "Friendship and Moral Growth," *Journal of Value Inquiry* 33, 1 (1989): 3–13.

———. "The Impracticality of Impartiality," *Journal of Philosophy* 86, 11 (Nov. 1989): 645–646.

———. "Moral Integrity and the Deferential Wife," *Philosophical Studies* 47, 1 (Jan. 1985): 141–150.

———. "Partiality," in *Encyclopedia of Ethics*, ed. Lawrence Becker with Charlotte Becker (New York: Garland, forthcoming 1992).

———. "Welfare Cuts and the Ascendance of Market Patriarchy," *Hypatia* 13, 2 (Summer 1988): 145–149.

———. "Women in Poverty and Welfare Equity," in *Poverty, Justice, and the Law: New Essays on Needs, Rights, and Obligations*, ed. George R. Lucas, Jr. (Lanham, Md.: University Press of America, 1977), pp. 91–104.

———, and Larry May. "Harming Women as a Group," *Social Theory and Practice* 11, 2 (Summer 1985): 207–234.

Frye, Marilyn. "History and Responsibility," in *Hypatia Reborn: Essays in Feminist Philosophy*, ed. Azizah Y. al-Hibri and Margaret A. Simons (Bloomington: Indiana University Press, 1990), pp. 300–304.

———. "Lesbian Perspectives on Women's Studies," *Sinister Wisdom* 14 (Fall 1980): 3–7.

———. "Lesbian 'Sex,' " *Sinister Wisdom* 35 (Summer/Fall, 1988): 46–54.

————. "Male Chauvinism—A Conceptual Analysis," in *Philosophy and Sex*, ed. Robert Baker and Frederick Elliston (1st ed. only; Buffalo, N.Y.: Prometheus, 1975), pp. 65–79.

————. "On Second Thought . . .," *Radical Teacher* 17 (Nov. 1980): 37–38.

————. "A Piece of the Pie," *Quest: A Feminist Quarterly* 3, 3 (Winter 1976–77): 28–35.

————. "The Possibility of Feminist Theory," in *Perspectives on Sexual Difference*, ed. Deborah Rhode (New Haven, Conn.: Yale University Press, 1990), pp. 174–184.

————. "The Possibility of Lesbian Community," *Lesbian Ethics* 4, 1 (Spring 1990): 84–87.

————, and Carolyn Shafer. "Rape and Respect," in *Feminism and Philosophy*, ed. Mary Vetterling-Braggin et al. (Totowa, N.J.: Littlefield, Adams, 1977), pp. 333–346.

Ginzberg, Ruth. "Feminism, Rationality, and Logic," *American Philosophical Association Newsletter on Feminism and Philosophy* 88, 2 (Mar. 1989): 34–39.

————. "Healing and Gender," in *Search of Science: Nursing's Pursuit of Its Scientific Identity*, ed. Anna Omery and Christine Kasper. (Berkeley: University of California Press, forthcoming).

————. "Reply to [Neil] Jahren ["Comments on 'Uncovering Gynocentric Science' "]," *Hypatia* 5, 1 (Spring 1990): 178–180.

————. "Teaching Feminist Logic," *APA Newsletter on Feminism and Philosophy* 88, 2 (Mar. 1989): 58–62.

————. "Uncovering Gynocentric Science," *Hypatia* 2, 3 (Fall 1987): 89–105.

Harding, Sandra G. "Feminism: Reform or Revolution?" in *Women and Philosophy*, ed. Carol C. Gould and Marx W. Wartofsky (New York: G. P. Putnam's Sons, 1976), pp. 271–284.

Held, Virginia. "Birth and Death," *Ethics* 99, 2 (Jan. 1989): 362–388.

————. "Feminism and Moral Theory," in *Women and Moral Theory*, ed. Eva Feder Kittay and Diana T. Meyers (Totowa, N.J.: Rowman & Littlefield, 1987), pp. 11–128.

————. "Non-contractual Society," *Science, Morality and Feminist Theory* (Calgary, Alberta: University of Calgary, 1987), pp. 111–137. (*Canadian Journal of Philosophy*, Supp. vol. 13.)

Hoagland, Sarah. "Androcentric Rhetoric in Sociobiology," *Women's Studies International Quarterly* 3, 2/3 (1980): 285–293.

————. "Coercive Consensus," *Sinister Wisdom* 6 (Summer 1978): 86–92.

————. "Dear Julia: On Racism and Separatism," *Lesbian Ethics* 1, 2 (Spring 1985): pp. 68–73.

————. " 'Femininity,' Resistance, and Sabotage," in *"Femininity," "Masculinity," and "Androgyny": A Modern Philosophical Discussion*, ed. Mary Vetterling-Braggin (Totowa, N.J.: Littlefield, Adams, 1982), pp. 85–98.

————. "Lesbian Ethics: Some Thoughts on Power in Our Interactions," *Lesbian Ethics* 2, 1 (Spring 1986): 5–32.

————. "Moral Agency under Oppression," *Trivia* 9 (Fall 1986): 73–90.

————. "Moral Agency under Oppression: Part II: Praise and Blame," *Trivia* 10 (Spring 1987): 24–40.

————. "Moral Agency under Oppression, Part III: Playing among Boundaries," *Trivia* 11 (Fall 1987): 49–65.

————. "A Note on a Bind," *APA Newsletter on Feminism and Philosophy* 88, 3 (June 1989): 39.

————. "A Note on the Logic of Protection and Predation," *APA Newsletter on Feminism and Philosophy* 88, 1 (Nov. 1988): 7–8.

————. "On the Re-education of Sophie," in *Women's Studies: An Interdisciplinary Collection.* Westport, Conn.: Greenwood, 1978.

————. "Sadism, Masochism, and Lesbian-Feminism," in *Against Sadomasochism,* ed. Robin Ruth Linden et al. (East Palo Alto: Frog in the Well Press, 1982), pp. 153–163.

————. "Violence, Victimization, Violation," *Sinister Wisdom* 15 (Fall 1980): 70–72.

————. "Vulnerability and Power," *Sinister Wisdom* 19 (Winter 1982): 13–23.

Houston, Barbara. "Caring and Exploitation," *Hypatia* 5, 1 (Spring 1990): 115–119. (Contribution to a symposium on Nel Noddings, *Caring: A Feminine Approach to Ethics and Moral Education* [Berkeley: University of California Press, 1984].)

————. "Rescuing Womanly Virtues: Some Dangers of Moral Reclamation," in *Science, Morality and Feminist Theory,* ed. Marsha Hanen and Kai Nielsen (Calgary, Alberta: University of Calgary, 1987), pp. 237–262. (*Canadian Journal of Philosophy,* Supp. vol. 13.)

Jaggar, Alison M. "Abortion and a Woman's Right to Decide," in *Women and Philosophy,* ed. Carol C. Gould and Marx W. Wartofsky (New York: G. P. Putnam's sons, 1976), pp. 347–360.

————. "Feminist Ethics," in *Encyclopedia of Ethics,* ed. Lawrence Becker with Charlotte Becker (New York: Garland, forthcoming 1992).

————. "Feminist Ethics: Some Issues for the Nineties," *Journal of Social Philosophy* 20, 1–2 Spring/Fall 1989): 91–107.

————. "Gendered Thinking and Nuclear Politics," in *Nuclear War: Philosophical Perspectives,* ed. Michael Fox and Leo Groarke (New York: Peter Lang, 1985), pp. 173–177.

————. "How Can Philosophy Be Feminist?" *APA Newsletter on Feminism and Philosophy* 2 (Apr. 1988): 4–8.

————. "Love and Knowledge: Emotion in Feminist Epistemology," *Inquiry* 32, 2 (June 1989): 151–176.

————. "On Sexual Equality," *Ethics* 84, 4 (July 1974): 275–291.

————. "Political Philosophies of Women's Liberation," *Feminism and Philosophy,* ed. Mary Vetterling-Braggin et al. (Totowa, N.J.: Littlefield, Adams, 1977), pp. 5–21.

————. "Prostitution," in *Philosophy of Sex: Contemporary Readings,* ed. Alan Soble (Totowa: N.J.: Littlefield, Adams, 1980), pp. 348–368.

————. "Relaxing the Limits on Preferential Treatment," *Social Theory and Practice* 4, 2 (Spring 1977): 227–235.

————. "Sex Inequality and Bias in Sex Difference Research," in *Science, Morality and Feminist Theory*, ed. Marsha Hanen and Kai Nielsen (Calgary, Alberta: University of Calgary, 1987), pp. 25–39. (*Canadian Journal of Philosophy*, Supp. vol. 13.)

————. "Sexual Difference and Sexual Equality," in *Theoretical Perspectives on Sexual Difference*, ed. Deborah L. Rhode (New Haven, Conn.: Yale University Press, 1990), pp. 239–254.

————. "Tenure, Academic Freedom, and Competence," *Philosophical Forum* 10, 2–4 (Winter–Summer 1978–1979): 360–370.

Ketchum, Sara Ann. "The Good, the Bad and the Perverted: Sexual Paradigms Revisited," *Philosophy of Sex: Contemporary Readings*, ed. Alan Soble. (Totowa, N.J.: Littlefield, Adams, 1980), pp. 139–157.

————. "Moral Redescription and Political Self-Deception," in *Sexist Language: A Modern Philosophical Analysis*, ed. Mary Vetterling-Braggin (Totowa, N.J.: Littlefield, Adams, 1981), pp. 279–289. (Response to Laurence Thomas, "Sexism and Racism: Some Conceptual Differences," *Ethics* 90, 2 (Jan. 1980): 239–250.)

Longino, Helen E. "The Ideology of Competition," in *Competition: A Feminist Taboo?* ed. Valerie Miner and Helen E. Longino (New York: Feminist Press, 1987), pp. 248–258.

Lugones, María. "Hablando cara a cara/Speaking Face to Face: An Exploration of Ethnocentric Racism," in *Making Face, Making Soul*/Haciendo Caras: *Creative and Critical Perspectives by Women of Color*, ed. Gloria Anzaldúa (San Francisco: Aunt Lute, 1990), pp. 46–54.

————. "Hispaneando y lesbiando: On Sarah Hoagland's *Lesbian Ethics*," *Hypatia* 5, 3 (1990): 138–146.

————. "Playfulness, 'World'-Travelling, and Loving Perception," *Hypatia* 2, 2 (Summer 1987): 3–19.

————. "Racism and Pedagogy," *Breaking Ground* 6 (Northfield, Minn.: Carleton College) (Spring 1984): 38–42.

————. "Structure/AntiStructure and Agency under Oppression," *Journal of Philosophy* 87, 10 (Oct. 1990): 500–507.

Lugones, María Cristina and Elizabeth V. Spelman. "Competition, Compassion, and Community: Models for a Feminist Ethos," in *Competition: A Feminist Taboo?* ed. Valerie Miner and Helen E. Longino (New York: Feminist Press, 1987), pp. 234–247.

————. "Have We Got a Theory for You! Feminist Theory, Cultural Imperalism and the Demand for "the Woman's Voice," in *Hypatia Reborn: Essays in Feminist Philosophy*, ed. Azizah Y. al-Hibri and Margaret A. Simons (Bloomington: Indiana University Press, 1990), pp. 18–33.

McFall, Lynne. "Bitter Love," *Story* 39 1 (forthcoming Winter 1991).

————. "Happiness, Rationality, and Individual Ideals," *Review of Metaphysics* 37, 3 (March 1984): 595–613.

———. "Integrity," *Ethics* 98, 1 (Oct. 1987): 5–19.

McKay, Nellie. "Afterword" to reprint of Jo Sinclair, *The Changelings* (New York: Feminist Press, 1986), pp. 323–337.

———. "Afterword" to reprint of Louise Meriwether, *Daddy Was a Number Runner* (New York: Feminist Press, 1986), pp. 209–234.

———. "Black Woman—White University," *Women's Studies International Quarterly* 6, 2 (Summer 1983): 143–147.

———. "Black Women's Autobiographies—Literature, History, and the Politics of Self," *Hurricane Alice–A Feminist Review* 3, 4 (Fall 1986): 8–9.

———. "Introduction" to reprint of Ann Petry, *The Narrows* (Boston: Beacon, 1988), pp. vii–xx.

———. "Response to 'The Philosophical Bases of Feminist Literary Criticism,' by Ellen Messer Davidow," *New Literary History* 19, 1 (Autumn 1987): 161–168.

———. "What Were They Saying? Black Women Playwrights of the Harlem Renaissance," in *The Harlem Renaissance Re-Examined*, ed. Victor Kramer (New York: A.M.S. Press, 1987).

Moody-Adams, Michele. "On the Alleged Methodological Infirmity of Ethics," *American Philosophical Quarterly* 27, 3 (July 1990): 225–235.

———. "On the Old Saw That Character Is Destiny," in *Identity, Character, and Morality: Essays in Moral Psychology*, ed. Owen Flanagan and Amélie Oksenberg Rorty (Cambridge, Mass.: MIT Press, 1990).

Moulton, Janice. "A Paradigm of Philosophy: The Adversary Method," in *Discovering Reality: Feminist Perspectives on Epistemology, Metaphysics, Methodology, and Philosophy of Science*, ed. Sandra Harding and Merrill B. Hintikka (Dordrecht: Reidel, 1983), pp. 149–164.

———. "The Myth of the Neutral 'Man,'" *Feminism and Philosophy*, ed. Mary Vetterling-Braggin et al. (Totowa, N.J.: Littlefield, Adams, 1977), pp. 124–137.

———. "Review Essay: Philosophy," *Signs* 2, 2 (Winter 1976): 422–433.

———. "Sex and Reference," *Philosophy and Sex*, ed. Robert Baker and Frederick Elliston (1st ed. only; Buffalo, N.Y.: Prometheus, 1975), pp. 34–44. Reprinted in *Sexist Language*, ed. Mary Vetterling-Braggin (Totowa, N.J.: Littlefield, Adams, 1981), pp. 183–193.

———. "Sexual Behavior: Another Position," *Journal of Philosophy* 73, 16 (1976): 537–546.

Noddings, Nel. "Ethics from the Standpoint of Women," in *Theoretical Perspectives on Sexual Difference*, ed. Deborah L. Rhode (New Haven, Conn.: Yale University Press, 1990), pp. 160–173.

———. "A Response [to Claudia Card, Sarah Hoagland, and Barbara Houston on Nel Noddings, *Caring*]," *Hypatia* 5, 1 (Spring 1990): 120–126.

O'Neill, Onora. "How Do We Know When Opportunities Are Equal?" *Women and Philosophy*, ed. Carol C. Gould and Marx W. Wartofsky (New York: G. P. Putnams's Sons, 1976), pp. 334–346.

Pierce, Christine. "AIDS and *Bowers v. Hardwick*," *Journal of Social Philosophy* 20, 3 (Winter 1989): 21–32.

———. "Can Animals Be Liberated?" *Philosophical Studies* 36, 1 (July 1979): 69–75.

———. "Equality: *Republic* V," *Monist* 57, 1 (Jan. 1973): 1–11.

———. "Eros and Epistemology," in *Critical Feminist Essays in the History of Western Philosophy,* ed. Bat-Ami Bar On. Albany: State University of New York Press, forthcoming.

———. "Natural Law Language and Women," *Woman in Sexist Society,* ed. Vivian Gornick et al. (New York: Basic Books, 1971; New American Library paperback, 1972), pp. 242–258.

———. "Review Essay: Philosophy," *Signs* 1, 2 (Winter 1975): 487–503.

Pierce, Christine, and Margery L. Collins. "Holes and Slime: Sexism in Sartre's Psychoanalysis," *Women and Philosophy,* ed. Carol C. Gould and Marx W. Wartofsky (New York: G. P. Putnam's Sons, 1976), pp. 112–127.

Pierce, Christine, and Sara Ann Ketchum. "Implicit Racism," *Analysis* 36, 2 (Jan. 1976): 91–95.

———. "Rights and Responsibilities," *Journal of Medicine and Philosophy* 6, 2 (Aug. 1981): 271–279.

———. "Separatism and Sexual Relationships," in *Philosophy and Women,* ed. Sharon Hill and Marjorie Weinzweig (Belmont, Calif.: Wadsworth, 1978), pp. 163–171.

Piper, Adrian M. S. "Higher Order Discrimination," in *Identity, Character, and Morality: Essays in Moral Psychology,* ed. Owen Flanagan and Amélie Oksenberg Rorty (Cambridge, Mass.: MIT Press, 1990).

———. "Moral Theory and Moral Alienation," *Journal of Philosophy* 84, 2 (Feb. 1987): 102–118.

———. "Pseudorationality," in *Perspectives on Self-Deception,* ed. Amélie Oksenberg Rorty and Brian P. McLaughlin (Berkeley: University of California Press, 1988), pp. 297–323.

———. "Two Conceptions of the Self," *Philosophical Studies* 48, 2 (Sept. 1985): 173–197.

Rich, Adrienne. "Compulsory Heterosexuality and Lesbian Existence," *Signs* 5, 4 (Summer 1980): 631–660.

———. "Women and Honor: Some Notes on Lying," *On Lies, Secrets, and Silence: Selected Prose 1966–1978* (New York: Norton, 1979), pp. 185–194.

Ringelheim, Joan. "Women and the Holocaust: A Reconsideration of Research," *Signs* 10, 4 (Summer 1985): 741–761.

Rumsey, Jean. "Constructing Maternal Thinking," *Hypatia* 5, 3 (Fall 1990): 125–131.

———. "The Development of Characer in Kantian Moral Theory," *Journal of the History of Philosophy* 27, 2 (Apr. 1979): 247–265.

Russ, Joanna. "The New Misandry," in *Amazon Expedition: A Lesbian-feminist Anthology,* ed. Phyllis Birkby, Bertha Harris, Esther Newton, and Jane O'Wyatt (New York: Times Change Press, 1973), pp. 27–33.

Scheman, Naomi. "Individualism and the Objects of Psychology," in *Discovering Reality: Feminist Perspectives on Epistemology, Metaphysics,*

Methodology, and Philosophy of Science, ed. Sandra Harding and Merrill B. Hintikka (Dordrecht: Reidel, 1983), pp. 225–244.

Simons, Margaret A. "Racism and Feminism: A Schism in Sisterhood," *Feminist Studies* 5, 2 (Summer 1979): 384–401.

———. "Two Interviews with Simone de Beauvoir," *Hypatia* 3, 3 (Winter 1989): 11–27.

Simons, Margaret A. "Racism and Feminism: A Schism in Sisterhood," *Feminist Studies* 5, 2 (Summer 1979): 384–401.

Spelman, Elizabeth V. "Anger and Insubordination," in *Women, Knowledge, and Reality: Explorations in Feminist Philosophy,* ed. Ann Garry and Marilyn Pearsall (Boston: Unwin Hyman, 1989), pp. 263–273.

———. "Aristotle and the Politicization of the Soul," in *Discovering Reality: Feminist Perspectives on Epistemology, Metaphysics, Methodology, and the Philosophy of Science,* ed. Sandra Harding and Merrill B. Hintikka (Dordrecht: Reidel, 1983), pp. 17–30.

———. "Combatting the Marginalization of Black Women in the Classroom," *Women's Studies Quarterly* 10, 2 (Summer 1982): 15–16.

———. "On Treating Persons as Persons," *Ethics* 88, 2 (Jan. 1978): 150–161.

———. "Plato on Women," *APA Newsletter on Feminism and Philosophy* 88, 3 (June 1989): 18–21.

———. "Theories of Race and Gender/The Erasure of Black Women," *Quest* 5, 4 (Spring 1982): 36–62.

———. "Woman as Body: Ancient and Contemporary Views," *Feminist Studies* 8, 1 (Spring 1982): 109–131.

Spelman, Elizabeth V., and Maria Cristina Lugones, "Competition, Compassion, and Community: Models for a Feminist Ethos," in *Competition: A Feminist Taboo?* ed. Valerie Miner and Helen E. Longino (New York: Feminist Press, 1987), pp. 234–247.

———. "Have We Got a Theory for You! Feminist Theory, Cultural Imperialism, and the Demand for the Woman's Voice." *Hypatia Reborn: Essays in Feminist Philosophy,* ed. Azizah Y. al-Hibri and Margaret A. Simons (Bloomington: Indiana University Press, 1990), pp. 18–33.

Thomas, Laurence. "Abortion, Slavery, and the Law: A Study in Moral Character," *Abortion: Moral and Legal Perspectives,* ed. Jay Garfield and Patricia Hennessey (Amherst: University of Massachusetts Press, 1984), pp. 227–237.

———. "Jews, Blacks, and Group Autonomy," *Social Theory and Practice* 14, 1 (Spring 1988): 55–69.

———. "Liberalism and the Holocaust: An Essay on Trust and the Black-Jewish Relationship," in *Echoes from the Holocaust: Philosophical Reflections on a Dark Time,* ed. Alan Rosenberg and Gerald E. Myers (Philadelphia: Temple University Press, 1988), pp. 105–117.

———. "Sexism and Racism: Some Conceptual Differences," *Ethics* 90, 2 (Jan. 1980): 239–250.

Thomson, Judith Jarvis. "A Defense of Abortion," *Philosophy and Public Affairs* 1, 1 (1971): 47–66.

Trebilcot, Joyce. " 'But Then What Is Liberation?' Hortense and Gladys on Sex," *Lesbian Ethics* 2, 3 (Summer 1987): 60–62.

——. "Conceiving Women: Notes on the Logic of Feminism," *Sinister Wisdom* 11 (Fall 1979): 43–50.

——. "A Course about Mothering and the Right to Resist It," *Women's Studies Quarterly* 11, 4 (Winter 1983): 32–34.

——. "Craziness and the Concept of Rape," *Womanspirit* 9, 23 (Winter Solstice 1982): 28–30.

——. "Craziness as a Source of Separatism," in *For Lesbians Only,* ed. Sarah Lucia Hoagland and Julia Penelope (London: Onlywomen Press, 1988), pp. 196–199.

——. "Dyke Economics: Hortense and Gladys on Money," *Lesbian Ethics* 3, 1 (Spring 1988): 1–13.

——. "Dyke Methods," *Hypatia* 3, 2 (Summer 1988): 1–13.

——. "Hortense and Gladys on Dreams," *Lesbian Ethics* 1, 2 (Spring 1985): 85–87.

——. "How the Health Care System Controls Women," *Subject to Change* 8, 4 (Apr. 1982): 10–11, 25, 30.

——. "In Partial Response to Those Who Worry That Separatism May Be a Political Cop-Out: An Expanded Definition of Activism," *Gossip: A Journal of Lesbian Feminist Ethics* 3 (Dec. 1986): 82–84.

——. "More Dyke Methods," *Hypatia* 5, 1 (Spring 1990): 140–144.

——. "Notes on the Meaning of Life," *Lesbian Ethics,* 1, 1 (Fall 1984): 90–91.

——. "Sex Roles: The Argument from Nature," *Ethics* 85, 3 (Apr. 1975): 249–255.

——. "Taking Responsibility for Sexuality," in *Philosophy and Sex,* ed. Robert Baker and Frederick Elliston (2d ed. only; Buffalo, N.Y.: Prometheus, 1984), pp. 421–430.

——. "Two Forms of Androgynism," *Journal of Social Philosophy* 8, 1 (Jan. 1977): 4–8.

——. "Women's Studies Ten Years Later," *off our backs* 9, 2 (Jan. 1980): 16, 33.

Winant, Terry. "The Feminist Standpoint: A Matter of Language," *Hypatia* 2, 2 (Winter 1987): 123–148.

——. "How Ordinary (Sexist) Language Resists Radical (Feminist) Critique," in *Hypatia Reborn: Essays in Feminist Philosophy,* ed. Azizah Y. al-Hibri and Margaret A. Simons (Bloomington: Indiana University Press, 1990), pp. 54–69.

Young, Iris Marion. "The Exclusion of Women from Sport," *Philosophy in Context* 9 (Fall 1979): 44–53.

——. "Self-Determination as a Principle of Justice," *Philosophical Forum* 11, 1 (Fall 1979): 30–46.

——. "Throwing like a Girl: A Phenomenology of Feminine Bodily Comportment, Motility and Spatiality," *Human Studies* 3 (1980): 137–156.

Zita, Jacqueline N. "Female Bonding and Sexual Politics," *Sinister Wisdom* 14 (Summer 1980): 8–16.

———. "Historical Amnesia and the Lesbian Continuum," *Signs* 7, 1 (Autumn 1981): 172–187. (Contribution to a symposium on Adrienne Rich," Compulsory Heterosexuality and Lesbian Existence," *Signs:* 5, 4, [Summer 1980]: 631–660.)

———. "Lesbian Angels and Other Matters," *Hypatia* 5, 1 (Spring 1990): 133–139. (Response to Joyce Trebilcot, "Dyke Methods," *Hypatia* 3, 2 [Summer 1988]: 1–13.)

———. "The Premenstrual Syndrome: Dis-easing the Female Cycle," *Hypatia* 3, 1 (Spring 1988): 77–99.

———. " 'Real Girls' and Lesbian Resistance," *Lesbian Ethics* 3, 1 (Spring 1988): 85–96.

———. " 'The Sex Question' and Socialist Feminism," *Sinister Wisdom* 31 (Winter 1987): 120–127.

Zita, Jacqueline N., and Susan Geiger. "White Traders: The Caveat Emptor of Women's Studies," *Journal of Thought* 20, 3 (Fall 1985): 106–121.

BOOKS: 1970–1991.

Adams, Carol J. *The Sexual Politics of Meat: A Feminist-Vegetarian Critical Theory.* New York: Continuum, 1990.

Addelson, Kathryn Pyne. *Impure Thoughts: Essays on Philosophy, Feminism and Ethics.* Philadelphia: Temple University Press, 1991.

Allen, Jeffner. *Lesbian Philosophy: Explorations.* Palo Alto, Calif.: Institute of Lesbian Studies, 1987.

Allen, Paula Gunn. *The Sacred Hoop: Recovering the Feminine in American Indian Traditions.* Boston: Beacon, 1986.

Anzaldúa, Gloria. *Borderlands:* La Frontera: *The New Mestiza.* San Francisco: Spinsters/Aunt Lute, 1987.

Atkinson, Ti-Grace. *Amazon Odyssey.* New York: Links Books, 1974.

Baier, Annette. *Postures of the Mind: Essays on Mind and Morals.* Minneapolis: University of Minnesota Press, 1985.

———. *A Progress of Sentiments: Reflections on Hume's Treatise.* Cambridge, Mass.: Harvard University Press, 1991.

Barry, Kathleen. *Female Sexual Slavery.* Englewood Cliffs, N.J.: Prentice-Hall, 1979.

Bart, Pauline B., and Patricia H. O'Brien. *Stopping Rape: Successful Survival Strategies.* New York: Pergamon, 1985.

Bartky, Sandra Lee. *Femininity and Domination: Studies in the Phenomenology of Oppression.* New York: Routledge, 1990.

Bleier, Ruth. *Science and Gender: A Critique of Biology and Its Theories on Women.* New York: Pergamon, 1984.

Brantenberg, Gerd. *Egalia's Daughters: A Satire of the Sexes.* Trans. from Norwegian by Louis Mackay, with Gerd Brantenberg. Seattle: Seal Press, 1985.

Cannon, Katie G. *Black Womanist Ethics.* Atlanta: Scholars Press, 1988.

Chase-Riboud, Barbara. *Sally Hemings: A Novel.* New York: Viking, 1979. (Based on the life of the slave woman owned by Thomas Jefferson, with whom she had five children.)

Chodorow, Nancy. *The Reproduction of Mothering: Psychoanalysis and the Sociology of Gender.* Berkeley: University of California Press, 1978.

Copper, Baba. *Over the Hill: Reflections on Ageism Between Women.* Freedom, Calif.: Crossing Press, 1988.

Cornwell, Anita. *Black Lesbian in White America.* Naiad Press, 1983.

Cortese, Anthony. *Ethnic Ethics: The Restructuring of Moral Theory.* Albany: State University of New York Press 1990.

Daly, Mary. *Beyond God the Father: Toward a Philosophy of Women's Liberation.* Boston: Beacon, 1973.

———. *Gyn/Ecology: The Metaethics of Radical Feminism.* Boston: Beacon, 1978.

———. *Pure Lust: Elemental Feminist Philosophy.* Boston: Beacon, 1984.

Davis, Angela Y. *Women, Culture, and Politics.* New York: Random House, 1989.

———. *Women, Race and Class.* New York: Random House, 1981.

Davis, Elizabeth Gould. *The First Sex.* Baltimore: Penguin, 1971.

Dworkin, Andrea. *Intercourse.* New York: Free Press, 1987.

———. *Letters from a War Zone: Writings 1976–1989.* New York: Dutton, 1988.

———. *Our Blood: Prophecies and Discourses.* New York: Harper & Row, 1976.

———. *Pornography: Men Possessing Women.* New York: Perigee, 1981.

———. *Right-Wing Women.* New York: Perigee, 1983.

———. *Woman Hating.* New York: Dutton, 1974.

Frye, Marilyn. *The Politics of Reality: Essays in Feminist Theory.* Trumansburg, N.Y.: Crossing Press, 1983.

Gilligan, Carol. *In a Different Voice: Psychological Theory and Women's Development.* Cambridge, Mass.: Harvard University Press, 1982.

Griffin, Susan. *Pornography and Silence: Culture's Revenge against Nature.* New York: Harper & Row, 1981.

———. *Rape: The Power of Consciousness.* San Francisco: Harper & Row, 1979.

———. *Woman and Nature: The Roaring inside Her.* New York: Harper & Row, 1978.

Grimshaw, Jean. *Philosophy and Feminist Thinking.* Minneapolis: University of Minnesota Press, 1986.

Held, Virginia. *Rights and Goods: Justifying Social Action.* New York: Free Press, 1984.

Hoagland, Sarah. *Lesbian Ethics: Toward New Value.* Palo Alto, Calif.: Institute of Lesbian Studies, 1988.

hooks, bell. *Ain't I a Woman: Black Women and Feminism.* Boston: South End Press, 1981.

———. *Feminist Theory: From Margin to Center.* Boston: South End Press, 1984.

———. *Talking Back: Thinking Feminist, Thinking Black.* Boston: South End Press, 1989.

———. *Yearning: Race, Gender, and Cultural Politics.* Boston: South End Press, 1990.

Hynes, H. Patricia. *The Recurring Silent Spring.* New York: Pergamon, 1989.

Jaggar, Alison M. *Feminist Politics and Human Nature.* Totowa, N.J.: Rowman & Allanheld, 1983.

Jones, Ann. *Women Who Kill.* New York: Fawcett Columbine, 1980.

Jordan, June. *On Call: Political Essays.* Boston: South End Press, 1985.

Kitzinger, Celia. *The Social Construction of Lesbianism.* London: Sage, 1987.

Klepfisz, Irena. *Dreams of an Insomniac: Jewish Feminist Essays, Speeches, and Diatribes.* Portland, Ore.: Eighth Mountain Press, 1990.

———. *A Few Words in the Mother Tongue: Poems Selected and New (1971–1990).* Portland, Ore.: Eighth Mountain Press, 1990.

Lorde, Audre. *The Cancer Journals.* Argyle, N.Y.: Spinsters, Ink, 1980.

———. *Sister Outsider: Essays and Speeches.* Trumansberg, N.Y.: Crossing Press, 1984.

———. *Zami: A New Spelling of My Name.* Watertown, Mass.: Persephone Press, 1982. Reprinted Trumansberg, N.Y.: Crossing Press, 1983.

McCunn, Ruth Lum. *Thousand Pieces of Gold: A Biographical Novel.* Boston: Beacon, 1981. (Based on the life of a Chinese-American pioneer woman who survived footbinding, poverty, and slavery to build a life of relative freedom in the northwest United States.)

Macdonald, Barbara, with Cynthia Rich. *Look Me in the Eye: Old Women, Aging and Ageism.* San Francisco: Spinsters, Ink, 1983.

McFall, Lynne. *Dancer with Bruised Knees.* New York: Atlantic Monthly Press, forthcoming 1993.

———. *Happiness.* New York: Peter Lang, 1989.

———. *The One True Story of the World: A Novel.* New York: Atlantic Monthly Press, 1990.

MacKinnon, Catharine A. *Feminism Unmodified: Discourses on Life and Law.* Cambridge, Mass.: Harvard University Press, 1987.

———. *Sexual Harassment of Working Women.* New Haven, Conn.: Yale University Press, 1979.

Martin, Jane Roland. *Reclaiming a Conversation: The Ideal of the Educated Woman.* New Haven, Conn.: Yale University Press, 1985.

Millett, Kate. *The Looney Bin Trip.* New York: Simon & Schuster, 1990.

———. *Sexual Politics.* Garden City, N.Y.: Doubleday, 1970.

Mohr, Richard D. *Gays/Justice: A Study of Ethics, Society, and Law.* New York: Columbia University Press 1988.

Morrison, Toni. *Beloved: A Novel.* New York: Knopf, 1987.

———. *The Bluest Eye: A Novel.* New York: Holt, Rinehart, & Winston, 1970.

Murdoch, Iris. *The Sovereignty of Good.* London: Routledge and Kegan Paul, 1970.

Noddings, Nel. *Caring: A Feminine Approach to Ethics and Moral Education.* Berkeley: University of California Press, 1984.

———. *Women and Evil.* Berkeley: University of California Press, 1989.

Nussbaum, Martha. *The Fragility of Goodness: Luck and Ethics in Greek Tragedy and Philosophy.* Cambridge, Eng.: Cambridge University Press, 1986.

Penelope, Julia. *Speaking Freely: Unlearning the Lies of the Fathers' Tongues.* New York: Pergamon, 1990.

Pierce, Christine. *How to Solve the Lockheed Case.* New Brunswick, N.J.: Transaction Press, Rutgers University, 1986.

Raymond, Janice G. *A Passion for Friends: Toward a Philosophy of Female Affection.* Boston: Beacon, 1986.

———. *The Transsexual Empire: The Making of the She-Male.* Boston: Beacon, 1979.

Rich, Adrienne. *Blood, Bread, and Poetry: Selected Prose 1979–1985.* New York: Norton, 1986.

———. *Of Woman Born: Motherhood as Experience and Institution.* New York: Norton, 1976.

———. *On Lies, Secrets, and Silence: Selected Prose 1966–1978.* New York: Norton, 1979.

Ruddick, Sara. *Maternal Thinking: Toward a Politics of Peace.* Boston: Beacon, 1989.

Rush, Florence. *The Best Kept Secret: Sexual Abuse of Children.* Englewood Cliffs, N.J.: Prentice-Hall, 1980.

Russ, Joanna. *Magic Mommas, Trembling Sisters, Puritans and Perverts: Feminist Essays.* Trumansburg, N.Y.: Crossing Press, 1985.

Schur, Edwin. *Labeling Women Deviant: Gender, Stigma, and Social Control.* Philadelphia: Temple University Press, 1983.

Solanas, Valerie. *SCUM Manifesto.* London: Matriarchy Study Group, 1983. (Reprint of Olympia Press edition of 1968).

Spelman, Elizabeth V. *Inessential Woman: Problems of Exclusion in Feminist Thought.* Boston: Beacon, 1988.

Stimpson, Catharine R. *Where the Meanings Are: Feminism and Cultural Spaces.* New York: Methuen, 1988.

Thompson, Karen, with Julie Andrzejewski. *Why Can't Sharon Kowalski Come Home?* San Francisco: Spinsters/Aunt Lute, 1988.

Walker, Alice. *The Color Purple: A Novel.* New York: Harcourt Brace Jovanovich, 1982.

———. *In Search of Our Mothers' Gardens.* New York: Harcourt Brace Jovanovich, 1983.

———. *Living by the Word: Selected Writings 1973–1987.* New York: Harcourt Brace Jovanovich, 1988.

Wittig, Monique. *Les Guerilleres.* Trans. from French by David Le Vay. New York: Avon, 1973.

———. *The Lesbian Body.* Trans. from French by David Le Vay. New York: Avon, 1976.

Yamamoto, Hisaye. *Seventeen Syllables and Other Stories.* Latham, N.Y.: Kitchen Table: Women of Color Press, 1988.

Young, Iris Marion. *Justice and the Politics of Difference.* Princeton, N.J.: Princeton University Press, 1990.

———. *Throwing Like a Girl and Other Essays in Feminist Philosophy and Social Theory.* Bloomington: Indiana University Press, 1990.

Zamora, Margarita. *Language, Authority and Indigenous History in the Comentarios Reales de los Incas.* Cambridge, Eng.: Cambridge University Press, 1988.

The Contributors

ANNETTE C. BAIER teaches philosophy at the University of Pittsburgh. She has also taught at the universities of Aberdeen, Auckland, and Sydney. She is the author of *Postures of the Mind: Essays on Mind and Morals* (1985) and *A Progress of Sentiments: Reflections on Hume's Treatise* (1991).

BAT-AMI BAR ON is an associate professor of philosophy at the State University of New York at Binghamton. Her major area of philosophical investigation is violence. She is currently working on a book entitled *Everyday Violence.*

CLAUDIA CARD is a professor of philosophy at the University of Wisconsin in Madison, where she is also a member of the Women's Studies Program and the Institute for Environmental Studies. She was a visiting professor at Dartmouth College in 1978–79 and at the University of Pittsburgh in 1980. She has published numerous articles on ethics, feminist theory, and lesbian culture and is writing a book on character and moral luck.

VICTORIA M. DAVION is an assistant professor at the University of Georgia, Athens, where she is also a member of the Environmental Ethics Graduate Certificate Program. She has published essays on ethics, feminist philosophy, and social and political philosophy. She is also an instructor in the Chimera self-defense program for women.

MARILYN FRIEDMAN's writings bring feminist perspectives to bear on issues of contemporary interest in "mainstream" ethics and social philosophy. Her papers have appeared in numerous journals, including *Hypatia, Journal of Philosophy,* and *Ethics.* She currently teaches philosophy at Purdue University, where she is finishing a book entitled *What Are Friends For? Essays on Feminism, Personal Relationships, and Moral Theory.*

MARILYN FRYE teaches philosophy and women's studies at Michigan State University. She roots her political and philosophical thought in her involvement in her local lesbian community. She is author of *The Politics of Reality: Essays in Feminist Theory* (1983).

RUTH GINZBERG is an assistant professor of philosophy at Wesleyan University, where she also teaches women's studies. She has written several articles, including "Uncovering Gynocentric Science," "Teaching Feminist Logic," "Eros in the Philosophy Classroom," and "A Feminist Looks at Women's Studies" and is currently writing a book, *Flirting with Survival.* She has been a member of the Society for Women in Philosophy since 1982.

SARAH LUCIA HOAGLAND is professor of philosophy and women's studies at Northeastern Illinois University in Chicago. She is author of *Lesbian Ethics* (1988) and coeditor of *For Lesbians Only: A Separatist Anthology* (1988).

ALISON M. JAGGAR is professor of philosophy and women's studies at the University of Colorado, Boulder. She has also taught at the University of Illinois at Chicago, the University of California at Los Angeles, and Rutgers University, where she held the Laurie New Jersey Chair in Women's Studies. Her books include *Feminist Frameworks* (coedited with Paula Rothenberg; 1984), *Feminist Politics and Human Nature* (1983), and *Gender/Body/Knowledge: Feminist Reconstructions of Being and Knowing* (coedited with Susan R. Bordo, 1989). She is currently working on a book *Feminism and Moral Theory,* supported by a fellowship from the Rockefeller Foundation. She is a founding member of the Society for Women in Philosophy and currently chairs the American Philosophical Association Committee on the Status of Women. She works with a number of feminist organizations and sees feminist scholarship as inseparable from feminist activism.

MARÍA C. LUGONES is a feminist philosopher and grass-roots radical political educator. Born in Buenos Aires, she has lived in the United States since 1967 and identifies as a U.S. Latina. She teaches at Carleton College during the academic year and at Escuela Popular Norteña in New Mexico during the summer.

LYNNE MCFALL teaches moral philosophy and philosophy of literature at Syracuse University. She is the author of *Happiness* (1989), a philosophical study, and *The One True Story of the World* (1990), a novel. She currently holds a National Endowment for the Arts Fellowship in Literature. Her second novel, *Dancer with Bruised Knees*, is forthcoming.

MICHELE M. MOODY-ADAMS is assistant professor of philosophy at Indiana University. Her research interests are in moral and political philosophy, the philosophy of law, and the history of modern philosophy.

CHRISTINE PIERCE is associate professor of philosophy at North Carolina State University, Raleigh, and a recent associate editor of *SIGNS: Journal of Women in Culture and Society*. Her articles on ethics and feminism have appeared in *The Monist, Philosophical Studies, Analysis,* and other journals and anthologies. She is coeditor of *People, Penguins, and Plastic Trees: Basic Issues in Environmental Ethics* (1981) and *AIDS: Ethics and Public Policy* (1988).

ELIZABETH V. SPELMAN teaches in the Philosophy Department and Women's Studies Program at Smith College. She is the author of *Inessential Woman: Problems of Exclusion in Feminist Thought* (1988) and is now at work on an examination of the treatment of human suffering in Western philosophy.

JOYCE TREBILCOT describes herself as "a white, middle-class lesbian feminist born in California in the thirties, educated in analytic philosophy, and abused into early rebellion by the institutions of patriarchy. I earn money as a teacher and coordinator of women's studies in St. Louis, Missouri."

Index